Craft Economies

Craft Economies

Edited by
SUSAN LUCKMAN AND NICOLA THOMAS

BLOOMSBURY VISUAL ARTS
LONDON • NEW YORK • OXFORD • NEW DELHI • SYDNEY

BLOOMSBURY VISUAL ARTS
Bloomsbury Publishing Plc
50 Bedford Square, London, WC1B 3DP, UK
1385 Broadway, New York, NY 10018, USA
29 Earlsfort Terrace, Dublin 2, Ireland

BLOOMSBURY, BLOOMSBURY VISUAL ARTS and the Diana logo are trademarks of Bloomsbury Publishing Plc

First published in Great Britain 2018
Paperback edition published 2023

Cover design: Olivia D'Cruz
Cover image: JamFactory Contemporary Craft & Design. Homewares collection featuring THROWN ceramics and
JAMJAR Storage Jar/Photographer: Andre Castellucci

A catalogue record for this book is available from the British Library.

A catalog record for this book is available from the Library of Congress.

ISBN: PB: 978-1-3503-5340-4
HB: 978-1-4742-5953-8
ePDF: 978-1-4742-5955-2
ePub: 978-1-4742-5956-9

Typeset by Deanta Global Publishing Services, Chennai, India
Printed and bound in Great Britain

To find out more about our authors and books visit www.bloomsbury.com and sign up for our newsletters.

Contents

List of Illustrations

Figures

Tables

Contributors

Jane Andrew is an educator and researcher working at the University of South Australia in the School of Art, Architecture, and Design, where she is Director of matchstudio, an interdisciplinary research and professional practice studio that supports students' transition from university to work. She is also co-convenor of The Art & Design of Health & Wellbeing research and innovation cluster and Research Associate to Professor Susan Luckman on the Crafting Self ARC project. Jane's early career as a designer-maker, together with her role as Executive Director of Craftsouth (now Guildhouse), inspired her teaching and research career that focuses on the contribution 'creative capital' makes to economic development. Her areas of research focus on creative enterprise development, collaborative inter-disciplinary communities of practice and understanding value networks.

Sonja Andrew is a senior lecturer in design at the University of Huddersfield. Crossing the disciplines of design, semiotics and narratology, she employs the creative process as a mode of research inquiry. Her main research focuses on textile semantics, communication and cultural memory, exploring multimodality through visual and tactile communication on cloth, and the influence of context on audience perception. In 2014, the Arts and Humanities Research Council selected her work on textile communication and visual narrative for an Image Gallery Award, and in 2016, her work 'The Ties That Bind (II)' received an award at the 'From Lausanne to Beijing' International Textile Art Biennial in China. Sonja exhibits internationally and her commissioned work includes pieces for the United Bristol Healthcare Trust, the Cancer Research UK Manchester Institute and Wells Cathedral. Her designs are featured in 'Textiles, The Art of Mankind', a global review of contemporary textile practice.

Jessica R. Barnes is a lecturer in human geography at Northern Arizona University. She teaches courses on regional geography, global development and surveillance. She earned her PhD and served as a teaching associate at the Department of Geography at Ohio State University. Her doctoral research was on how crafters' work fits into lives and livelihoods in Columbus, Ohio. She published an article in *Aether: the Journal of Media Geography* on her master's research, which examined how print journalists localized climate change for regional publications. In 2016, she completed a research project funded by the NAU Department of Geography, Planning, and Recreation on the virtualization of iconic music studio production spaces.

Julia Bennett is the head of Research and Policy in Crafts Council. She develops policy and advocacy strategies, writes about craft and manages research projects, strengthening evidence to improve the conditions for craft. Recent research commissions include Studying Craft 16 (TBR 2016), an analysis of trends in craft education and training, *Innovation through Craft: opportunities for growth*, that describes how collaboration drives innovation and growth, and Measuring the Craft

Economy (TBR 2014), a set of proposals which resulted in Department of Media, Culture and Sport including craft data for the first time in its economic estimates. As an experienced researcher, research manager, policy specialist and strategist, Julia has worked independently with small charities and arts organizations, as well as for the Local Government Association, the Learning and Skills Improvement Service, the Minority Rights Group and a number of local councils.

Chantel Carr is a researcher in the School of Geography and Sustainable Communities at the University of Wollongong, Australia. Her research examines industrial cultures, material labour and skill. Chantel trained and worked in architecture prior to undertaking her PhD, and has taught environmental performance and design studios since 2008.

Zhen Troy Chen, PhD, FHEA, is a senior lecturer in Digital Advertising, London College of Communication, University of the Arts London. He is also an Adjunct Research Fellow of the Griffith Centre for Design and Innovation Research at Griffith University. His research interests are in digital media and advertising, cultural and creative industries, cultural and media policy, journalism and experience design. His recent research monograph is entitled *China's music industry unplugged: Business models, copyright and social entrepreneurship in the online platform economy* (Palgrave Macmillan, 2021). His research papers have appeared in *Journal of Consumer Culture, International Journal of Cultural Policy, Ethics and Information Technology, Social Semiotics, Asian Journal of Women's Studies, SAGE Research Methods* and *Global Media and China*.

Lisa Ann Daily is a graduate assistant at George Mason University whose work focuses on the intersection of consumer and commodity culture, global capitalism, visuality and media, and in/justice. Her dissertation, 'Ethical Inc. Ethical Commodity Formations and the Rise of a Conscious Capitalism™', critically examines the contemporary proliferation of an ethical capitalist reconfiguration, which seeks to mobilize privatized solutions for 'public benefit'. Examples abound from the recent passing of Benefit Corporation legislation in states throughout the United States and organizations such as Conscious Capitalism™ to consumer activism and commodities that espouse to 'do good' with every purchase.

Hélène Day Fraser is the Associate Dean, Master of Design, Jake Kerr Faculty of Graduate Studies at Emily Carr University of Art + Design. Her textile/garment-based work addresses concerns and developments in the areas of sustainability, new digital technologies, craft and legacy practices of making and generative systems. Day Fraser's research explores social engagement, identity construction and clothing consumption habits; it is informed by her design education, and a previous professional career in fashion, design and manufacturing. Day Fraser is the lead investigator of the cloTHING(s) as conversation research initiative. She is a co-founder of the Material Matters research centre and the manager for Emily Carr's DESIS lab.

Kandy Diamond is a designer, artist and lecturer with a specialism in knitted textiles. In 2006, Kandy set up her brand 'Knit and Destroy', with which she has seen international success. 2013 brought the release of *Knit and Destroy … Gets Handy!*, a book containing twenty hand-knit patterns of Kandy's designs. Crafting products that blur the lines between product and art, Kandy has made a natural progression to making non-wearable art pieces as well as products, with work that aims to challenge cultural preconceptions by offering an alternative representation of knitting, creating pieces that are at odds with the embedded stereotype.

Keith Doyle is an assistant professor of industrial design, Faculty of Design + Dynamic Media, Faculty of Graduate Studies, Emily Carr University of Art + Design. Doyle is the lead/co-lead investigator on university research initiatives like cloTHING(s) as conversation research project and the XX1T Triennale di Milano Liminal Labs. Doyle is affiliated researcher of GRAND NCE and founding faculty member and director of Material Matters research centre at Emily Carr University of Art + Design. He holds both a BFA and an MFA in sculpture. He maintains an active design and material practice presenting scholarly works and exhibitions locally and abroad.

Chris Gibson is Professor of Human Geography at the University of Wollongong, Australia. His research interests are in cultural economy, economic geography and the future of making things amid climate crisis.

Xin Gu is a lecturer in the School of Media, Film and Journalism at Monash University, Australia. Xin has been prominent in the attempt to contextualize contemporary Western debate around cultural economy in Asia. Her recent research investigates the interrelationship between process of 'digitalization' and 'material culture' through the emergence of maker culture in Australian and Chinese cities. She is currently contracted by Routledge for a joint authored book on *Culture and Economy in the New Shanghai*.

Ella Harris is a PhD candidate in geography at Royal Holloway, University of London. Her thesis looks at the ways in which space-time is imagined and distributed within pop-up culture and uses interactive documentary as a methodological tool to explore non-linear spatiotemporal imaginaries. Ella has published on pop-up's spatiotemporal logics (*Geography Compass*; 2015), immersive pop-up cinema (*Journal of Urban Cultural Studies*; 2016, *Live Cinema*, Forthcoming) and interactive documentary (*Area*; 2017). She is also working on an ongoing collaborative project called 'Precarious Geographies', which includes a special issue currently in preparation.

Charles Heying is Professor Emeritus of Urban Studies and Planning at Portland State University, Portland, Oregon, United States. He has co-authored a book and numerous articles on the politics and development of Olympic cities. Professor Heying's current research combines his interest in art and craft with his passion for community-based economic development. His 2010 book, *Brew to Bikes: Portland's Artisan Economy*, describes how the transformation from an industrial to a post-industrial economy is being articulated in the trend-setting edges of Portland's artisan production. Heying participated in a Kauffman Foundation–funded project investigating the entrepreneurial ecosystems of the 'maker movement' in three US cities. He is co-author of The Maker Movement and Urban Economic Development (2017) published by the *Journal of the American Planning Association*.

Gail Kenning is a researcher at the University of Technology Sydney (UTS); Design United Research Fellow at University of Technology, Eindhoven (TU/e), Netherlands; Honorary Reader in Design for Ageing and Dementia at Cardiff Metropolitan University, Wales, UK; and Visiting Fellow at the Museum of Applied Arts and Sciences, Sydney (MAAS). Gail works across art, craft and design. Her artistic practice uses extended textiles, photography and video, programmed animations and data visualization. She has exhibited and screened works internationally and nationally, and has published in journals including *Continuum, Media International Australia, Textile: Cloth and Culture* and *Leonardo*. She is Chief investigator on projects including Arts Engagement for Livable Communities, Making It Together (a co- and participatory design project for people living with dementia), Arts access evaluation with Art Gallery New South Wales and is an international co-investigator on a design for dementia AHRC (Arts and Humanities Research Council)-funded project in the UK: LAUGH (Ludic Artefacts Using Gesture and Haptics).

Katve-Kaisa Kontturi is a senior lecturer in Art History at the University of Turku, Finland, where she co-directs a transdisciplinary project on 'New Economies of Artistic Labour' (Kone Foundation, 2020–2024). She also serves as an Honorary Fellow at the Faculty of Fine Arts and Music, The University of Melbourne, where she previously held a post-doctoral fellowship under which research work for the article included in this book was conducted. She has published widely on New Materialisms and the arts, including the monograph *Ways of Following: Art, Materiality, Collaboration* (2018) and articles in journals such as *Journal of Aesthetics & Culture, Cultural Studies Review* and *Nora: Nordic Journal of Feminist and Gender Research.*

Jo Law leads the Media Arts curriculum at the University of Wollongong that investigates the transformative potential of art and technology. Her transdisciplinary research focuses on creative practice's relationship with changing sociocultural and political environments. In particular, she is interested in how the textual imprints of media and materials in artworks shape human experience. Her current research includes the project Material Science, Slow Textiles, and Ecological Futures – a collaboration between contemporary arts, material science and climate science that examines the interconnectedness of social, environmental and technological transformations through art.

Susan Luckman is Professor of Cultural and Creative Industries and Director of the Creative People, Products and Places Research Centre (CP3) at the University of South Australia. She has been Chief Investigator on 5 ARC and 4 EU awarded projects including the current Australian Research Council Discovery Project 'The value of craft skills to the future of manufacturing in Australia'. Susan is the author of *Craftspeople and Designer Makers in the Contemporary Creative Economy* (Open Access – Palgrave, 2020), *Craft and the Creative Economy* (Palgrave Macmillan, 2015) and *Locating Cultural Work: The Politics and Poetics of Rural, Regional and Remote Creativity* (Palgrave Macmillan, 2012).

Sophia Maalsen is the Ian Fell Postdoctoral Research Fellow at the University of Sydney, where she is researching the role of technology in 'smart homes' as a locus to address future environmental and social challenges. Prior to joining the University of Sydney, Sophia was a postdoctoral researcher on the EU-funded Programmable City Project where she investigated the digital transformation of cities and urban governance. Sophia has also worked in the Enabling Built Environments Program at the University of New South Wales, specifically on a project that investigated how and why people with a disability were undertaking DIY home modifications. Her particular expertise is in understanding the intersection of the material, digital and the human and how these effects lived experience.

Steve Marotta is a doctoral candidate in urban studies and planning at Portland State University. His research is broadly at the intersection of culture and political economy, and has focused empirically on craft production, media representations of cities, narratives of localism, and the 'maker movement' in four American cities. His dissertation examines the relation between place imaginaries and value circulation (e.g. 'Made in Detroit') with an eye towards the modes of belonging such relationships produce alongside rapidly changing urban environments.

Marzia Mortati is Associate Professor in Design at the Department of Design, Politecnico di Milano. Her main research focus lies in the relationship between design and innovation, looking in particular at design for policy and the public sector, the role of data and artificial intelligence in the design process, and in applying social and systemic innovation to the public sector. She is one of the Executive Directors at the European Academy of Design, and Vice-Director of the International Master in AI for public services. She teaches strategic and service design since 2007 both at graduate and at post-graduate levels, and is involved in international research concerning design for policy, design and AI, and social innovation.

Gabriele Oropallo was Senior Lecturer in Critical and Contextual Studies at the School of Art, Architecture and Design, London Metropolitan University. His research examined how the environmental crisis altered practice and mediation of design and technology. He was a founding member of critical design practices Repair Society and Arquip é lagos Urbanos, with which he participated respectively in the Istanbul Design Biennial and São Paulo Architecture Biennial. In 2017, he was a convenor of the Design History Society Annual Conference on 'Making and Unmaking the Environment', and he regularly contributed to *form* design magazine and *The Bloomsbury Encyclopedia of Design*.

Sung-Yueh Perng is Post doctoral Researcher on the ERC-funded Programmable City project at Maynooth University, Ireland, after receiving his PhD in sociology from Lancaster University, UK. His current research is concerned with the incorporation of digital and data-driven innovations into urban life and governance. He has conducted case studies in Dublin and Boston, examining if civic hacking can meaningfully address community problems and also exploring concerns that emerge from the processes.

Philip Robbins is faculty within the Division of Creative Arts and Industries at Langara College, a co-founder of the Material Matters Research Centre at Emily Carr University, and a former lead investigator. His work explores the crossover and collisions between digital and analogue, legacy and emergent. Robbins collaborates on a variety of industry and academia facing, multidisciplinary research partnerships. His current research, published in the proceedings of the 2016 CUMULUS conference in Nottingham, explores the place of digital technologies and the legitimacy of the maker's hand in a digitally mediated process.

Angelina Russo is an MBA-Higher Education Management graduate of the University College London and is an invited associate scholar in the Centre for Research in Digital Education, Moray House, University of Edinburgh. She was also a chief investigator in the ARC Centre of Excellence for Creative Industries and Innovation (2005–11). Professor Russo is a co-founder of the 4,000-member social network Museum3 and is the chief investigator on the newly established multi-institutional project Mobile Makers. She is a member of the Fulbright Scholarship Committee an ARC assessor, an academic representative of the Unisuper Consultative Committee and a member of the Australian Institute of Company Directors.

Ezra Shales, Professor in the History of Art at Massachusetts College of Art and Design, focuses on the productive confusion that lies at the intersection of design, craft and art. He is the author of the book *Made in Newark* (Rutgers University Press, 2010), in which he explores craft as an anchor of regional identity in Progressive-era New Jersey. He has written on artisans who built the

Empire State Building and is an active curator whose exhibitions have travelled to the Museum of Arts and Design (NYC) and the United States's National Museum of Women in the Arts. He has a PhD from the Bard Graduate Center.

Sarah Teasley is Reader in Design History and Theory and Head of Programme for History of Design at the Royal College of Art, and a historian concerned with design, technology and society, particularly in modern and contemporary Japan. Her current book project explores relationships between the state, manufacturers, scientists, educators and designers working with wood in twentieth-century Japan. Teasley's publications include *Global Design History* (Routledge, 2011). Grants and fellowships include support from the British Academy, the Arts and Humanities Research Council, the Association of Asian Studies and the Design History Society.

Nicola Thomas is Professor of Historical and Cultural Geography at the University of Exeter. She has developed a body of work around craft geographies, situating contemporary and 20th century craft practice within the broader creative economy. Her approach addresses the intersection of material, historical, cultural, social, political and economic contexts through an exploration of craft makers' livelihoods and the spatial dimension of their labour. Her research always attends to the historicity of cultural production and consumption, bringing a historical sensitivity to critical understandings of the cultural and creative economy.

1

Crafting economies

Contemporary cultural economies of the handmade

Susan Luckman and Nicola Thomas

Craft Economies seeks to capture craft's current 'moment in the sun' through an exploration of the configuration in ways craft intersects with debates, practices and worlds beyond craft making itself. We wish to locate this discussion within the larger picture of its implications for our understandings of the contemporary cultural economy which we recognize to be a diverse landscape of encounters, exchanges and relations between producers, consumers, intermediaries, communities, policy, skills, materials and technologies. However, this crucially includes questions around *qui bono?*, that is 'who benefits?', and what is at stake – including for craft practice itself – as craft (broadly conceived) experiences a zeitgeist moment of popularity as part of 'turn toward the tactile' (*Crafts* p. 34) in the digital age.

Since the 1980s a huge shift in the commercial landscape has seen creative entrepreneurial cultural production shoot to centre-stage of government and corporate planning, research and development. This shift has paralleled the increased aestheticization of everyday life and the rise of the design and lifestyle sectors of the economy. Craft in its many forms both does and does not smoothly feed into these larger policy and commercial trends. Hence, the plurality indicated in the title to this collection – *Craft Economies* – very deliberately signals not only the multiplicity of craft itself, but also the complexity of its relationships with the economic field, including its fraught status as a creative industry. The debate around this most famously came to a head in the UK in 2013 when the Department of Media, Culture and Sport (DCMS) floated the idea of deleting craft from its list of creative businesses. The DCMS argued that as craft-based enterprises tend to be sole trader operations (88 per cent according to a 2012 United Kingdom Crafts Council-commissioned study: BOP Consulting 2012, p. 4), they are frequently thus 'too small to identify in business survey data' (DCMS 2013, p. 14). Ironically, many artists and craftspeople have been at the forefront of critiques of the shift from 'cultural' to 'creative' industries, principally on account of the economically rationalist way it can enable the measurement and qualification of the value of a creative practice in largely, if not purely, economic terms. The very idea that craft could potentially be strategically removed from a national listing of creative industries is in and of itself evidence of how far the British model in particular has sought to move away from traditional understandings of the cultural industries. The neo-liberal economic and geo-political specificity of this move comes to the fore when we consider whether such a move to distance craft from official governmental narratives around creativity could occur in Japan, India, China, Finland, South Africa or Germany, who all variously champion craft, making and the artisanal in their own policy rubrics.

Thus, while it has become almost a cliché in the Global North to see high-street shopfronts deploying macramé, retro sewing machines or other signifiers of craft making to denote cool or bespoke cachet, the mobilization of craft in current economic discourses has far deeper and more profound implications. Craft work is being championed by individuals, communities and governments as the answer to complex and profound issues of economic and social inclusion. On the plus side, this has seen the rise of various craft-based social enterprises, including many which enable displaced or otherwise marginalized peoples to use traditional skills in new contexts as both a source of income as well as identity and belonging. More concerning, however, are the ways that craft work is part of the wider trend towards increasingly precarious creative employment across much of the Global North. Despite social welfare safety nets, together with many of the grants, allowances, scholarships, apprenticeships, residencies, prizes and other kinds of practice and income support available to craftspeople being wound back in some locales, we are ironically seeing an increase in the numbers of graduates being produced by the educational sector. Emerging from degrees heavy on book learning but not studio practice, these graduates emerge into an employment landscape where self-employment is encouraged in governmental policy as a quick fix to creative un- or under-employment. Alongside a growing number of career changers, down shifters and 'e-retirees' as well as established makers, these graduates find themselves setting up their digital shopfront, complete with polished artists' statement and Instagram-able images, in the desperate hope that they will manage to achieve cut-through and a sustainable income in an already over-crowded online marketplace. That people continue to be willing to make the sacrifices required to establish and maintain a life working in craft is evidence of the seductive power of making, for as Tanya Harrod has succinctly reminded us: 'Craft is a condensed way of suggesting that there is production as well as consumption, that work need not be an alienating affair' (Harrod 2001, quoted in Harrod 2015, p. 39).

Beyond the individual and at the institutional and inter-sectoral level, globalization and advanced manufacturing are today breathing interesting new life into craft's relationship with industry and larger-scale production. In his book the *Invention of Craft* (2013), leading craft curator and scholar Glenn Adamson convincingly argues that 'craft' as we know it today came into being in the mid-nineteenth century when it was cast as the Industrial Revolution's 'Other', deliberately rupturing links between artisanal making and manufacture; craft and technology. In so doing, new distinctions and boundaries within craft's field came into being which privileged the small-scale, authentic, transparent and organic. Clearly, therefore, 'there is no way of talking about modern craft that is neutral. It was invented at a time of conflict between the ranks of the skilful and others involved in production, who recognized the unique potency of skill and therefore wanted to contain and control it' (Adamson 2013, p. xxiv). Significantly, Adamson's words echo those of Adorno over a century earlier who cautioned: 'Whenever handicraft is established as a norm today, one must closely examine the intention. The concept of handicraft stands in close relationship to function. Its functions, however, are by no means necessarily enlightened or advanced' (Adorno

1979, p. 36). Today, 'craft' clearly remains an ideologically loaded term, deployed differently by agents in particular contexts.

Thus, one of the interesting sites around which to explore its meaning and value is presented by the re-suturing of 'craft' to 'production' at play around the rise of the 'designer maker' whose market is today facilitated by the very globalization that the Industrial Revolution enabled. The rise internationally of greater numbers of affluent consumers, but also the very sameness of a consumer goods marketplace centralized in a few sites of production (China in particular), is driving the demand for bespoke, niche products. Moreover, highly localized studio production models are being re-invigorated by rapid prototyping, demand production and the often cost-effective scalable affordances of new digital making technologies. Such technologies are often those championed by the maker's movement: laser cutting and additive manufacturing (AM), more commonly known as 3D printing. Ironically, while the 'new' is all too frequently championed in relation to craft's industrial relationships, not surprisingly given the historical erasures ensuing from the hegemonic Western construction of craft as the Industrial Revolution's 'Other' outlined by Adamson, any emphasis on the 'newness' of links between craft, design and manufacture also does a tremendous injustice to much iconic and still influential, though nonetheless often fraught, twentieth-century innovation in this space.

Today, contemporary localized craft economies, variously integrated into global flows of people, materials and goods, offer products which are sought after points of difference in a flooded consumer marketplace. Local governments, business and tourist developments, makers themselves and visitors look to the handmade as part of wider strategies of local differentiation in a world where increasingly across much of the industrialized world high streets, malls and their products look more and more the same. Sadly, despite this, hands-on craft training is under profound threat from higher education funding pressure. Increased student numbers alongside budget cuts have led to the winding back of expensive studios, workshops and supervised practical tuition in universities. Again, all this is occurring against a backdrop where global production of ever more stuff is progressively dominated by fewer and fewer nations, with the loss not only of local jobs but also of knowledge.

These collections – *Craft Economies* and *Craft Communities* – grew out of conversations the editors started on a UK 'craft road trip' which started at the Carpenters' Hall, London, which was the venue for the 2014 annual conference of the British Heritage Crafts Association (HCA). The HCA is a not-for-profit organization whose primary concern is to be 'the advocacy body for traditional heritage crafts. Working in partnership with Government and key agencies, it provides a focus for craftspeople, groups, societies and guilds, as well as individuals who care about the loss of traditional crafts skills, and works towards a healthy and sustainable framework for the future' (http://heritagecrafts.org.uk/what-we-do/). Their work in recent years has drawn attention to crafts which are at risk in the UK, particularly those with skills being held in the hands of an ageing population with no visible route for being passed on to another generation. 'The Radcliffe Red List of Endangered Crafts' (Heritage Crafts Association 2017) lists 'extinct crafts', which are no longer carried out such as sieve and riddle making, and 'critically endangered crafts', where there is serious danger of them no longer being practiced including piano making, paper marbling and metal thread making (http://heritagecrafts.org.uk/redlist/categories-of-risk/). Of the endangered crafts, bicycle making sits in the list, alongside the making of ladders and precision instruments. Within this list there are over ninety crafts listed that are currently viable, from armour and helmet making to tatting. This review of heritage craft sits alongside the work of the UK Crafts Council in taking stock on a regular basis of the health of contemporary craft. While these different foci are sometimes held in tension (Jakob and Thomas 2015), both the Heritage Crafts Association and the Crafts Council are advocating strong government interventions to support the UK craft economy and education of children and students in making skills. As universities and technical training facilities in countries that have prioritized the knowledge economy have cut back practical training in the face of decreased economic demand and thus funding for graduates with practical making skills, it is salutary to give thought as to what kinds of craft skills may become 'heritage' in the not-too-distant future.

Already the realities of the distance of the actual labour of making from the head offices of the companies which commission it are coming home to roost in areas of artisanal making that have otherwise been with us for millennia. For instance, shoemaking. The following example is from the transcript of an interview between one of the editors and a British shoemaker who now lives in Australia. She recounts in turn a conversation she had with a British elder statesman of shoemaking, a maker of around eighty years of age in her estimation:

> He told me who he was and his job is to go around, he goes into major shoe factories and talks to managing directors of _____ and all these different shoe making companies. You'd think 'oh well, they know all about shoes' but they know nothing about the construction of a shoe and he, he's been in the industry all his life and he talks [to them] about the components of the shoe, so that they are more knowledgeable about a shoe, so that they can talk to their manufacturers in China about how shoes are constructed. … It's a bit like farm managers who know nothing about straw and hay. (Luna Newby, Shoemaker, February 2017)

Without makers not only keeping skills alive, and transmitting them to the next generation, all craft can potentially become at risk. Digital technology is offering one key trajectory along which craft knowledges and skills can play an essential role in the future development of manufacturing, especially high-end scalable and customizable production, and some of the possibilities for this are explored in the chapters featured in this volume. But as indicated in the example of shoemaking offered just above, not everything is so rosy for the future of craft, especially in the English-speaking world with its cut-backs to craft training. So despite craft's apparent seemingly everywhere visibility, we are living in interesting, and potentially dangerous, times. It is precisely how craft bumps up against and intersects with these kinds of wider geo-political and socio-economic imperatives that the chapters in this volume explore across its five sections.

Craft, making and the creative economy

Craft's economic place in circuits of production and consumption involves more than just the selling of handmade goods; rather it represents the movement, circulation and dissemination of multiple inputs, outputs and skills. It also represents a particular way of being in the world – including as located in economies – and how we negotiate our often fraught relationship with this larger field. For this reason, many of the contributors to this volume, and especially this section, explore craft as an enabler of new relationships and alternate understandings of relationships in the Global North to the mainstream economy. Katve-Kaisa Kontturi's chapter proposes that contemporary craft practices offer an alternative to the all-consuming, disembodied and individualist logic of cognitive capitalism. Drawing upon the ideas of Semper, Riegl, Simondon, Deleuze and Guattari, and both the writings and activist art of Erin Manning, Kontturi explores how craft embraces 'passive time' instead of profit-driven and maximized temporality, and focuses on material and bodily collaborations instead of individual and disembodied labour. Similarly, drawing upon Ivan Illich's understanding of conviviality as 'opposite of productivity' yet as essential to social lives together, in her chapter Marzia Mortati offers a reflection on the behavioural change in creativity and engagement that is branching in and out of design to generate new connections to craft and inform new ways to work, produce, socialize and innovate. In particular, she explores this in terms of new products and services that are proposing novel design scenarios linked to personal manufacturing, peer production, crowd funding and micro-entrepreneurship. Thus, we can see that craft makers overlap with multiple other creative and making sectors, and require inputs sourced both locally and from around the world. Handmade items as final products too are distributed via global networks enabled by the internet. But the sector also retains a strong focus upon direct selling through various forms of local fairs and markets. Buying direct from the maker in this way thus fits in with larger lifestyle and ethical consumption practices with a focus on local economies and short circuits of production or, at the other end of the spectrum, as part of fair-trade systems of transnational ethical consumption, as is explored by Lisa Daily in her contribution to this collection.

For makers, the direct selling process can be both a boon and a curse, robbing them of weekends with family, and often requiring significant logistical investment in travel, inventory and stall fixtures, not to mention the mental effort of retail work. But it is also the case that craft fairs are a tried and true means by which to 'get out there' and start selling: 'that one can get started for relatively little money, receive feedback from customers, and build a clientele. ... From the customer's perspective, the personal nature of the transaction is also key' (Kelly 2003, p. 234). But as we have already seen, the craft economy is not just about the final (handmade) product with most craft workers having to cultivate a diverse portfolio of activities to piece together an income stream. Some are able to do so within the space provided by their practice, for instance, through teaching, offering apprenticeships, designing patterns and selling making kits; others still work in other sectors of the economy or seek social security payments as a means by which to top up or subsidize their creative work. A rare few have their practice subsidized through arts or other practice-specific grant programmes. In her chapter, Xin Gu outlines many of these complexities, locating craft within contemporary debates around the creative industries, including the ways in which craft work has been profoundly impacted by digital technologies, and the ways in which craft start-ups have been a means of socio-economic inclusion, often for young people, as well as located at the forefront of urban renewal strategies, such as Renew Newcastle in Australia.

Craft, the 'handmade' and contested commodification

Adamson's cautionary warning referred to earlier comes into its own in this collection in those chapters specifically exploring craft and the contests that come into play once it enters the economic sphere. Craft is notable in the contemporary consumer marketplace for its connection to the skill of particular makers and the claims around being 'handmade' it can make. The post-Etsy online craft marketplace represents a profound expansion of the market, one enabled in part by new kinds of digital making tools which present a particular challenge to conventional understandings of the handmade. Of note here too is the contemporary strength of the figure of the designer-maker. The emphasis on 'design' as well as 'making' here flags the possibility of legitimated modes of scaling up production lines of 'bread and butter' work, which may or may not be produced by the actual hands of the given designer-maker. Or indeed anyone's hand in the case of the on-demand customized production made possible by 3D printing and companies such as Shapeways (https://www.shapeways.com).

What is lost or gained through the current bringing together of 'design' and 'craft', on the back of the previous iteration of status sought through a greater alignment of craft with the world of art, remains to be fully seen, though some challenging trends are clearly emerging. For example, in his contribution, Ezra Shales drawing upon some high-profile British case studies explores how contemporary throwers of prototypes on the wheel – 'ghost potters' – perceive their labour, especially when their job is to exaggerate signs of craftsmanship. More positively, digital tools, scalable design and localized small-scale production also offer up potential responses to making and living in an age of climate change. Using as a starting point economist E. F. Schumacher's 1960s era ideas around appropriate technology (AT), Gabriele Oropallo engages with the idea of 'enoughness' to trace a genealogical connection between AT and contemporary practices such as the repair and making movements. Both favour labour-intensive approaches to manufacturing as opposed to capital-intensive ones as the basis for a more sustainable way of being. Also with a focus on craft's links with niche manufacturing, Chris Gibson and Chantel Carr similarly challenge those of us in the Global North to consider what we really need to make and the conditions under which things are made, given the spectre of economic and environmental crisis. They seek to bring culture and creativity into greater dialogue with material work and production to consider what kinds of reconfigurations of labour-capital-technology relations niche and craft-based forms of manufacturing creativity bring with them, and how such smaller scale manufacturing might engage with the skills of those made redundant from more traditional manufacturing industries.

Certainly, digital technologies such as additive manufacturing, Computer Numerical Control routing and laser sintering all operate quantitatively to potentially enable makers to speed or scale up whole production processes or parts thereof. But beyond their newness, do such technologies actually represent a qualitative paradigm shift jeopardizing the very nature of what it means to make something by hand, or will they eventually settle down to be considered just another tool, like a hammer or kiln, in the maker's repertoire? Sonja Andrew and Kandy Diamond draw upon their own textile practices to reflect upon how digital technology can be integrated with more traditional textile skills and practices. In so doing, they make the case for digital making as part of an authentic approach to craft and offer strategies for its incorporation, while also acknowledging the ambiguous status of digital tools as part of hand making processes in the eyes of audiences and consumers. But even if and when what are now new digital making technologies settle into the continuum that is contemporary craft practice, complex questions around skill, value, scale and the essence of hand making remain. What skill is and means, and how a global market accustomed to cheap mass-manufactured goods and able to choose between a similar handmade product from a maker in a high cost of living country to someone in a lower one values skilled practice, are further issues facing contemporary craftspeople. The geographic distance from the actual 'hand' of the maker can today be substantial. Maintaining price points in such a marketplace is a complex balancing act, a situation exacerbated by the entry into the market of many new consumers untrained in identifying quality even when an object is in the hand, let alone over the distance of the internet.

The work of craft

Clearly, we can see here that contemporary craft economies are bringing into being new models of work, alongside work practices that have persisted for millennia. The training required to prepare graduates and the support needed by all craft practitioners today concerns not only their creative practice per se, but also a full gamut of understanding about how to locate oneself in this complex economic and artistic landscape, and the potential implications of one's decisions. All the while, as Julia Bennett writes in this volume drawing upon a study commissioned by the UK Crafts Council into the British crafts education sector, across much of the Global North we are seeing a de-skilling of craft makers as tertiary education providers seek to cut costs by winding back expensive, supervised studio-based training, instead bringing craft students into more conventional theory-based classrooms together with visual arts, architecture and/or design students. Moving forward, to fill this gap Bennett makes the case for the kinds specialist support provided by sectorial organizations such as the Crafts Council programmes Hothouse, Injection and Firing Up.

Despite its ambiguous status as a recognized creative industry, craft has long been an iconically precarious form of work, which in its emphasis on the need to piece together multiple income streams, making identities and even jobs, exemplifies the kinds of vulnerable protean (Bridgstock 2005) or portfolio careers now mainstreamed across the creative economy. Gender is key here. Not only is such precarity and casualization widely referred to as the 'feminisation' of the workforce, but also craft's often devalued status as both an artistic field and a serious occupation has long been challenged by the predominance of women as craft makers (Parker 1984). Nonetheless, alongside wider governmental policy encouragement for individualized risk-taking via self-employment, women's craft micro-enterprise is very much on the rise. As Jakob's has observed, 'No longer a sequestered and quaint domestic leisure activity, crafts and DIY ... have redefined their images and social stigmas with progressive agendas of emancipation, individualization, sub-cultural identification and anti-commercialism as well as emerged as a multibillion-dollar industry' (Jakob 2013, p. 127). That is, 'Crafts are currently being rediscovered not only as a hobby but also as a desirable enterprise' (Jakob 2013, p. 127). And not only for women, as Banks has observed craft labour appears 'to be becoming more, rather than less, significant to creative industry production and policy-making' in an economic climate where creation chains are increasingly constituted by smaller, contingently linked sites of production (Banks 2010, p. 306).

Especially factoring in global practices of craft production (including both traditional and modern as well as social enterprise forms), what craft work looks like today, and what a craft career may look like and how it might be built, all operate across a diverse field of opportunity and risk. Despite the winding back of many of the governmental grants programmes previously supporting craft art practice, the shift to a focus on entrepreneurial creative industries does indeed enable a different set of possibilities today. On the upside, the barriers to entry are lower with the internet, and social media in particular, enabling many makers to bypass traditional gatekeepers. On the down side, however, as with much of the rest of the creative economy, this is a crowded marketplace, notable for its high risks and low returns. It is also a marketplace that requires new forms of business skills development alongside practice-based expertise, including the capacity to brand, market and sell the self as part of the value of your work. Thus, drawing upon findings from a major three-year study of Australian designer-makers, Susan Luckman and Jane Andrew critically explore the kinds of new 'self-making' skills required to succeed in this competitive environment.

The entrepreneurial possibilities for craft being touted above are not limited to wealthy economies. Craft-based social enterprises, long supported by global development agencies such as UNESCO, are also experiencing substantial growth in the global marketplace for craft and design. New organizations can themselves set up global shopfronts on the internet, selling local 'world craft' (Murray 2010) products transnationally, either directly or through agencies. First, nations and traditional artists are thus able to find new markets for their skills (e.g. Bima Wear, http://bimawear.com/about/; the Tjanpi Desert Weavers of Central Australia, https://tjanpi.com.au; Cooper-Hewitt's 'Design for the other 90%', http://www.designother90.org), albeit into markets and with products often mediated by external (Western/minority world) designers. Notably too, such initiatives also flourish in the Global North itself, often as a means to provide socio-economic inclusion to displaced peoples, including migrant and refugee communities (CUCULA, https://www.cucula.org/en/; The Social Outfit, https://thesocialoutfit.org; Livstycket, http://www.livstycket.com/01.start/start_eng.htm). Arguably less well known are similar initiatives targeting peripheral workers (such as poor crafters) in postindustrial regions of the Global North who have been marginalized by dominant understandings of the economy. In her chapter, Jessica Barnes explores two such US arts entrepreneurship models: Etsy's The Craft Entrepreneurship Program (targeting crafting microbusinesses in economically depressed areas in the Bronx, New York, and Rockford, Illinois), and a Columbus, Ohio, group called Women Crafting Change. She finds mixed success, but similarly to Jakob's own US studies (2013), a clear pattern of low wages and women seeking out craft as a family-friendly alternative to conventional employment.

Craft-driven place-making and transnational circuits of craft practice

Celebrating place-specific associations has become a prominent feature of the current craft zeitgeist, with the desire to support local economies and makers part of a response to economic and environmental challenges. Unpicking discourses of the 'local' can lead us to challenge an inward, parochial, place-bound understanding of the local, instead pointing to the way in which 'place' is always formed in relationships that extend well beyond any perceived boundary (following the arguments of Doreen Massey 1991). The archaeological and contemporary record of handmade objects frequently reminds us that the exchange and trade of ideas, materials, process and forms has always bound together makers and consumers, whether living in the same settlement or many thousands of miles apart. These relations become visible as the maker sources their materials from suppliers, or as they sell their work to customers through direct or online sales. Exchanges in aesthetics and form become visible, for example, within the transnational market as a potter, who draws inspiration from the Japanese Mingei folk movement, sends their work to be sold overseas in a Japanese department store. The production of fairly traded handwoven cloth, made into fashionable garments, designed for a particular market, captures a complex relationship that binds producers, designers and consumers in a symbolic and economic relationship that reaches across continents. Many of these social and material relationships are fused with an ethics of care that unites the desire for good labour and the aesthetics of work that the Arts and Crafts Movement espoused.

What is sometimes more difficult to judge is the provenance of materials and the supply chains that enable the 'local' or ideas of 'authenticity' to be produced, and the value the market places on less visible forms of labour. Within this volume Stephen Marotta and Charles Heying interrogate ideas of localism, to explore what 'Made in' really means. The challenge for makers working with ideas of the local, selling into 'authenticity' and making within a local market, is the need to sustain their businesses over a longer time period and to maintain a dynamic interest in their own work, while feeding a marketplace that comes to expect a certain style. Craft practice in local areas is often porous because practitioners in the craft economy have long recognized the need to source materials and distribute their work far and wide, in order to achieve a good livelihood.

The dominant marketing narrative of crafted work involves telling the makers' story and how they produce the work they have for sale. The 'hand of the maker' is a key narrative in such stories, placing attention on the skilled work and hours of labour that go into making an item. These 'making stories' are often woven into place-based narratives with evocative tours of studios, daily practices of observing, sketching and collecting, bound into making landscapes that feed the consumers' imagination with ideals of a handcrafted life. Consumers might buy into this handcrafted life, through their own practice, noted through the rise of classes and tuition, or through the acquisition of items that can be styled in their own homes. Consumers might access makers' work and stories in increasingly complex ways. What is ever-present, in pop-up initiatives as described by Ella Harris in this volume, or at fairs, festivals, open studios, trade shows, online shops or virtual exhibitions, is the maker, with attention placed on their skilled labour, and often an opportunity to witness (in real life or through film) the process of making.

The symbolic value of crafted objects that have come to be associated with specific places, perhaps through the quality of the product, the dogged determination of generations of makers, the rarity of the process or the cachet associated with it has resulted in associations of place that are entangled with the product itself. These associations have long histories supported by 'industrial atmospheres' noticed by economist Alfred Marshall in 1919 that have enabled the interdependencies between competing firms or makers to generate a sustained presence that secures a places' reputation for quality of a product and the associated market over many generations. In this volume Troy Zhen Chen addresses the example of Sanbao in Jingdezhen, Jiangxi Province in China, famed for the production of porcelain, and which is now navigating the emergence of a strong creative industries agenda supported by the Chinese government.

The place of craft within the contemporary creative economy, as we have noted, is a contested one. Where a place has a deep history of craft practice, with an associated contemporary craft sector, the decisions made by those creating policy to support the sector are revealing of the value placed on the craft sector and those that work within it. Craft as a tool for economic regeneration has been present throughout the twentieth century and continues to be turned to in the hope of supporting local and regional industry (Thomas, Harvey, and Hawkins 2012). Within this volume Sara Teasley steps inside the networks of crafts manufacturers in Yamagata, Japan, to explore the interplay of the longer history of craft production in the area with recent attempts to promote and develop the craft industry through formal policy routes. The promotion of economic development through place-based approaches such as the denotation of 'Craft Towns' as a form of destination marketing, or through tourism initiatives and awards, needs to be placed alongside other initiatives which do not primarily prioritize market exchange, but value the skills and knowledge of the makers themselves.

The UNESCO 2003 Convention for the Safeguarding of Intangible Cultural Heritage is one such example of international action to secure the intergenerational knowledge and skills to produce traditional crafts. In safeguarding skills and knowledge, UNESCO aims to ensure the viability of the transferring of skills and meaning across generations, not just the specific form of skilled practice itself (UNESCO, n.d.). In this respect it allows for change within the community of practice, countering the charge of stifling innovation through observance of a fixed practice. It is interesting to consider the effect of such schemes as they feed back into the creative economy. Japan adopted the scheme of 'Holder of an Important Intangible Cultural Property' in 1950 and made the first designations for crafts in 1955 to individuals practicing with high levels of mastery. Referred to as 'Living National Treasures' these individuals are charged with passing on their skills in areas of the craft and the performing arts. As Goto (2013, p. 581) notes, the approach adopted within Japan has been to support the ongoing utilization of materials, techniques and skills which are 'allowed to evolve adjusting to industrial surroundings and the market', and are acknowledged as a 'very important source for creative industry and high-tech industries'. Thus, the intangible gains a highly tangible place in the contemporary market place.

Technology, innovation and craft

With an eye to the future, the final section of the *Craft Economies* collection returns to many of the themes of technology and crafting futures prefigured otherwise throughout the volume. Valuably, following the rupture around the Industrial Revolution identified by Adamson earlier, the section's authors (re)connect craft with its origins in strong relationship to making and manufacturing, technology and science. That is, to the long history of craftspeople working with high technology, and especially in materials innovation: prototyping and making maquettes for industry, customized prosthesis design, glass blowing for scientific instruments. The potentialities of legacy materials intermixed with emergent technologies and processes is a core exploratory focus of Material Matters, a research cluster within the Intersections Digital Studios of Emily Carr University of Art+Design. In their contribution to the volume, Keith Doyle, Hélène Day Fraser and Philip Robins detail two avenues of their recent work within ceramic and textile methodologies: 3D printing developments and their potential relationship to ceramic-based processes (mould making, slip casting, encaustic tile production) and initial 'proof of concept' work tying the inherent build quality of filament-based 3D printers with traditional woven/knit/sewn (threaded) structures.

Today craft continues to exist alongside both niche and mass manufacturing: in the car industry, engineering and aeronautics. Materials innovation is occurring around new fibres and smart materials (e.g. the production of new fibres from algae). Women have played a long and proud part in the history of fabric (material) science and have often come from different backgrounds to extend the boundaries of materials and making. The celebrated weaver Theo Moorman worked on technical fibres in the Second World War in the Ministry of Aircraft Production (Moorman 1999), and, in another context, Kevlar was created by Stephanie Kwolek in the labs of DuPont. As we have seen across this collection, the skills of craft traverse into and across other fields of production, including manufacture, and vice versa. As just one example, Gail Kenning and Jo Law's chapter explores how digital media and computational technologies can be used to mimic and, more importantly, remediate and extend craft-based textiles. Thus, in this and a myriad of other ways, rather than diluting the uniqueness of craft, its people, skills, materials and practices variously sit along a long continuum of tools and ways in which the engagement of craft with technology has long been fluid. Importantly here today we are starting to see a revaluing of craft skills and understandings within the innovation context, including for the contribution it can make to sustainable climate futures (such as lower-impact production-consumption-recycling cycles).

Additive manufacturing/3D printing is poised to revolutionize rapid prototyping, craft customization and on-demand production, on small- as well as large-scale making. It will potentially reverse 'perhaps the greatest blow against the artisan two centuries ago, namely the establishment of means of production too large and complex for any individual to afford' (McCullough 2010, p. 315). Thus, one of the key challenges moving forward is access to not only the technologies but also the skills to engage meaningfully with these emerging possibilities. The collective has a long and proud history and present in the story of craft; today social enterprises, co-working spaces, artist-run initiatives and co-operatives sit proudly alongside emergent sites of making such as Fablabs and have much to teach them about shared making spaces. The maker's movement still remains too distant from craft, with the effect that such facilities remain largely ahistorical, not benefitting from the lessons of the past around the challenges of genuine social inclusion around making. One such legacy to learn from was the nineteenth-century Mechanics Institute movement, which was influential across much of the British Commonwealth. It failed when it became a middle-class social salon, not a genuinely inclusive facility though which to share useful knowledge across the population. Craft has much to offer the maker's movement around what organizational models work for the range of collectivized spaces available, how people access tools and equipment they need only infrequently and what happens when these commercialize. To this end, Angelina Russo's chapter considers the questions: What innovations must occur in maker expertise so that designers and craftspeople can engage most productively with emerging digital fabrication practices, and how can these new making practices be embedded all the way through new modes of knowledge production in order to achieve innovations in product development? Meanwhile, the final chapter in this collection takes a slightly different tack to the others, using craft as a set of practices and metaphor by which to organize a more socially inclusive computer coding community. Drawing upon their experience with the Dublin Pyladies coding group, Sophia Maalsen and Sung-Yueh Perng intersect gender, relations of making and places of making nested firmly within the digital world to 'craft' a digital making space in which women feel included and valued, thus 'hacking' into the male gendered spaces of coding and open source communities.

But this is not all about the 'new' as fetish as the return to traditional and sustainable materials such as indigo dyes and willow indicates. Importantly, craft's value as it intersects across the craft economy is part of a larger re-connection to making and a sensibility towards innovation in the popular public imaginary. It is also part of a larger call to ethics, including to thinking about the interconnected relationships that are experienced globally through production, recycling and reprocessing. Making and materials innovation is clearly needed. This is why we need to see craft economies as not simply one-way chains leading to closed-off consumption, but as part of larger circuits of use and reuse, where demand increasingly drives more ethically attentive practices of production and consumption, and thus why this connection has as its core focus around craft and the social and material relations of economic value.

Acknowledgements

While this two-volume collection has morphed into something (epically) larger, it has its origins in the 'Placing Cultural Work: (New) Intersections of Location, Craft and Creativity' symposium held at the Open University's London (Camden) campus in November 2013. Jointly funded by the Open University, UK, and the University of South Australia, the event was co-organized by Susan Luckman and Mark Banks, now Professor of Culture and Communication and Director of CAMEo Research Institute for Cultural and Media Economies at the University of Leicester, and we would very much like to thank Mark for making this event, and this collection, possible. We also owe a huge thanks to Rebecca Barden, Claire Constable, Abbie Sharman, and the team at Bloomsbury UK. They have been incredibly supportive of this highly ambitious two-volume collection from the very beginning, and beyond patient with all the delays and complexities involved in bringing together work from so many people. We can't thank you enough. We of course also wish to thank all the contributors for being willing to share their work with us here. Similarly, a big thank you also goes to the JamFactory Contemporary Craft & Design, and Andre Castellucci and Sophie Guiney in particular, for letting us use Andre's photo of the JamFactory's homewares collection featuring THROWN ceramics and JAMJAR Storage Jar on the cover. Finally, Susan would like to acknowledge the funding provided by the Hawke EU Centre for Mobilities, Migrations and Cultural Transformations at the University of South Australia in 2016 to visit Exeter to work with Nicola on the finishing editorial touches, and also the Australian Research Council's Discovery Project funding scheme (project number DP150100485), which supported the research from which the quote used above in the Introduction is drawn. Finally, words cannot describe the debt owed to Martin and Rob; as always, thank you.

References

Adamson, G. (2013), *The Invention of Craft*, London: Bloomsbury.
Adorno, T. (1979), 'Functionalism today', *Oppositions*, 17: 30–41.
BOP Consulting. (2012), *Craft in an Age of Change*, Commissioned by Crafts Council, Creative
    Scotland, Arts Council of Wales, and Craft Northern Island, London: BOP Consulting.
Bridgstock, R. (2005), 'Australian artists, starving and well-nourished: What can we learn from the
    prototypical protean career?', *Australian Journal of Career Development*, 14 (3): 40–8.
Department for Culture, Media & Sport. (2013), *Classifying and Measuring the Creative Industries:
    Consultation on Proposed Changes*, London: Media & Sport Department for Culture.

Goto, K. (2013), 'Policy for intangible cultural heritage in Japan: How it relates to creativity', in I. Rizzo and A. Mignosa (eds.), *Handbook on the Economics of Cultural Heritage*, Cheltenham: Edward Elgar Publishing.

Harrod, T. (2015), *The Real Thing: Essays on Making in the Modern World*, London: Hyphen Press.

Heritage Crafts Association. (2017), *The Radcliffe Red List of Endangered Crafts*, http://heritagecrafts.org.uk/redlist/ (accessed 30 May 2017).

Jakob, D. (2013), "Crafting your way out of the recession?: New craft entrepreneurs and the global economic downturn", *Cambridge Journal of Regions, Economy and Society*, 6: 127–40.

Jakob, D. and N. J. Thomas. (2015), "Firing up craft capital: The renaissance of craft and craft policy in the United Kingdom", *International Journal of Cultural Policy*, 23 (4): 495–511.

Kelly, M. (2003), "Seeking authenticity in the marketplace", *The Journal of Popular Culture*, 37 (2): 220–43.

Marshall, A. (1919), *Industry and Trade*, London: Macmillan.

Massey, D. (1991), 'A global sense of place', *Marxism Today*, (38) June: 24–9.

McCullough, M. (2010), "Abstracting craft: The practiced digital hand", in G. Adamson (ed.), *The Craft Reader*, Oxford: Berg.

Moorman, T. (1999, first published 1975), *Weaving as an Art Form: A Personal Statement*, West Chester: Schiffer Publishing Ltd.

Murray, K. (2010), "Outsourcing the hand: An analysis of craft-design collaborations across the global divide", *Craft + Design Enquiry*, 2: 59–73.

Parker, R. (1984), *The Subversive Stitch: Embroidery and the Making of the Feminine*, London: The Women's Press.

Thomas, N. J., D. C. Harvey and H. Hawkins. (2012), "Crafting the region: Creative industries and practices of regional space", *Regional Studies*, 47 (1): 75–88.

UNESCO. (n.d.), *What is Intangible Cultural Heritage?*, https://ich.unesco.org/en/what-is-intangible-heritage-00003 (accessed 30 May 2017).

PART ONE

Craft, making and the creative economy

2

Crafts community

Physical and virtual

Xin Gu

Introduction

In an article in the *New Yorker*, 'Making It – pick up a spot welder and join the revolution' (2014) Evgeny Morozov argued that the current 'Maker movement' was less about revolution and more in line with neo-liberal capitalism, being all about 'middle-class lifestyles', 'consumerism' and 'D.I.Y. tinkering'. By placing too much hope on materials, tools and the skills they require, he argued we lose focus on the real problem, that of *capitalist* industrialization. Making disguises the fact that we are normalizing a practice of 'doing more with less' (Morozov 2014).

'Doing more with less' was evident in the promotion of creative entrepreneurship associated with the 'creative industries', a landmark piece of cultural policy introduced by the New Labour government in the UK in 1997 and has been criticized lately for its neo-liberal agendas (cf. Hewison 2014). As O'Connor (2010) argued, the idea of the creative industries was more than just being innovative in your own bedroom. It sought to address some key problems of postindustrial Britain – how to promote new industries and jobs and re-tool the workforce now that industry policy levers had been abolished by Margaret Thatcher. But the creative industries were 'policy lite' (O'Connor 2016). The emphasis on individual creativity and entrepreneurialism was also about making the most of your resources in order to survive in an increasingly competitive and rapidly changing society. The widespread promotion of creativity focused on people's ability to self-educate and self-direct as part of that 'entrepreneurship of the self' that, as Angela McRobbie (2016) has argued, has now become almost second nature. The flip side of this injunction to 'be creative' has been the erosion of more traditional social values embedded in 'cultural work'. Sennett has argued this for contemporary work as a whole (Sennett 2008), as has McRobbie (2016) and others in specific field of cultural work (Banks 2007, Hesmondhalgh et al. 2015), where 'networking' becomes parasitical on other, longer term, forms of social bonding.

The 'sociality of creative industries' (Grabher 1997) has not just been about oiling the wheels of an agglomeration economy but is also essential to the independent arts and craftsperson's ability to survive in difficult market conditions (Gu 2014). The precarious market in which small-scale independent cultural workers operate – and crafts workers represent a classic case here – are exacerbated by the lack of union representation and labour protection. Social networks here operate to create a sense of 'community' as much as they facilitate information flows and the efficient arrangement of project working. The 'community effects' of the sociality of cultural workers have been ignored in the turn to creative industries as about ideas and innovation (exemplified in the absorption of 'crafts' into a wider 'design sector'). This has been a process of de-materialization which has focused on 'creativity' as IP and 'design' as styling, at the expense of complex cultural economies of production and making, and their real socio-spatial contexts. Cities, which in the 1990s were positioned as centres of agglomerated production, witnessed this de-materialization as a shift from production to consumption economies, with networks of production displaced by chains of consumption. The workshop becomes boutique display. However the consumption chain was organized, it paid little attention to the sociality of those who supplied it.

As if in compensation for this spatial displacement of production by consumption, from the turn of the millennium, craftspeople were offered a new direct, democratic access to a global market no longer marked by the exclusionary tyranny of distance. If the 1970s and 1980s 'countercultural revolution' has dreamed about the possibility of the equality of the big and the small, peer-to-peer (P2P) websites like *Etsy* began to present real possibilities for empowering independents and consumers. The internet was seen as a democratizing tool, offering opportunities for 'indies' to be taken more seriously by connecting them with global markets. According to ABS data, craft is a high-growth area in Australia's cultural economy (ABS 2007). The number of people involved in the sector nearly doubled between 2004 and 2007. A total of 960,000 people were involved in craft activities accounting for most of the 200 per cent growth in the overall visual art sector (ABS 2007). Etsy is a key factor in the growth as it significantly lowers market entry for SMEs.[1] But what is ironic in the 'Etsyfication' of the crafts sector is, as Luckman pointed out, the 'analogue' versus the 'digital' (Luckman 2013). As the material qualities of making, of craftsmanship and of an appreciation of tradition and quality become instrumental in the recent revival of the crafts economy, the physical distance between consumers and makers has never been so wide. In Australia, the over-reliance on Etsy by local small crafts producers keen to sell internationally exemplifies new tendencies in the 'globalization of cultural economy' (Appadurai 2006). This is already a key shaping force for the local fashion industry, that is, the increasing emptying out of what it meant to be 'local' (Weller 2007). When conducting research on the crafts sector in Newcastle, NSW, Marcus Westbury discovered that over 70 per cent of Australian Etsy sales are to international markets (Westbury 2015b). However, with its increasing popularity, Etsy also has to face increasing criticism from indie communities as to how well the politics of the crafts community can be matched by the platform's need to extract value from the unique individual identity of these independent makers. I will address this as a key changing condition of cultural work in the sector – that is, the need for local craftspeople to coordinate a globally networked 'niche' cultural economy. This will have implications for other cultural sectors operating at the interface of the 'digital' and the 'analogue'.

Towards a renewed understanding of work in the crafts economy

Scholarly observations on cultural work linking to the 'independents' seem to agree on the nature of work in the sector, namely precarity tied to various forms of self-exploitation (cf. Ross 2010; McRobbie 2016). Mark Banks (2007) argues that this problem can be related to a 'Foucauldian' model where 'labour discipline' does not come from external coercion but from an internalization of wider organizational or social goals. The construction of an independent, entrepreneurial identity where one's career emerges out of one's own creativity and commitment is precisely the route by which industrial organizations shift responsibility for success and failure onto the shoulders of individuals (McRobbie 2002). For writers such as Boltanski and Chiapello (2005), this points to the capture of the whole artistic critique of capitalism – the worker's need for self-fulfilment, individual expression, meaningful work and so on – by newly restructured 'connexionist' capitalism, where the self becomes an individual enterprise. Within this environment, creative producers take responsibility for their own failure, and work harder than ever, only to fall further into self-exploitation. The arrival of 'digitalization' was supposed to change the fundamental condition of cultural work via the eradication of market barriers, which in turn changes the organization of work that is increasingly organized throughout globalized networks such as Etsy. It is a complex issue and beyond the scope of this chapter. However, it is possible to see the limitation of the process of digitalization in solving the labour problem in the crafts economy. Through the development of Etsy, we can observe forces taking place in the crafts economy that could potentially worsen the condition of work, and I will start by re-assessing the notion of 'creative entrepreneurship'.

The rise of SMEs, micro-businesses and freelancers within the craft, as well as other sectors of the creative economy, was a key characteristic of the broadly identified creative industries. Leadbeater's *Living on Thin Air* (2000) argued that talent would always shine through in this economy that places a premium on human capital. Values such as 'choice, autonomy and satisfaction' have attracted many creatives, and democratizing technologies have made self-employment more possible than ever before.

This notion of creative entrepreneurship was largely criticized by labour studies in the creative industries blaming it for self-exploitation when measured against the rewards that are gained from this kind of work (Banks 2007; Gill 2007; Ursell 2006). Ursell's (2006) work revealed that the passion, resilience and determination of people in these work situations were based on their belief that their identity can be secured only through self-actualization, creativity and social recognition. This is the route to self-exploitation as the individual takes on an increased number of responsibilities (Banks 2007). There is also the sheer excitement and vitality of a scene – 'the intoxicating pleasure of leisure culture' (McRobbie 2002) – which is easily overlooked but which animates many creative people and secures their sense of identity (Currid 2007).

The digital revolution in the creative industries has made the most out of the notion of 'creative entrepreneurship' and the democratization of 'creativity' (Hartley 2005). But many have questioned the 'success' that digitalization has brought (Taylor 2014). Digital platforms may provide easier market access for SMEs but market success (whether online or offline) was never the sole criterion of cultural value, nor its sole motivation (O'Connor 2016). The reliance on digital 'tools' such as Etsy risks the loss of the ability to identify these cultural values, as the platform simply registers sales made. These platforms also make the local market less important to the activities of local makers and further de-couples makers from personal interaction with their markets and their immediate social contexts.

The notion of craft was never just about skills and quality of work – or rather, these were always linked to socially embedded ethical practices. Richard Sennett in *The Craftsman* (2008) argued for a valuation of the skills involved in the handling of the inherent qualities of the material, of the performance of a task 'for its own sake'. He also emphasized the social space and time required for such craftsman-like attention and that this was being eroded in contemporary capitalism. In any approach to the crafts economy we have to address the kinds of social space and time (or lack thereof) in which this takes place. I suggest here that the tendency of digital platforms to flatten time and space will exacerbate the problems experienced by SMEs in the crafts economy.

First, despite the globalization of local crafts market, making is still very much a local phenomenon. The crafts sector has a reputation as a cottage industry with most of the work carried out in-house by makers themselves. There is a strong sense of being 'plugged in' to a scene. The pleasure of being 'part of something' is a promise of being true to oneself and one's ambitions, of continuing to be an active player in a world one has made one's own. It is true that the ambitions that drive many craftspeople interweave artistic and commercial success. However, their sense of what is aesthetically 'right' and their ability to have control over this is crucial to their identity. There is an equally strong sense of doing something because it is 'good' and giving something back to the local community was a part of that. Such 'irrational' consideration (irrational in the sense that the pursuit of these values may impede the economic performance of these businesses) also contributes to the vibrancy of a local creative scene further strengthening the symbolic value of the crafts economy. All of the above are often projects of self-construction embedded in local cultural tradition and customs. To the extent that digitalization replaces the 'local' with the 'global', it threatens to further undermine the independent's ability to establish the sociocultural space of the local.

Secondly, the key organizational structure for the crafts economy is social networking – the formation of the local crafts communities through which people can meet and exchange ideas. It is exemplary of the sociality of creative industries. These are not simply spaces in which new entrepreneurs can form and come through to success, part of the classic creative industries churn; what they provide is a cultural and social value in itself. It is the strong sense of wishing to contribute towards producing something locally distinct, and recognized as such, by their peers that animates many craftspeople. This is what drives them despite the potential economic cost of staying in this industry, but nor is this mere compensation for economic failure. Digital platforms are not equivalent to the kinds of social spaces that local crafts communities provide. For example, many craftspeople have expressed concern about the shoddiness, the misuse of materials and the cutting of corners that some wholesale Etsy businesses have engaged in, practices deeply opposed by independent craftspeople. These anxieties find no expression within Etsy and other such digital spaces.

In the virtual world, community peer pressure is less able to form a collective identity with values that can be brought to bear in the global marketplace. What's the difference between a cute pinnable object made by a Melbourne maker and one from a maker from Newcastle, Australia, to a buyer from London? This has increasingly become a problem for the Etsy crafts community – how to communicate local cultural and ethical 'brand' value on a global trading platform. The success of Etsy is predicated on similar values to those in physical communities, claiming similarly to be a space within which a shared cultural understanding of particular tastes, ethical standards and lifestyle choices can be communicated and appreciated. As the Etsy mission statement has it,

> In an Etsy Economy, creative entrepreneurs can find meaningful work selling their goods in both global and local markets, where thoughtful consumers can discover those goods and build relationships with people who make and sell them.[2]

But these intangible values become increasingly unattainable as Etsy ascends to global success story. The gradual change in the philosophy of Etsy from promoting the more laid-back cottage industry style towards more professional self-marketing strategies was a key problem here. The difference between doing business in a local market and doing business on Etsy lies in its 'randomness'. But as has already been acknowledged, crafts businesses have never been just about business; personal values also play an important role. The producer–consumer relationship here is ideally a choice based on personal values rather than on an abstract concept of 'transaction'. In the virtual world, it is difficult to layer those values with business transactions. Such alliances are further formed and influenced by shared interests, lifestyles and other social and cultural values. Interpersonal relationships here are more 'narrative' than 'informational' (Wittel 2001); that is, they build on shared stories developed over time and they are more likely to survive through the ups and downs of economic conditions. The identity of the maker may be turned into a business opportunity, but the exchange between makers and their clients could be a long-term one, living on through the object even beyond ongoing direct contact. In this way, a kind of brand loyalty can be achieved by aligning it with the concept of 'friendship'. But on *Etsy*, customer loyalty is fluid and hard to guarantee.

Lastly, it is important to recognize the craftspeoples' ultimate desire for defending their commitment to a certain level of craft skill. It gives them a sense of purpose, a kind of justification, for their persisting in difficult circumstances. The commitment to doing the job properly is rooted in a social context, as is the recognition of the craftsman's skills and his/her valuation as an ethical model. This was not compensated when moving online. In the virtual marketplace, it is the ability to 're-invent oneself' – the marketing and PR skills that count. This entrepreneurial principle ('sell yourself') in the virtual space based on the flattening of time and space constantly runs in conflict with a commitment to refining a specific set of aesthetic and technical skills. Writing about her own experience with Etsy, Grace Dobush expressed how the maker's identity becomes secondary to sales figures, heralding an absorption by the mainstream market: '*Etsy* has grown from a startup built by crafters and for crafters to a juggernaut on the verge of an IPO … So while *Etsy* maintains a hipster façade, they lost their indie cred years ago' (Dobush 2015). Comments like those from Grace might be conceived as 'irrational' by mainstream business practitioners, but are common within the crafts community operating as it is in a restrictive market.

Though many crafts businesses continue to use Etsy in order to make a living, they simultaneously attempt to distance themselves from Etsy's profit maximization strategy, one that many feel threatens to undermine their integrity as craftspeople. Craftspeople like Dobush are not reacting against 'the market' as such, but against what they perceive as the wrong kind of market. While the internet has opened up new global markets, it has 'disembedded' those markets both from the spatial and the communal context in which the objects are made, and from the close relationship between buyer and seller so important for maker cultures. This does not have to be a fetishization of the face-to-face transaction, just a recognition that the internet brings new challenges in terms of establishing shared aesthetic and ethical values. Without attention to these, as increasingly is the case with Etsy, the market follows a logic of economies of scale and of marketing, which drives out a lot of the quality. As Dobush (2015) exclaimed, the market for independent designs is not in Etsy but elsewhere!

Following recent debates on Etsy has prompted me to move beyond the question of whether digitalization democratizes the creative industries playing fields, as the answer is now clearly demonstrated by the continuing power of the big corporations and the fact that, despite a few creative industry 'lottery winners', the majority of the businesses remain at survival levels. I think it is time to take back some of the hopes invested in digital platforms and try to reclaim some of the time required to make great work. Renew Newcastle has been presented below in order to illustrate some of my views. At the same time, I believe that it proposes a possible future without overriding the already ubiquitous 'digitalization' in many creative industries.

Crafts community as urban renewal: Renew Newcastle

The key relevance of Renew Newcastle (RN) to the above debate is that it shows processes of localization interlaced with globalization, 'digital' with 'analogue'. Many RN crafts businesses sell through Etsy to international markets. However, it is at the local city level that other important cultural and social values of the crafts economy are sustained and nurtured. Because of the 'materialization' of these other non-economic values at the local levels, the local crafts economy is able to achieve a certain economic success. Unlike the traditional 'creative clusters' development model now well understood by cities globally, RN, I argue, has presented another possibility in the age of digitalization and globalization. Taking the crafts economy as a whole, the economic outcomes might be insignificant to the city of Newcastle. However, the role the local crafts economy plays through its ability in positioning the city, as a nodal point of the global cultural economy, is important.

RN was set up in 2008 to help local arts and craftspeople to secure short-term cheap retail and work space in the city centre of Newcastle. One of Australia's oldest industrial cities, Newcastle suffered badly from the decline of traditional industries in the 1980s. The centre of Newcastle faced massive disinvestment and dereliction about which neither the city council nor the various developer-led schemes of the past twenty years seemed able to do anything. RN as a community-based enabling body was set up to act as an intermediary between the independent cultural sector and property owners in order to convince the latter to license their property for use to the former. It aimed to identify vacant buildings and to strike a deal for the short-term reactivation of these spaces by local maker communities. It should be noted that this position of 'intermediary' was not officially mandated by the cultural sector, the city nor the real estate sector, but was a task growing out of Westbury's long-term involvement with local craftspeople.

RN happened at the time when market for local crafts economy had increasingly shifted into the virtual market place. This has meant for many their work (as labour rather than product) is becoming increasingly 'invisible' and that the intersection of work and play, business and shared values has become disarticulated in social media platforms. Unlike high-street brands capable of

FIGURE 2.1 *The Stage* is managed by Renew Newcastle to provide cheap exhibition space for short-run local creative projects. Photo credit Edwina Richards c/o Renew Newcastle.

relocating mass manufacturing to cheaper labour markets, local craftspeople are in more need of physical spaces for small-scale in-house production and exhibition (see Figure 2.1). The increasing competition of retail spaces both online and offline leaves little room for the independents. This is the primary goal of the RN project – to resolve some tension between the local and the global, the aesthetic and business knowledge, and the 'intrinsic' and 'instrumental' dimensions of these communities. One of the key outcomes of the RN in achieving this goal is in how the local crafts community is able to build a collective identity through this process of urban renewal, to give something back to the city.

RN has been very successful in reducing vacancy rates in the Newcastle city centre, and doing so in a way that has boosted the image of the city. But some commentators have accused RN of being complicit with the city council in using artists for boosterish purposes (Munzner and Shaw 2014). However, the wider arts and crafts community in Newcastle broadly shared in this regeneration narrative, but they did so in a context of trust and mutuality of interest brokered through RN's clear commitment to addressing the spatial needs of that community. RN had always been upfront about its attempt to create a 'shared urban narrative' between the local community, the arts and crafts sector, the city council and the real estate industry, while acknowledging that the idea of working within an economic development agenda doesn't always sit comfortably with many arts and craftspeople. Westbury argued that an independent non-for-profit body representing the local cultural community was the only way to develop its potential to contribute to the long-term sustainability of Newcastle and to build trust across the different partners (Westbury 2015a). The provisional and multifaced regeneration narrative worked because of the way in which the aesthetic values of the craft community were positioned as the central voice in this narrative. The task of keeping this voice and the values it articulated central is one which RN has to constantly struggle with, across the normal vicissitudes of funding cuts, changes in council policy and personnel, various floated development schemes, and the persistent tendency in creative cities and creative industries policy discourses to become primarily economic (cf. O'Connor and Shaw 2014). Out of it all, the city certainly got an enhanced brand and a very successful regeneration narrative, but this was founded on an explicit recognition of the value of the 'creative' community to the city. Such recognition was taken as a validation of the real contribution of small independent arts and craftspeople to the city.

Neither RN nor those who were involved in the new spaces saw this as primarily about 'delivering economic growth'. Rather, they saw RN as allowing them to take a first step out of their bedrooms towards a potential career. As RN CEO Christopher suggested, RN is about removing market barriers for small-scale arts and crafts businesses in the real world. And what keeps the tensions of business and creativity in check is the sense of meaning and validation needed to survive outside of the mainstream economic context, for in these restricted economic circumstances, opportunities are scarcer, so to become part of the community one has to buy into the aesthetic and ethical commitment. This becomes more important in the era of digitalization when it is harder to 'rationalize' the uncertainty in the global market and local 'know-how' is the only thing which supplies any substance to the kinds of work they are involved in. Such understanding intersects with the urban context at a number of levels – occupying redundant inner-city shops and sponsoring a stand at the local marketplaces are the common practices. In the case of RN, through these creative practices, they were to help bring a derelict city centre back into active use.

Derelict city centres are not just a problem for city councils and property developers but represent a sense of collective failure and an absence of future (O'Connor and Gu 2010). Bringing back a historic CBD into active use through a maker culture represented an aesthetic and ethical validation of the values this community of practitioners held dear. Thus, the creation of a new spatial infrastructure also provided the sociocultural context for a revived creative ecosystem in Newcastle. The marginal spaces in which these crafts networks can form are crucial, despite their seemingly uneconomic dimension. These spaces are not simply workspaces but part of the 'affective community' that Pratt (2000) identifies with the urban spaces emerging out of the organization of a niche market. The close affiliation of lifestyle and identity with business practices has led to the emergence of an alternative urban space in which to identify with like-minded people. These communities have strong aesthetic and ethical bonds that are underpinned by spatial co-presence.

The success of RN rests to a large extent on its understanding that shared narrative works best when it is felt to represent not just 'industry needs' but also the social and cultural aspirations of the sector. This is not just about recognizing the reality of their business practices and tailoring services to help them, but also having a space in which to express anxieties about the dynamics of the sector itself. RN is therefore not just about brokering empty space but also about validating their contributions beyond 'economic impact'. It facilitated a shared narrative involving a claim to cultural validation based around a sense of the collective equity embedded in the urban built fabric, one that could act as a source of collective identification for the city as a whole. RN had a cultural political agenda, that it would represent the needs of the independent crafts sector not just to provide workspace but to represent the aspirations of the crafts sector at the wider city level. In terms of the economy of the crafts sector, the enhancement of the city's image would certainly strengthen this. But it has been very easy for the overly economic focus of creative industries strategies to ignore the social and cultural values that underpin creative ecologies.

Conclusion

Writing about the post-Etsy pro-am economy, Luckman reminded us it would be naïve to presume the current 'consumer-oriented' maker culture will bring real social changes (Luckman 2013, p. 265). Such thinking seems to echo the increasing scepticism around the democratizing power of the internet by Morozov (2014). But there are other issues here. Since the late 1980s, a combination of New Labour's 'creative industries' and Richard Florida's 'creative class' (Florida 2005) promoted creative industries as the driver of a new urban economy. In both of these policy agendas, usually under the broad rubric of 'design', craftspeople and latterly 'makers' have been centrally positioned as some kind of interface between art and commerce, aesthetics and materiality (O'Connor 2012). If the creative industries policy agenda has been increasingly, even exclusively, about economic growth (Foord 2009) then 'design' has often borne the brunt of the expectations for such growth. This has been particularly marked in the urban context where this growth is sought less in direct employment impacts and more in the symbolic value they bring to buildings, 'quarters' and even whole cities: symbolic value which translates into brand value for cities and real estate value for property developers.

Initiatives such as RN have further attempted to mobilize 'makers' for urban regeneration, but this is a regeneration defined in much broader terms than economic growth or city branding. It recognizes the role of arts and craftspeople in regeneration, in terms both of the quality of the 'urban' this regeneration seeks to produce and of the aesthetic and ethical qualities which they bring to it. At the same time, it aims to provide the spatial infrastructure required by this maker community, that is, access to cheap, flexible work and retail space which almost every commentator now highlights as coming under increasing threat in all creative – and not so creative – cities (cf. Shaw 2013). RN's spatial intervention inevitably raises issues around the complex matrix of economic, social and cultural imperatives at work in the arts and crafts sector. Most pointedly, it highlights the intersection of these imperatives with urban life at different levels, not just the reuse of space but also the collective identification with the built environment, and the ways in which the commitment to making interesting, beautiful, skillful, authentic new things can feed into the wider self-esteem of the city as a whole.

The contrast between the RN community and that of Etsy is not simply one of physical and virtual. Both kinds of community are easily inserted within more disembedded, or 'deterritorialized', economies that have little to do with the values their commodities claim to embody: the first that of the global real estate, the second, an aggregation of personal data that marks the new internet companies. Each has its challenges, but this is not about the authenticity of the real versus the 'fake' communality of the virtual. In both it is about a recognition of the social and cultural, the ethical and aesthetic values, at stake in crafts and maker culture. The demonization of the 'machine' in the earlier arts and crafts movement, the fetishization of the technological in the latter-day maker movement and the claims for the democratizing power of the internet – all in their different ways ignore the ways in which it is *capitalist* industrialization and postindustrialization that is at stake. From this perspective we can see the crafts movement completely differently to those promoters of the creative industries who see the 'design' industries as the interface between creativity and commercial innovation (cf. NESTA 2013). It can be seen as an attempt to retrieve a way of making a living through a certain kind of aesthetic production and exchange, one that has links to a sense of material qualities and skills, of tradition and community, as well as of creativity and innovation. It is certainly haunted by temptations of nostalgia, of smug overpriced middle-class consumption, of the aesthetic banalities of 'designer' goods. But, to return to Luckman's point, somewhere in here is a source of social change and renewal, of a culture of ends and means that can be of very great value.

Notes

1 This research is part of the Monash University Arts Faculty Seed Funding 2016 'maker culture in Melbourne', and interviews with local craftspeople have revealed the correlation between Etsy and the increase of SMEs.

2 See Etsy's mission statement. Available at https://www.etsy.com/au/mission. Last checked 18 September 2016.

References

ABS. (2007), 'Work in selected culture and leisure activities, Australia', *Australian Bureau of Statistics*, April 2007. Available online: http://www.abs.gov.au/Ausstats/abs@.nsf/lookupMF/D86A9FF41EC1D574CA2568A900139430 (accessed 1 April 2016).

Appadurai, A. (1990), 'Disjuncture and difference in the global cultural economy', *Theory, culture & society*, 7 (2): 295–310.

Banks, M. (2007), *The Politics of Cultural Work*, Basingstoke: Palgrave.

Boltanski, L. and E. Chiapello. (2005), *The New Spirit of Capitalism*, London: Verso.

Currid, E. (2007), *The Warhol Economy: How Fashion, Art, and Music Drive New York City*, Princeton: Princeton University Press.

Dobush, G. (2015), 'How Etsy alienated its crafters and lost its soul', *Wired*, 19 February. Available online: http://www.wired.com/2015/02/etsy-not-good-for-crafters/ (accessed 1 August 2015).

Florida, R. (2005), *Cities and the Creative Class*, New York: Routledge.

Foord, J. (2009), 'Strategies for creative industries: an international review', *Creative Industries Journal*, 1 (2): 91–113.

Gill, R. (2007), *Technobohemians or the New Cybertariat? New Media Work in Amsterdam a Decade after the Web*, Amsterdam: Institute of Network Cultures.

Grabher, G. (1997), 'Organizing diversity: evolutionary theory, network analysis and postsocialism', *Regional Studies*, 31: 533–44.

Gu, X. (2014), 'Developing entrepreneur networks in the creative industries – a case study of independent desginer fashion in Manchester', in E. Chell and M. Karata (eds.), *Handbook of Research on Small Business and Entrepreneurship*, 358–73, Cheltenham: Edward Elgar.

Hartley, J., ed. (2005), *Creative Industries*, Oxford: Wiley-Blackwell.

Hesmondhalgh, D., et al. (2015), *Culture, Economy & Politics: the case of New Labour*, London: Palgrave Macmillan.

Hewison, R. (2014), *Cultural Capital. The Rise and Fall of Creative Britain*, London: Verso.

Leadbeater, C. (2000), *Living on Thin Air: The New Economy*, Harmondsworth: Penguin.

Luckman, S. (2013), 'The aura of the analogue in a digital age – women's crafts, creative markets and home-based labour after Etsy', *Cultural Studies Review*, 19 (1): 249–70.

McRobbie, A. (2016), *Be Creative: Making a Living in the New Cultural Industries*, Cambridge and Malden: Polity.

McRobbie, A. (2002), 'Clubs to companies: Notes on the decline of political culture in speeded up creative worlds', *Cultural Studies*, 16 (4): 516–31.

Morozov, E. (2014), 'Making it – pick up a spot welder and join the revolution', *The New Yorker*, 13 January. Available online: http://www.newyorker.com/magazine/2014/01/13/making-it-2 (accessed 1 August 2015).

Munzner, K., and K. Shaw. (2014), 'Renew who? Benefits and beneficiaries of renew newcastle', *Urban Policy and Research*, 3 (1): 17–36DOI:10.1080/08111146.2014.967391.

NESTA. (2013), *A Manifesto for the Creative Economy*, London: NESTA. Available online: www.nesta.org.uk/sites/default/files/a-manifesto-for-the-creative-economy-april13.pdf (accessed 9 October 2014).

O'Connor, J. (2016), 'After the creative industries: Why we need a cultural economy', *Platform Papers* 47, Currency House: Melbourne.

O'Connor, J. (2012), 'From allure to ethics: Design as a 'creative industry', in E. Felton, O. Zelenko, and S. Vaughan (eds.), *Design and Ethics: Reflections on Practice*, 33–42, London: Routledge.

O'Connor, J. (2010), *The Cultural and Creative Industries: A Literature Review*, 2nd edn. London: Creative Partnerships.

O'Connor, J., and X. Gu. (2010), 'Developing a creative cluster in a post-industrial city: CIDS and Manchester', *The Information Society*, 26 (2): 124–36.

O'Connor, J., and K. Shaw. (2014), 'What next for the creative city?' *City, Culture and Society*, 5 (3): 165–70.

Pratt, A. (2000), 'New media, the new economy and new spaces', *Geoforum*, 31 (4): 425–36.

Ross, A. (2010), *Nice Work If You Can Get It: Life and Labour in Precarious Times.* NYU series in social and cultural analysis, New York: NYU Press.

Sennett, R. (2008), *The Craftsman*, London: Allen Lane.

Shaw, K. (2013), 'Independent creative subcultures and why they matter', *International Journal of Cultural Policy*, 19 (3): 333–52.

Taylor, A. (2014), *The People's Platform: Taking Back Power and Culture in the Digital Age*, New York: Metropolitan Books.

Ursell, G. (2006), 'Working in the Media', in D. Hesmondhalgh (eds.), *Media Production*, 133–72, Maidenhead: Open University Press.

Weller, S. (2007), 'Beyond 'global production networks': Australian Fashion Week's Trans-sectoral synergies', *CSES Working Paper No. 33*. Available online: http://www.vises.org.au/documents/wp33.pdf (accessed 1 May 2016).

Westbury, M. (2015a), 'Fostering local creativity to revitalize struggling cities', *New Cities Foundation*, 19 May. Available online: http://www.newcitiesfoundation.org/fostering-local-creativity-to-revitalize-struggling-cities/ (accessed 1 August 2015)

Westbury, M. (2015b), *Creating Cities*, Melbourne: Niche Press.

Wittel, A. (2001), 'Towards a network sociality', *Theory, Culture & Society*, 18 (6): 51–76.

3

Fast forward

Design economies and practice in the near future

Marzia Mortati

This chapter proposes a reflection and discussion on the behavioural and attitudinal change in creativity and engagement that is branching in and out of design to generate new connections to industry and to inform new ways to work, produce, socialize and innovate. Recently, new channels are being experimented with to create products and services that, linked to the new socio-economic and technological drivers, are proposing novel design scenarios. These encompass emergent drivers and phenomena such as personal manufacturing, peer production and crowd-funding, and are influenced by greater societal, political and environmental factors, such as the green imperative, the need for more sustainable productive practice and behaviours, and the budget cuts in public administrations derived from the 2008 economic crisis. The chapter begins from the understanding that firms, people and the public sector are being challenged by the drivers mentioned above, and asks the question: How is design evolving to respond to this new landscape? The answers hope to open discussions that investigate the emergence of a new type of creative firm and entrepreneur, the characteristics of a new kind of designer or a designer-citizen, and a renewed type of connection between designer, user and organization.

Although seemingly now pervasive within understandings of the future of design, this topic has just begun to be explored, both from an academic perspective and from the perspective of practitioners, as it underlines a revolution that touches upon work and human practices and reforms traditional proprietary processes towards more participative arenas for proposing and sharing ideas. Designers are contributing to the wide experimentation connected to these topics both through direct creative input – for example, experimenting with new ways to design objects collaboratively with people through digital tools – and through facilitating processes that enable all stakeholders to address problems directly – for example, experimenting with new approaches to support the public sector in developing new participative processes for decision-making. Design and creativity can give meaning to tools and technologies that help people understand and develop processes of collaboration, and inspire a different way to be entrepreneurs and citizens. Here this is explored through the idea of a more resilient and convivial society as an essential ingredient for creating stronger design systems. According to Illich (1975), a convivial society is based on invention and promotes people as co-creators of social processes. This idea is extremely relevant to the imagining of new socio-economic and industrial systems while offering the starting point to educate new types of citizens. How can the new organizational processes trigger different entrepreneurial models and innovation in products and services? How can collaborative making practices, enabled by social technologies, be properly explored and practised? How is this contributing to re-shaping and upgrading the design process? These are but a few of the questions this chapter seeks to briefly investigate without looking for definitive answers, but rather aiming at contributing to the wider dialogue already unfolding around the future of design.

Setting the scene

As a function of humans, design is shaped by and interested in social and civic behaviours, from political issues to economic development, from the renovation of the public sphere to the meaning of progress, trust and optimism. Recently, this breadth of discourses has stretched the practice of design between two main issues: the necessity to prove its value in economic terms while bearing a greater social responsibility and the opportunity to re-invest in making and experimentation by taking advantage of the new manufacturing technologies and possibilities for peer and distributed collaboration. A phase of regeneration seems under way that links design, on the one side, to the imagination of a better world through the enhancement of people's life (social innovation, service design, transformation design all envision this type of scope) and, on the other, to the reform of industrial production, manufacturing models and systems, distribution logics and characteristics of markets (digital fabrication and an idea of industrial renaissance are especially connected with these interests).

The causes of this expansion in design are to be found in the larger socio-economic and technological drivers that are leading society through a large transition, which includes a substantial change in how people live, communicate, relate to one another, and think about the physical and virtual things they own. For example, from an economic standpoint, the budget cuts in all areas of the public spending across much of the Global North determined by the 2008 economic downturn have determined the need for a profound rebalancing of activities, from research and education to tourism and culture. In Europe especially, the past few years have witnessed a shift in how governments invest in different assets, from the plan for a Big Society released by the Cabinet Office in the UK (Cabinet Office 2010) to wide reforms in jobs and education made in Italy (Il Sole 24 Ore 2015), as well as the investments made by the European Union towards an inclusive, sustainable and smart society (EC 2010). The new situation has underlined the interconnectedness of the systems governing the world – a financial flaw in a US banking system collapses, affecting the world and triggering a ripple effect in many other systems showing publicly the high level of interdependency of people, economies and societies. Although the importance of societal, economic and productive connections and relationships have long been influential in the social sciences, interconnectedness today is far more outreaching, thanks to the distribution of digital technologies. These have made evident and accessible a potentially infinite network of contacts, thus revolutionizing how people live, socialize and share experiences and goods. Through virtual social networks and social platforms, music, food, clothes, experiences and opinions have become a matter of 'followers' and 'likes' expressed in a click or, as in the case with Twitter, 160 characters. Further, technologies are democratizing atoms, creating an industrial and manufacturing renaissance, of which personal fabrication and 3D printers are just the tip of the iceberg. As Chris Anderson (2012) commented, the internet has democratized publishing, broadcasting and communications, thus provoking a massive increase in the range of both participation and participants in everything digital. This has created the 'long tail of bits'. Now the same is happening to manufacturing, thus creating the 'long tail of atoms'.

These drivers uncover a global reality where technological possibilities are huge and unpredictable, economic resources are scarce and markets turbulent, and social concerns are daunting and necessitate radical changes in how we use Earth's resources. All these extremes demand but also offer a great potential for people, governments and businesses to try and rethink the way they are organized and operate. The evolution of the digital has provided the first tools – globally wired platforms that greatly ease the connection between people while offering the possibility of a wider overview of systems and phenomena – to understand the importance of connectivity, at both technical and social levels. This is now multiplied through collaboration and creativity that are proposing radical new ways to look at the future. For instance, new channels are being experimented with to rebalance and amplify the weak signals of otherwise positive transformations. These include crowdfunding, peer production, collaborative services and other modes of creative experimentation and inputs. Many call this a networked society (Castells 2002; Mulgan 2013) that will increasingly push people towards openness, sharing, collaboration and global self-organization, thus changing the way we innovate, design sustainable goods and services, and govern. In the search for the next big paradigm that can drive industry success, the Ericsson industry observatory reports:

Technological revolutions lead to new ways of thinking about techno-economic issues. Such transformations reach beyond the industry in question to society at large, and evolve to become the shared basic principles of the period. In the era of cars and mass production, the shared principles were related to mass production and mass markets, economies of scale, standardization, centralization and hierarchies. In contrast, the guiding principles of the information age are decentralized integration, network structures, adaptability, agility, customization, knowledge as capital, clusters and economies of scope. (Ericsson 2013, p. 3)

Organizational linear systems have evolved into network-based structures and constellations of value far more outreaching and impacting, but also far less graspable, than old economic, business and managerial logics. Creative processes have extended ownership and innovation, handing over authorship to self-organized communities using their collective intelligence, while involving people in the creative process directly, whether it be the process of designing a t-shirt or a policy.

These traits profoundly touch upon design and the creative industries: as civic behaviours change, design seeks to understand the desires of people and the solutions that can enhance their life; as manufacturing unlocks systems and technologies, it works to make them meaningful and accessible while provoking reflection for industry. In this vision framed by systemic evolution, design participates in the jam session of innovation, contributing to the generation of original socio-productive configurations (Mortati 2013). Further, as the current socio-economic phenomenology evolves, design looks to upscale its role and practice. Therefore, the intent of the next paragraph is to try and capture some of the main traits of this evolution by identifying relevant current experiments linked to the development of new processes and phenomena, such as micro-creative firms, new value constellations and temporary communities of makers. In these examples, design can no longer be considered solely a tool or an output of certain kinds of processes, but it is acknowledged as a triggering subject. This could be described as a designer-citizen or a (political) engine of cycles of construction/destruction of new solutions for socio-economic growth.

Novel design scenarios

Design is guided by the ambition of imagining a desired state of the world, and as such it is recognized to happen first of all in the world of imagination, as events are envisioned and manipulated before any real action (Rittel 1987). Traditionally, the visions produced by designers are linked to manufacturing, industrial goods produced in large scale, consumer taste, function, price and so on. The logic of incorporating it in innovation as an output or driver of the process is very much in line with this tradition. This approach can be described very well through reference to important moments in German design history, for example, when Walther Rathenau imagined a new sense for the offer of AEG (a German electro-technical company), as an alternative to stalling technological development. In 1907 Rathenau, owner of AEG and the son of its founder, called in artist Peter Behrens to re-shape his firm. Behrens intervened not only on the shape of products, but also on the architecture (the organizational structure) of the company and on its coordinated image, re-designing brochures, catalogues and advertising posters. The underlying intuition of Rathenau has been a founding one in the design profession and in its relationship to industry: since technological research was proceeding slowly and all of his competitors were selling products with similar performances, he decided to trust an unusual factor, namely art – aesthetics, image and communication. Therefore, Rathenau decided to create value, increasing the intensity and the quality of the design project in AEG. This intuition has steadily acquired importance through other similar examples, affirming that design could be applied in a company to define a mission, a vision, a brand identity and equity, as well as the socio-economic exchange relationships of the company inside and outside its boundaries. But despite the changes it has undergone through the years, design has always kept one fixed point: its focus on giving shape to things, where 'things' are either material – like products – or immaterial – like services.

However, as in the scenario described in the previous paragraph, design has begun to look well beyond consumers' taste and price. Two dimensions are crucial when seeking to frame this complex landscape within the lens of design. The first one is organizational, and focuses on the way in which companies establish their collaborations and arrange their supply chain. This is relevant to design because it disrupts the traditional iconic relationship of a singular designer with one singular entrepreneur or company, as one of the main levers of successful designs in the past. One example for all is the case of Italian designers and entrepreneurs that, building *enlightened one-to-one relationships* (Mortati and Cruickshan 2011), have endeavoured to make 'Made in Italy' a worldwide marker of design distinction. The current structure of this value chain is quite different: digital technologies have multiplied links and exchanges so as to evolve the traditional designer–entrepreneur–consumer connection into a network of networks, where each stakeholder represents a complex system of interchanges. Linear and networked organizational systems are thus currently crucial opposites in design practice.

The second dimension looks at how the design process has been opened up for wider participation. Traditionally, designers are stand-alone talented individuals carrying out their function in a hierarchical line; increasingly, however, designers participate in multidisciplinary teams comprising experts and non-experts, as both other professionals and users. In many cases the team never meets in person, and is made up of people who contribute an idea leaving to others the task of adjusting and multiplying its value. According to Paul Atkinson (2006), the transition from an era of vertical flow to a collaborative and open one has been possible mainly because of the possibility of using technologies that allow designing through code, so that a product design no longer needs to be sent to a factory to be produced to be rendered and circulated. The code allows wider collaboration both in sharing knowledge (e.g. making the code available online for anyone else to modify and reproduce an object) and in experimenting together with people around the world. Enabling digital technologies are multiplying the possibilities for the democratization of design, and are therefore central to the search of new scenarios opposing a proprietary and a collaborative idea of the design process.

Reflecting on these conditions, many recent examples of design projects, initiatives, experiments and businesses can be axiomatically mapped in a system to spot the most relevant areas in which design economies and practice are changing, and how. For this purpose, the author has reviewed about 100 cases, looking for the most interesting and diverse experimentations linked to how design practice is changing in terms of process and organization. The initial pool has included a wide array of examples with no geographic specificity, and spanning from interesting projects and experimentations from individuals or groups looking at designing and producing products differently up to cases of innovative business and public sector institutions incorporating design and design capabilities in meaningful ways. Further, the author has selected twenty-five for their relevance and difference from traditional design practice to look at their *what, how, who and where?* Finally, they have informed the development of, and been positioned within, the framework outlined in Table 3.1. Further, the analysis performed on each case has served to extract the characteristics of each of the scenarios proposed, and thus the cases selected are used in the narrative to explain the scenarios themselves.

Community-driven services are entrepreneurial ideas that innovate particularly by reorganizing a specific value chain by means of digital technologies. Such projects often propose an alternative way of linking the traditional stakeholders in a process, making this the major strength of the business idea. For example, SFMade (http://www.sfmade.org/) has identified a new way to empower local manufacturers and potentially transform the city (San Francisco). By connecting

Table 3.1 Map of novel design scenarios

Networked	Community-driven services	Open and distributed ecologies
Linear	Controlled cooperations	Generative environments
	Proprietary	Collaborative

local businesses in a larger system, they envision a sustainable local economy where companies who design and manufacture products locally thrive and create quality jobs.

Controlled cooperations describe the evolution of the more traditional forms of design experimentation and are especially focused on products. The main drivers are the novelty of new materials – often self-created and self-produced – and an alternative exploration of traditional production methods. Biocouture (http://www.biocouture.co.uk/) is a biocreative design consultancy that works to help brands imagine their 'biodesigned future', especially by creating new materials out of experimentation with microorganisms. Out of collaboration with new scientific fields (in this case, biotechnology), design helps firms imagine how they can evolve for the future.

Generative environments stem from ideas derived out of a more open, generative design process, where people are invited to modify plans and codes for their own purpose or to contribute substantially to the collective end result. The success is based on the wide collaboration of users to help the idea have an impact, and follows a process of 'one-to-many'. It encompasses examples as different as platforms for crowdfunding (https://www.kickstarter.com/), collaborative policy making (https://openpolicy.blog.gov.uk/category/policy-lab/) and nature-inspired generative design (http://n-e-r-v-o-u-s.com/).

Open and distributed ecologies are systems where both design and organizational processes are network based and ideas are built 'many-to-many', that is, by engaging a wide number of passionate users to collaborate both in proposing ideas and in contributing to their success and amplification. This is the scenario of collective intelligence serving grand societal challenges, thanks to pioneering cases like Linux and Wikipedia, and has nowadays evolved into cases like D-Cent where collective intelligence and digital technologies are explored to foster open democracy (http://dcentproject.eu/).

Takeaways and discussions

The four scenarios presented besides framing the current reflection on the present and near future of design economies and practice are preparatory for wider discussions about how design and creativity are giving meaning to tools and technologies.

On the one side, design is confronted with an emergent reform of production that is shifting part of its concerns away from the development of serial and standard goods and towards small-scale and personalized manufacturing. This reform – although very recent – is already involving machines and technologies as well as human social behaviours, all of which are converging towards the creation of new types of *micro-creative firms*. The left side of Table 3.1 especially represents this. Designers are experimenting in this field mainly through the establishment of collaborative service networks and new productive chains based on human making capabilities. Moving into homes, cities and wider service environments, these systems could create new types of factories that are at the same time urban and rural, real and virtual, wired around a 'zero miles' digital system.

On the other side, the ambition of design to imagine a new and improved world is leading towards using its capabilities to serve higher societal challenges. The strength of collective intelligence has widened the access to the role of facilitator once assigned to individual designers alone. In many arenas, these emergent formations are now serving as triggers of critical thinking and sparks of collaboration, that is *designers-citizens,* and this trend is especially manifest in those enterprises operating more on the right side of the table. This has expanded the object of design to incorporate many new and more intangible areas of practice, from public services looking for radical efficiency (NESTA 2010) to policy seeking people-centred approaches for problem solving and setting (Bason 2014).

These two sides can be considered the areas leading the most interesting experimentation in design work and practice now. The remainder of the chapter will try to provide an initial overview of the new key agents involved in these processes, in the hopes of provoking further thinking about them.

Open discussion: The micro-creative firm

The first open discussion concerns the possibility of envisaging a new type of creative firm, capable of valuing differently the potential of networks beyond the organization of contacts and resources. This includes the capacity/possibility to rethink the mechanisms of production using new technologies, to imagine new paths to growth beyond turnover and to give new roles to users along the innovation process by means of ICTs.

Firms have always been considered economic objects from which profit had to be gained. The value of these artefacts is reflected in the concept of the stock price, and their main asset is identified in management as the core activity aimed at satisfying the investors' interests. This idea has held true for centuries; however, recently pilot projects are blooming which investigate new network-based business models and the business value of positive social impact. For example, the European Commission is paying attention to social innovation and its systemic nature[1] by funding initiatives aimed at defining metrics to evaluate their contribution to the well-being of a nation or an industrial system. However, this field of investigation is still fragmented. Few models have tried to envisage new answers, but often remaining anchored to old value creation systems. The theory referred to as Open Innovation (Chesbrough 2006), for example, is an attempt to open up proprietary innovation funnels, which remain though an old innovation paradigm, common in traditional hierarchical and multinational firms. On the contrary, new types of firms should be looking for original and looser mixes of tools and competences, control and flexibility, personal and professional life. In particular, creativity and digital tools are leading designers and creative people in general towards the establishment of micro-firms, or firms consisting of a single sole trader. These are becoming possible because of desktop manufacturing tools and connective mobile technologies that are engaging an increasing number of people (professionals as well as amateurs) and enabling them to transform their idea into reality and test it directly with the market. Designers are approaching this possibility by building self-managed manufacturing plants and relying on outsourcing for all types of operations through using online services that offer ready-made productive relationships. A new type of productive process is crucial to this description, demonstrated by examples like 'Custommade' (http://www.custommade.com/) and SlowD (http://www.slowd.it/) platforms, which try to create new business through connecting craftsmen and people looking for producers. Micro- or sole trader firms are collaborative service networks requiring almost no internal specialist physical assets. The core is not the hardware, for example, the productive plant. This represents only a technical means. Rather the heart of the enterprise is ability, motivation and opportunity, that is the social exchange necessary to connect places, resources, necessities and opportunities. This emergent innovation model affects design as well as economy, sociology and management: it talks of new business models and new entrepreneurial profiles (i.e. the digital craftsman), and highlights the need of including design capabilities differently in a business or an organization, as its ability for problem setting and solving using models of reality becomes central to understanding complex connections. This is quite important in the firm of the twenty-first century that is increasingly based on the strength of relationships, the importance of manual work and the value of local resources, small numbers and excellence.

Open discussion: The designer-citizen

Increasingly, designers are facilitating direct creative input from citizens into many arenas of public life previously not considered the purview of the designer. One of the most important and discussed examples in this area is the public sphere, where services and policies are looking for creative approaches to problem setting and -solving. In the design process, participation is becoming more than the consultation of users during one or all of the project development phases. Marco Steinberg (2014) talks of *stewardship* as the concept of evolving the traditional idea of facilitation to incorporate a non-neutral design position. This is referred to as the acknowledgement of the political and ethical position that designers play when embedded in a process, like any other professional, which crucially challenges the idea that he/she can be a neutral facilitator. Steinberg proposes to move beyond this by seeing the designer as a steward in a process, thus recognizing the need that in these arenas he/she should embody an ethical role of responsible management rather than trying to be a *superpartes* facilitator. This raises the challenge of declaring political values in order to offer transparent help to enable direct democracy and public service development. Building on Steinberg's concept, in a facilitated process, design should be seen not only as responsible guidance, but as one of the actors in the process, with own interests and ambitions. While the designer can succeed in becoming a steward for certain types of processes, in the majority of cases, however, he/she is first and foremost one of the stakeholders engaged, thus lacking the overview and decisional power necessary to be a responsible guide. He/she can/should, therefore, be first of all a responsible citizen, as an informed and non-neutral source of critical thinking and debate. When these types of characteristics are found also in a designer, the figure of a socially responsible design(er) or designer-citizen could be formed, who is described through the characteristics of both a craftsman and an entrepreneur. Sennett (2008) describes the craftsman as the special human condition of being engaged. The labourer with a sense of craft is engaged in the work in and for itself; the satisfactions of working are his/her own reward; the details of daily labour are connected in his/her mind to the end product, and work is connected to the freedom to experiment. These vision and characteristics are complemented by the 'joy' of entrepreneurial action as the starting point for transformation that is wished because of the peculiar psychological characteristics of the entrepreneur, as the dream and will to establish a private empire complemented by the will to fight and the joy of creation (Schumpeter 1911). This vision pushes design(er) beyond facilitation: it makes them a citizen, in the highest sense of the word, because through his/her dreams and visions he/she can propose the original connection of technology, economy and society, to offer solutions leading to more responsible social and economic development.

Towards a convivial and resilient economy

The emerging innovation framework described here has acknowledged the complex and shifting nature of design work as a networked and collaborative practice. The interconnectedness of the world is currently one of the most prominent features of social and economic facts, which encompasses physical links; flows of goods, money, ideas and people; the culture; and the environment, and therefore, it affects design in unexpected ways. Highly creative systems are becoming central to the increasingly intertwined relationship between economy and society, because they are capable of offering disruptive perspectives to old challenges. These are resilient and convivial systems, where designers participate responsibly to improving daily lives rather than trying to steer them. Resilience is the capacity of a system to adapt flexibly to change without being destroyed (Homer-Dixon 2006). It is the capacity to evolve and survive disruptive events, because each node (people, firm, community) is self-sufficient. Resilience is thus a key quality for future growth together with conviviality. The last is, in Ivan Illich's idea (1975), the essential ingredient in relationships and aims at creating a social life together. According to Illich, a convivial society is based on invention and promotes people as co-creators of social processes. This idea is central to the reimagining of new socio-industrial systems and the evolving role of design(ers) in the networked society. This is currently an exciting field of inquiry for design as well as other disciplines concerned with the future of society and the improvement of the conditions of life for all people.

Note

1 Social innovations are driven by a social mission and create value that is at once social and economical. BEPA differentiates them in social, societal and systemic, according to the scope. Social is defined as 'social demands that are traditionally not addressed by the market or existing institutions and are directed towards vulnerable groups in society' (BEPA 2011, p. 43); societal is defined as 'societal challenges in which the boundary between "social" and "economic" blurs, and which are directed towards society as a whole' (ibid., p. 43); systemic is described as 'reshaping society' (ibid., p. 42) 'in the direction of a more participative arena where empowerment and learning are sources and outcomes of well-being' (ibid., p. 43).

References

Anderson, C. (2012), *Makers: The New Industrial Revolution*, London: Random House.
Atkinson, P. (2006), 'Do it yourself: Democracy and design', *Journal of Design History*, 19 (1): 1–10.
Bason, C., ed. (2014), *Design for Policy*, Farnham: Gower Publishing Limited.

BEPA. (2011). 'Empowering people, driving change social innovation in the European Union'. Available online: http://ec.europa.eu/bepa/pdf/publications_pdf/social_innovation.pdf (accessed 30 July 2015).

Cabinet Office. (2010), 'Building the big society'. Available online: https://www.gov.uk/government/publications/building-the-big-society (accessed 30 July 2015).

Castells, M. (2002), *La nascita della società in rete*, Milano: EGEA.

Chesbrough, H. W., J. Vanhaverbeke, and J. West, eds. (2006), *Open Innovation: Researching A New Paradigm*, Oxford: Oxford University Press.

Commission of the European Communities. (2010), 'Europe 2020 flagship initiative. Innovation union'. Available online: http://ec.europa.eu/research/innovation-union/index_en.cfm?pg=keydocs (accessed 5 August 2012).

Ericsson Industry Observatory. (2013), 'Industry transformation in the networked society'. Available online: http://www.ericsson.com/res/docs/2013/industry-transformation-in-the-networked-society.pdf (accessed 30 July 2015).

Homer-Dixon, T. (2006), *The Upside of Down: Catastrophe, Creativity and the Renewal of Civilization*, USA: Island Press.

Il Sole 24Ore. (2015), 'The jobs act is an important step towards the reduction of long-term inequality, OECD says', 10 July. Available online: http://www.italy24.ilsole24ore.com/art/business-and-economy/ (accessed 30 July 2015).

Illich, I. (1975), *Tools for Conviviality*, London: Fontana.

Mortati, M. (2013), *Systemic Aspects of Innovation and Design. The Perspective of Collaborative Networks*, Milano: PoliMI SpringerBriefs.

Mortati, M., and L. Cruickshank. (2011), 'Design and SMEs: The trigger of creative ecosystems', Conference Proceedings, DPPI11, June 2011, Milan, Italy.

Mulgan, G. (2013), *The Locust and the Bee. Predators and Creators in Capitalism's Future*, New Jersey: Princeton University Press.

NESTA. (2010), 'Radical efficiency: Different, better, lower cost public services'. Available online: http://www.nesta.org.uk/publications/reports/assets/features/radical_efficiency (accessed 30 September 2013).

Rittel, H. (1987), 'The reasoning of designers', Proceedings of the International Congress on Planning and Design Theory, Boston, August 1987.

Schumpeter, J. A. (1911), *Theorie der wirtschaftlichen Entwicklung*, Leipzig: Duncker und Humblot.

Sennett, R. (2008), *The Craftsman*, USA: Yale University Press.

Steinberg, M. (2014), 'Strategic design and the art of public sector innovation', in C. Bason (ed.), *Design for Policy*, 87–101, Farnham: Gower Publishing Limited.

4

Craft, collectivity and event-time

Katve-Kaisa Kontturi

In 2012, artist and philosopher Erin Manning exhibited her collectively created fabric-installation *Stitching Time* at the Sydney Biennale. *Stitching Time* consisted of 2,000 earth-coloured, irregularly shaped and shimmering, translucent pieces of fabric. The fabrics were connected to each other with magnets, buttons and buttonholes so that they could fold into new constellations, such as garments, time and again. Each piece of fabric produced had taken around five hours of collective work in sewing circles across North America, Europe and Australia that took place during the twelve months preceding the biennale. In the installation these fabrics hanged from light netting constructions, low enough to be touched by the biennale guests. They were also piled in baskets to encourage participation – to lure people to spend time with them, to create something new.

When attending to the installation almost daily during its three-month existence, Manning (2015a, pp. 67–8) realized that the issue at stake was not how to get people to participate but rather the quality of participation. The installation that was designed 'to give people time' turned out to be something else – not for everyone, but for many. While some people took their time, lingering in the space enjoying its subtle movements or crafting imaginative outfits by attentively joining a new set of fabrics together, for many others participation seemed to mean just quickly doing something to leave their mark on the installation. Often garments were put together in a hurry and simply left on the floor when the visitors moved on.

What led to this turn of events was an apparent clash between different understandings and experiences of time and, consequently, also between modes of participation.[1] While the co-creators of the fabric pieces, including Manning and the architect Sam Spurr, who designed the hanging construction, had spent thousands of hours crafting the installation, a random exhibition visitor could walk in and in her or his hasty actions transform and hence disintegrate the installation astonishingly quickly, especially as this way of interacting seemed to encourage others to do so too (ibid., pp. 57–8). Since time was not spent in sensing what the installation was and could be about, the interaction thus carried out became rather an instrumental sort of participation, just changing or 'adding something' (ibid., p. 58).[2] Manning (ibid., p. 64, 70) later reflected that the rushed actions to 'get something done' were driven by the contemporary capitalist ethos that urges people to act without paying attention to the complexities involved. It is the same logic that values the production of the *new* without offering genuinely new openings, or reflection, on what has changed. Needless to say, this logic of time is driven by productivity and profit-making.

As Italian media theorist and activist Franco 'Bifo' Berardi (e.g. 2005, 2010) claims, we have internalized the logic, economy and time of capitalism; it is absorbed in the way we know ourselves, and it unconsciously directs our actions. The cognitariat, a derivate of Marx's proletariat, have incorporated the demand of working all the time, and not only during office hours; they have become their own bosses, making themselves constantly available for interactions which contemporary mobile technologies readily enhance (2010, pp. 88–90).[3] In his *24/7: Late Capitalism and the Ends of Sleep*, Jonathan Crary (2014) addresses the same phenomenon, the capitalist takeover of time. He writes that the new norm of 24/7 temporality praises activity for its own sake: 'to always do something, to move, to change' (ibid., p. 15). Importantly, this apprizing of activity is done at the cost of more *passive* actions such as sleep (ibid., p. 10).

It is in this context of the capitalist 'theft of time' that Manning and her collaborators wanted to offer something different, namely a different experience of time. Manning (2013, p. 206; 2015a, b) calls such time bereft of 'clock-time's' profit- and achievement-driven linearity, *event-time*. The concept links with an understanding of contemporary art as mobile architecture, where art emerges as relational event exceeding its form and the linear execution of a predetermined choreography (Manning 2013, p. 79–80; 101). It is also incited by process philosophies of Alfred Whitehead, Gilles Deleuze, Brian Massumi and Arakawa and Gins (see 2013, pp. 101–2, 106). Manning explains that 'to enjoy [this] processual force of time, it is necessary to take time, and to give time', to feel what the work seeks to give (2015a, pp. 58–9). Event-time also means that the subject cannot be an outsider to the event she participates in (2015b, p. 8): she cannot master the event like the participants who just added to or removed something from the installation. For event-time to occur, careful attention to the rhythm, materials and participating elements – whether human or non-human – has to take place. Event-time, then, is necessarily a collective experience. It is time *and* event simultaneously felt in their co-emerging complexity.

As a participatory installation that encourages time-consuming creative participation, *Stitching Time* relates to the growing investment in collective craft activities. It is not a coincidence that the popularity of craft activities including sewing circles has steadily grown as neo-liberalism has tightened its hold across the world over the past fifteen years. It is widely acknowledged today that crafting can offer an alternative mode of practice and duration: a retreat from the speed and efficiency of capitalist logic (e.g. Cvetkovich 2012, p. 168; von Busch 2013). The new coming of crafting, knitting at its forefront, received wide media attention already in the early 2000s, when celebrity knitters such as Madonna, Courtney Cox and even Russell Crowe paved the way for public awareness (Parkins 2004). Then, however, the focus of the crafting discourse was more on the care of the self (ibid., pp. 434–5) than on collective action. The calming 'zen-qualities' of knitting were praised and connected to other slow-life activities like cooking and 'cocooning' – home-making. On the other hand, trendy knitting cafés were founded in the metropolises of the Western world to offer calming spaces of inspiration and collective working. While the self-care discourse is certainly not altogether gone, today more and more emphasis is put on collective making, especially in relation to activism. Craftivism, a form of activism that uses craft as its medium, is burgeoning and can be encountered regularly in urban spaces, where 'yarnbombs' takeover trees, fences and even public memorials. As a form of activism, craftivism is *slow* and softly subversive: it appeals to the senses by way of its tactile medium, and the time put into the making of colourful crocheted, cross-stitch banners, for example, often attracts special attention, activating people to join in the process of collective making (Fitzpatrick and Kontturi 2015; Corbett 2013, pp. 5–6).

In the rest of the chapter, I will map some different practices of contemporary craft-makers by focusing on the ways they address and foster alternative understandings of time, how they offer quiet, tactile and 'long-durance' counter actions for the capitalist economy of time. In other words, I am interested in how they compose event-time. As suggested above, event-time is always a 'collective refashioning' (Manning 2015a, p. 56). Hence I will also ask how the artists in question call on collectivities to emerge even if they work alone. I will offer three case studies that map the current craft-based practices of two Australian contemporary artists, Kate Just and Casey Jenkins, and one Indigenous collective, the Tjanpi Desert Weavers.

'Favourite chicks' in stitch: Knitting a feminist genealogy

Ten stitches in pearl grey, six in a fleshy peachy skin colour, two in a slightly darker tone to mark the armpit hollow, then three chocolaty ones for underarm hair, and again come the fleshy peachy stitches and a few brown ones for the curling ends of her hair. Double this and you have one row of Kate Just's remake of Hannah Wilke's self-portrait all done! But this knitted portrait, a reproduction of one of the many in Wilke's *Intra-Venus* series, consists of 120 rows or so. Moreover, the knitted portrait belongs to a series that currently includes twelve pieces with over forty pieces planned. The series represents the global history of feminist art from Frida Kahlo to Pussy Riot (Russia) and Femen (the Ukraine), their Chinese and Japanese counterparts, the Americans Carolyn Schneeman and Cindy Sherman, Australian Tracy Moffatt and Sarah Lucas of the Young British Artist's generation. When completed, that will be altogether over half a million stiches around the world and across time.

It takes a long-time professional artist with experience of large-scale knitting projects and a history of numerous private exhibitions and community projects to take up such a demanding, ever-growing task as the *Feminist Fan* series. And even for the US-born, Melbourne-based artist Kate Just, who possesses all this knowledge and proficiency, the project has been quite a challenge – though an enjoyable one. The first of her knitted *Feminist Fan* portraits took three months to be completed and it was preceded by almost a year of studying and formulating a functional technique for its rendering (Just K. 2015a, pers. comm., 10 May). Knitting hundreds of thousands stitches, endless rows of knitting and purling, is not for the faint-hearted, or -handed. It is not surprising that several colleagues have jokingly suggested to Just that she should outsource her knitting (Just K 2015b, pers. comm., 12 Oct) time-consuming as it is and, in this sense, not profitable at all. Therefore, for all these precious hours spent, another method, or even a machine, could be more cost-effective.

However, Just (2015b, pers. comm., 12 October) feels very strongly against outsourcing: you never know what will come up in the process of knitting, and there are so many elements in the event of knitting that one could never simply follow given instructions. Also, devoting countless hours making feminist portraits has a very specific purpose. It is a deliberately laborious way of creating a genealogy of feminist art – bringing together a bunch of women makers and activists that she adores from the early twentieth century up to today, and across the globe. They are her 'favourite chicks' (Just 2015a, pers. comm., 10 May), and the series *Feminist Fan* is homage to their work that continues to be under-represented in museum collections, canons of art history

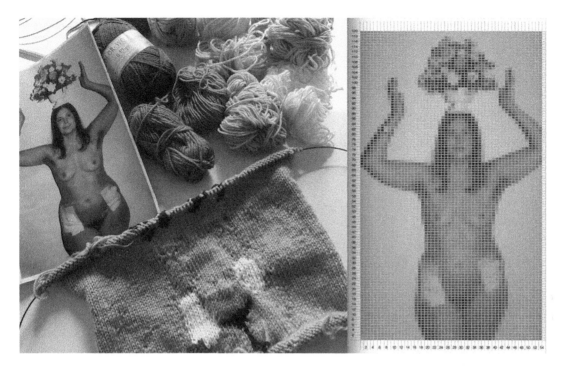

FIGURE 4.1 Kate Just's portrait of Hannah Wilke in the making, June 2015. *Feminist Fan Series* © Kate Just 2015. Reproduced with the permission of Kate Just.

and the media. Importantly, it is a handmade and time-consuming homage to the hard work that feminist artists have done over the decades.

By knitting a gathering of feminist artists and activists, Just is doing much more than a series of remade portraits. She is knitting an *event* that extends beyond its object-boundaries, 'across times and continents' (Just 2015a, pers. comm., 10 May). In the making of the *Feminist Fan* series, knitting does not exist alone; the virtual world of the internet is its indispensable connective companion. Just sources the portraits she knits by browsing the Web, as well as documents her work via her Twitter, Instagram and Facebook accounts. She has also encouraged her online community to suggest new portraits to be knitted. In addition, the event has its own designated hashtag, #feministfan, that connects images of feminist artists across the time zones and decades, beyond their physical being, through which the event can be recomposed over and over again.

However, knitting still bears a particular purpose for the artist herself. Just (2015a, pers. comm., 10 May) explains her bodily connection to the artists whose portraits she knits: it is 'through knitting I'm connecting with these women, I'm a fan, it's almost like I'm wearing them'. Importantly, this bodily connection involves getting the rhythm of knitting really going – flowing – otherwise it would be impossible to commit to forty more portraits or so. In the rhythmical movement of a knitting flow, 'everything happens as it's happening' (ibid.), images and stitches follow each other without the necessity to pay attention to technical details or the quantity of stitches anymore: they are now integrated into the bodily movement. This is how Just's working process opens itself from linear time to event-time. As Manning (2015a, p. 62) suggests, event in itself is a temporal concept: 'The event is *the how* of its unfolding, and this includes all participatory aspects in its relational movement' (emphasis added). By giving her time and body movement to the project, Just is creating an event that comes with a multiple bodily presence and layers of time actualized through knitting. According to her (2015a, pers. comm., 10 May), it is the very bodily nature of knitting that viewers often find appealing. Knitted fabrics are something that we have all worn close to our bodies; thus we are familiar with their specific material touch even without concretely touching them. This is how *Feminist Fan* affectively links – stitches – its viewer-participants with the decades of feminist art they might not otherwise be aware of.

Times and bodies of vaginal knitting

'*Attention whore*'. '*#gross*'. These phrases are popular with the commentators of Casey Jenkins's twenty-eight-day performance *Casting Off My Womb* that she did in October–November 2013 in Darwin, Australia. In the performance, Jenkins daily inserted a ball of white wool thread into her vagina and used it for knitting a month-long work of art. As the performance was as long as Jenkins's menstrual cycle, the knitting in the making naturally acquired and was infused by the varying shades of her menstrual blood (Figure 4.2). For centuries women have used all sorts of absorbent natural materials – from papyrus to sponge, from wool and linen to cotton – to keep menstrual blood from flowing, but to directly produce an artwork from the blood-infused material is quite something else. Art is public, especially when publicly performed, while menstruation is still understood as a private bodily procedure to be hidden, to the level that in television commercials for sanitary towels the liquid used to highlight their excellent absorbing qualities is blue. The blurring of the boundaries between the private and the public, and the bringing together of these different and gendered realms – and times – of creativity, seems to be one of the reasons behind the repulsive reactions to the work.

Interestingly, as Jenkins (2013) tells, not so many people saw the actual performance, and when they did, they were in fact encouraging in their feedback. It was when a video documentation of the performance started to circulate widely across the globe that the list of negative commentators started to grow – thousands and thousands (the YouTube viewer calculator reaching seven and a half million) – and 'dislikes' overpower 'likes' three times over. Jenkins says that she knew to expect outrageous comments, but the quantity of them came as a surprise: the same phrases were repeated endlessly like the commentators were robots and not human beings with genuine, subjective experiences (Jenkins in Galligeros 2015). When performing the piece, her wish was that the initial shock might eventually turn into new understandings of women's bodies and creativity as visitors would question their negative associations with the vulva. As this unfortunately was not the case, Jenkins decided to act on and produce a new artwork, a meta-commentary on the online harassment she had encountered: this machine-knitted work again uses wool soaked in her menstrual blood. Taking these works' title from the criticism, in *Attention whore* and *#gross* that were exhibited at the *F generation exhibition*, George Paton Gallery, Melbourne, in 2015, the bloody letters stand out from the white background.

The comments Jenkins received contrast with her perception that the process of vaginal knitting was an intimate experience, 'really natural and uneventful' (Vaginal Knitting [Feed], 2013; emphasis

FIGURE 4.2 Casey Jenkins knitting at Darwin Visual Arts Association (DVAA), *Casting Off My Womb*, © Casey Jenkins 2013. Reproduced with the permission of Casey Jenkins.

added). She admits, however, that knitting was much tougher when she was menstruating, when the thread was damp with blood, and stitches took more time and effort. In this way not only the blood but her natural bodily rhythm – the time of her body – was weaved into the knitted fabric. Noteworthy, Jenkins's understanding of uneventfulness is not in contradiction to the concept of event-time but rather supports it. Event-time is not time consciously performed, or overtly pre-planned: it has no time for decision, 'because the decision is immanent to the event's recomposition' (Manning 2015a, p. 106). In this sense, it might be described, as the artist does, as 'uneventful'.

Julia Kristeva's (1981) famous essay 'Women's Time' ('Les Temps des Femmes', 1979) offers another, more distant context for the timely matters of Jenkins's 'bloody' artworks. In her essay, Kristeva contrasts the linear time of the patriarchy (and capitalism) with its milestones and central figures to the cyclic time of women that in itself stretches between the natural time of the body, its cycles and the monumental time of myths and cults, that of the motherhood and the Virgin Mary, for example. What is important in terms of Jenkins's work is that Kristeva's essay is not all about reclaiming motherhood or the natural and psychic structures attached to it; it also acknowledged and called for new aesthetic practices that would contest the hegemonic, often language-based, expressions of linear time (Apter 2010, pp. 3–4). This is precisely what Jenkins does in her uneventful events of vaginal knitting: there is a mythical and solemn monumentality to her repetitive task reminiscent of Penelope in *Odyssey*, and the all-white surroundings of the cubic gallery space only add to this while the cyclic rhythm of her biological body reminds of its presence in the form of menstrual blood turning, staining the woven fabric reddish brown.

However, event-time as Manning writes about it is certainly not about 'natural' or biological bodies per se or their inherent capacities as Kristeva may have it. Rather it emerges in surprising and relational unfoldings of both corporeal and incorporeal entities, humans and objects. Event-time is about experiencing potentials immanent in the present that necessarily move you towards the future while carrying the 'pastness' along (Manning 2013, pp. 94–6). In the event-time of vaginal knitting, where the menstrual cycle is but one participant, the educated moves of a craftivist body with its histories of feminist art and activism another,[4] and where blood marks both the past and the future as it is knitted into the white yarn coming from Jenkins's vagina and forming a growing fabric. The layers of time weaved into event-time. As such, event-time offers a model for an aesthetic practice, where time is not 'willed by individuals' (ibid., p. 98) or restricted by the laws of industrial production, but enabled by moving relations. When Jenkins says, 'I can only do what my body allows me to do. That will shape the work, rather than thinking about what I'm going to make' (in Gallimari 2015), she speaks of the uneventfulness of event-time. And when she knits the offending comments about her work with the yarn soaked and dyed inside her menstruating body, or chants the repetitive verbal offences so that they make a song of their own as in her recent performance *Programmed to Reproduce* (2016), she literally and critically embodies the criticism and offers it a feminist future.

Weaving passive time, creating extinct species

In August 2014, I was waiting in the foyer at the Victorian College of the Arts at the University of Melbourne with students and staff members for the Tjanpi Desert Weavers master class to begin. Tjanpi Desert Weavers are an Indigenous social enterprise and art collective bringing together around 400 women from communities in Central Australia that at the time had just celebrated its twentieth anniversary. They were in Melbourne to present their admired grass sculptures at the Tarrawarra Biennale. While waiting, we had to complete a form granting rights to reproduce our image as this historical event was to be documented and the material might be used later in University publications. However, when the doors opened, we left the world of bureaucracy and stepped into a different experience of space and time: the women were there surrounded by piles of tjanpi (grass) and colourful raffia – the materials had been brought all the way from the Central Desert, from where the grass was also picked. Inside, not many introductions were made or instructions given: we were there to learn by making.

Already holding the materials in our hands, we sat in circles close to one another to watch our teachers knot the raffia heart of a basket and to skilfully introduce tufts of spiky and hard tjanpi to be woven inside each round layer (Figure 4.3). In this process of learning, there were no chronological steps to be followed; it was all about learning to feel the potential of the fibre and about yielding to collaboration with it. This is to say that we had to pay extraordinary attention to the materials we worked with. By making we learnt to choose raffia that was not too dry and 'sharp' as that would soon break. Or if anything else was not available, the technique of weaving had to be altered, stitches sown more densely. During the master class our sole attention was in the processes of weaving; we did not chat much nor make friends as one often does when crafting together – we socialized only within the confines of making: 'Could you hand me the scissors', 'Where would I find more green raffia'. The rhythm of making created its own time. We did not check our watches or phones: the event was too precious for 'efficient' time-keeping. What we did was to keep the process going quietly, repeating the stages, tending, caressing the process of weaving.

This kind of experience of time can be called passive (Kontturi 2012, pp. 172–3; see also Mahler 2008, pp. 65–78; Deleuze 1994, pp. 70–85). A lot happens, takes place, but not in an actively controlled manner: passive time is about material-relational immediacy. The concept of passive

FIGURE 4.3 Tjanpi artists Molly Miller (in the foreground) and Roma Butler (in the background, left), and Tjanpi Arts and Culture Field Officer Claire Freer (in the middle) teaching the Tjanpi Desert Weavers' master class at the Victorian College of the Arts, the University of Melbourne, August 2014. © Katve-Kaisa Kontturi. Reproduced with the permission of Katve-Kaisa Kontturi.

time emphasizes that it is the quality of time that matters, not what is calculable, nor when something ends or begins. Thus, what is essential to passive time is that it cannot be quantified or hurried up – it has to take its own time, otherwise it loses its most essential character. The careful tending of fire, or the lengthy process of seeking, carrying and purifying potable water, and religious processions that can take days, are all activities characterized by passive time (Mahler 2008, pp. 65–78). What is common to these passive time-consuming activities is that they often happen outside the availability of modern supplies and infrastructure. To occur, they all necessitate a long-duration affective relation between humans, materials and bodies, such as the one that co-occurred when weaving with the Tjanpi women. Importantly, this experience of passive time was not an individual 'zen' haven. It was certainly a collective occurrence that could not have taken place without its various participants, both human and non-human.

During the master class I focused on the pleasures of basic basket-weaving while some people moved on to composing tjanpi animals as our teachers did. As stated previously, the Tjanpi women were in Melbourne to present their work at the Tarrawarra Biennale, and it was there that they first exhibited their animal sculptures that were also on display at the Australian Pavilion of the 56th Venice Biennale (2015). The Venice Biennale work titled *Kuka Irititja (Animals from Another Time)* was part of a large-scale work by Fiona Hall called 'Wrong Way Time' – an installation critical of global capitalism and its overpowering governance of life: time, culture, people, money, what not. In these sculptures, Tjanpi artists combined their traditional materials with the camouflage clothing used by contemporary Australian and British military forces that Hall had provided them with. In the weaving process, strips of army clothing signifying colonial history became an essential part of the extinct animals revived or re-imagined through art-making. In this way, the series of animals that the women had never seen and which they had to therefore imagine based on the stories they had heard came to express the powers of colonization and capitalism on the ecologies of the natural environment (Michael 2015, p. 31).

Importantly, *Kuka Iritja* was not executed in studios but during a communal desert camp in which Tjanpi women worked and lived together with Fiona Hall. The camp took place in Pilakatilyuru, a region where West and South Australia meet Northern Territory, not far from where nuclear bombs were tested by the British after the Second World War. During the camp, the natural environment and its changes interwove and infused into the tjanpi sculptures. And inseparably to them came the ancestral stories about animals that no longer exist. These ancestral stories are part of *Tjukurpa* (dreaming): they belong to the dreamtime that is still actualized through traditional cultural and religious practices, such as basket-weaving with its history as long as its people, over 40,000 years. However, the women are equally aware of a different layer of (more recent) history and its influences on the extinction of many important 'meat animals'. They acknowledge not only atomic bomb testing but also the introduction of Western, capitalist food trade with its marketing of white flour, sugar and tea that they have a single word to describe, *mai*, as nourishment preferable to the bush food (Tjanpi Desert Weavers 2015, pp. 52–3). While atomic bombs can stop time and make whole species extinct at once, the pressure that the combination of colonialism, capitalism and global finance puts on the environment is even more overwhelming. Through their *Animals from Another Time*, the Tjanpi Desert Weavers tell about our fragile relatedness to the world. But they also offer hope: in the creative processes of grass weaving, old species can be revived, and new ones born. This, however, necessitates – as described above – passive actions and collective efforts emerging in the event-time.

Conclusion

In this chapter, the processes of craft making have offered access to event-time, to an experience of time that embraces the immediacy of material-relational, intensive qualities instead of quantifiable entities, collectivity emerging between both the human and the non-human participants.[5] As such, event-time can be perceived as a counter-power to capitalist forces including the 'theft' of time and individualization. By discussing the specificities of Kate Just's, Casey Jenkins's and the Tjanpi Desert Weavers' art projects, I have woven a map of alternative understandings and experiences of linear, profit-driven time – the time economy of capitalism. This mapping consists of deliberately time-consuming practices of making, women's time, passive time and, in passing, Indigenous dreamtime. What brings all these timely aspects together is careful sensitivity: attentiveness to process, to what is happening, becoming. Often this sort of production activity is connected not only to the crafts but to the pre-industrial life, to the times when time was not yet governed by capitalist concerns. Yet the contemporary crafting activities mapped in this chapter are not so much motivated by nostalgia about the past than by the desire towards a better future.

Notes

1 Manning (2015a, p. 68) suggests that the mismatch also related to the exhibition construction: as it offered fabric to be constructed into garments, it was too object-oriented and product-centred, and thus encouraged the audience to act accordingly.

2 In August 2015, I curated an exhibition titled 'Handmade Politics' for Titanik Gallery in Turku, Finland, and – interestingly – encountered similar sorts of issues with participation. In the press release as well as in the event description, I wrote that 'multiple colours and textures invite participation' hoping that exhibition would have its effect on visitors and change something in their thinking–being. I learnt soon that exhibition guests were indeed especially eager to engage in sometimes lengthy discussions about the works, but then other things began to happen too. For several occasions, artworks were moved, removed or even stolen; also new elements were added. In these cases, participation – or vandalism – was of *instrumental* sort. It did not attend to the complexity of the art piece in question, or the exhibition as whole. Also, these interactions were executed as quickly as possible to avoid attention, yet they were the ones that received a lot of media attention.

3 Another important aspect of cognitive capitalism is that today work is of different nature than it used to be: more and more people work in the services of information society – their work is rather cognitive than embodied. According to Berardi (2010, pp. 98–103), the overwhelmingly extended working hours, the logic of competition that encourages individualization and 'overcommunication' have caused panic and depression as people live their lives without actual bodily relationality. This, again, is something that crafting can offer (e.g. Cvetkovich 2012, pp. 21, 154–202).

4 Here, a reference to two iconic feminist performances using the muscle forces of the vagina creatively is evident: Carolee Schneeman's famous *Interior Scroll* (1975), a performance in which she pulled a written scroll from her vagina and read it too, and Shigeko Kubota's vaginal painting (1965).

5 These are also concerns that are considered as 'new materialist'; see Tiainen, Kontturi and Hongisto (2015).

References

Apter, E. (2012), '"Women's time" in theory', *Differences: A Journal of Feminist Cultural Studies*, 21 (1): 1–18.

Berardi, F. (2005), 'Cognitariat: Work, desire, depression', *Cultural Studies Review*, 11 (2): 57–63. Available online: https://epress.lib.uts.edu.au/journals/index.php/csrj/article/view/3656 (accessed 15 July 2014).

Berardi, F. (2010), *Soul at Work: From Alienation to Autonomy*, Los Angeles: Semiotext(e).

von Busch, O. (2013), 'Zen and the abstract machine of knitting', *Textile*, 11 (1): 6–19.

Calligeros, Marissa. (2015), 'Melbourne Artist Casey Jenkins' vaginal knitting prompts social media disgust', *Sydney Morning Herald*, 6 August. Available online: http://www.smh.com.au/entertainment/art-and-design/melbourne-artist-casey-jenkins-vaginal-knitting-prompts-social-media-disgust-20150807-giszij.html (accessed 7 September 2015).

Corbett, S. (2013), *A Little Book of Craftivism*, London: Cicada.

Crary, J. (2014), *24/7: Late Capitalism and the Ends of Sleep*, London and New York: Verso.

Cvetkovich, A. (2012), *Depression: A Public Feeling*, Durham and London: Duke University Press.

Deleuze, G. (1994), *Difference and Repetition*, Trans. P. Patton, New York: Columbia University Press.

Fitzpatrick, T., and K.-K. Kontturi (2015), 'Crafting change: Practicing activism in contemporary Australia', *Harlot of the Hearts: A Revealing Look at the Arts of Persuasion, No. 14*. Available online: http://harlotofthehearts.org/index.php/harlot/article/view/290/185 (accessed 15 October 2015).

Jenkins, C. (2013), 'I'm the "Vaginal Knitter" Performance Artist and I defend my Work', *The Guardian*, Tuesday 17 December 2013. Available online: http://www.theguardian.com/commentisfree/2013/dec/17/vaginal-knitting-artist-defence (accessed 13 October 2015).

Kontturi, K.-K. (2012), *Following the Flows of Process: A New Materialist Account of Contemporary Art*, Annales Universitatis Turkuensis, Ser. B – Tom. 329, Humaniora, Turku: Turku University.

Kristeva, J. (1981), Women's Time, Trans. A. Jardine and H. Blake, *Signs*, 7 (1): 13–35.

Mahler, J. (2008), *Lived Temporalities: Exploring Duration in Guatemala*, Bielefield: Transcript Verlag.

Manning, E. (2013), *Always More than One: Individuation's Dance*, Durham and London: Duke University Press.

Manning, E. (2015a), 'Artfulness', in R. Grusin (ed.), *The Nonhuman Turn*, 45–80, Minneapolis: The University of Minnesota Press.

Manning, E. (2015b), 'Pragmatics of the Useless: The Infrathin', A keynote lecture presented at the 6th International Conference on New materialisms, Transversal Practices: Matter, Ecology, Relationality, The University of Melbourne, 27–29 September.

Michael, L. (2015), 'Wrong way time', in L. Michael (ed.), *Fiona Hall: Wrong Way Time*, 23–37, Sydney: Piper Press and Australia Council of the Arts.

Parkins, W. (2004), Celebrity knitting and the temporality of postmodern, *Fashion Theory: The Journal of Dress, Body and Culture* 8 (4): 425–41.

Tiainen, M., K.-K. Kontturi, and I. Hongisto. (2015), 'Framing, following, middling: Towards methodologies of relational materialities', *Cultural Studies Review* 21 (2): 14–46. Available online: http://dx.doi.org/10.5130/csr.v21i2.4407 (accessed 15 December 2015).

Tjanpi Desert Weavers. (2015), 'Artists' statement' [an interview with Jo Foster and Linda Rive], in L. Michael (ed.), *Fiona Hall: Wrong Way Time*, 49–57, Sydney: Piper Press and Australia Council of the Arts.

Vaginal Knitting (Feed). (2013), video, SBS2 Australia, Available online: http://www.sbs.com.au/ondemand/video/74525763791/vaginal-knitting-the-feed (accessed 10 October 2015).

5

'Buy a hat, save a life'

Commodity activism, fair trade and crafting economies of change

Lisa A. Daily

A palpable simplicity, a comfort even, comes from slogans such as 'buy a hat, save a life'. Others too reassure consumers that their small quotidian acts of economic exchange provide life-changing tangible good for individuals and a societal whole: 'buy a pair [of shoes], give a pair to a child in need', 'this bag provides 185 school meals around the world', 'have a pint, change the world' or 'change your underwear, change the world'.[1] Each form of commodified aid, or what Roopali Mukherjee and Sarah Banet-Weiser deem *commodity activism,* circulates as a trifecta of good wherein '"doing good" and being a good consumer collapse into one and the same thing (2012: 12). Commodity, image and text all mobilize in the name of a new morally inclined capitalism that demonstrates that 'profit is achieved not by ruthless, inhumane practices or by unrestrained avarice but, rather, by both the corporation and the consumer acting "virtuously"' (Mukherjee and Banet-Weiser 2012: 11). In this model, consumption represents the individualization of an economic form of citizenship, or put another way, social activism morphs into marketable commodities and ideas about the world. What precisely is being consumed varies wildly from handmade hats and craft beers to fair trade dresses, mass-produced shoes and underwear, each with equally diverse interpretations of 'good'. In this chapter, only one avenue of 'doing good' is considered – that which focuses on the handmade crafted object as a source of empowerment for its artisan producer.

Evidenced in quips such as 'buy a hat, save a life', the chapter argues that craft economies reliant upon linking the commodity-form to acts of doing good depend upon a particular *optics of ethics.* This term frames how commodities, along with their images and texts, work to create imagined bonds of collectivity that enable the consumer – who is undoubtedly genuine in his/her desire to do good – to feel connected to a distant other in need. Most specifically for this chapter, optics of ethics unites affluent consumers from the Global North with female artisan producers in the Global South, who are seemingly reliant on the goodwill and gift of empowerment from the virtuous consumer and conscientious business or organization. I do not suggest that these practices are inherently bad, but rather that they are predicated upon a heightened neo-liberal logic wherein 'all dimensions of human life are cast in terms of market rationality' (Brown 2003). By situating social justice and the problems of the contemporary era in ready-made consumerist practices, it negates any criticism that would challenge the capitalist regime. Even ethical practices of fair trade '[do] not include the choice of not buying' (Johnston 2002: 46). The chapter cements these trends in three interrelated but distinct examples, some weighted more than others: Krochet Kids International, a US-based non-profit organization; Sudara, formerly known as the non-profit organization International Princess Project; and lastly, Global Girlfriends, an American for-profit business selling women-made, fair-trade products.[2] Each of these companies sells artisan products with claims of fair trade (whether following certification or not) and exists as a pathway towards empowerment for the distinctly female producers. The products themselves, as well as the images and text that circulate in their name, embody what Matthias Zick Varul deems a *symbolic use value*. This term emerges from Marx's notion of use value, but encompasses how commodities may take on symbolic forms. Within fair trade, symbolic use value saturates objects with the 'romantic commodification of the act of production itself', meaning that commodities function most usefully as the conduit of imagination so consumers may envision distant people and places (Varul 2008: 660). As it pertains to fair trade, many scholars refer to this process as a fetish for de-fetishization, which underscores how the movement strives to remove the original Marxian commodity fetish by unveiling the social relations of production (Lyon 2006; Binkley and Littler 2008). Social media and advertising most easily enact these processes with hashtag campaigns, online videos and photographs, and storytelling. Krochet Kids International goes so far as to brand its products with QR codes that allow consumers to find the artisan who made their product so they may 'write her a thank you note'.[3]

The moralization of trade and commodity activism

The blurring of familiar antinomies is ever present with politics, humanitarianism and social movements entering markets through the proliferation of not only non-profit organizations (which have dramatically increased over the past four decades), but also for-profit industries. Most companies that sell artisan fair trade products often frame the organization or business as a story of awakening – discovering a truer sense of self, moral outrage at a particular tragedy in a faraway place and the belief that the crisis is solvable through a simplistic act of entrepreneurship. For example, Sudara founder Shannon Keith retells her trip to India 'that opened her eyes to a tragedy occurring daily to women and girls throughout the country. She could hardly believe what she witnessed in India's Red Light Districts – modern day slavery' ('Our Story'). Her solution was to start PUNJAMMIES™, a line of loungewear 'made with hope by women in India who have escaped human trafficking' ('Punjammies'). The name itself – PUNJAMMIES – comes from the (un)clever decision to combine the word 'pajamas' with 'Punjab', a region in India. Like many companies and organizations that seek to 'empower' those who are in need, Sudara founder Shannon Keith is not a native of India, but rather travelled there from the United States.

Similarly, three young men from Spokane, Washington, who travelled during school breaks to volunteer in developing countries, started the non-profit organization, Krochet Kids International. All had learnt how to crochet, selling their own beanies for a while, and then after a trip to Uganda decided that teaching locals how to crochet would act as a way to empower the artisans to rise above poverty. Like Sudara, the intention to start a non-profit organization emerges from a place of concern, but its actions do little to stymie the broader structures that entrench communities in poverty. Instead, in the neo-liberal era social justice itself becomes a marketable idea, tangible in the commodity-form and the supporting images and text that simplify the consumer's activism. 'Changing the world' or 'saving a life' operates as a supposed recuperative frame that challenges the domineering abuses of a global capitalism gone awry with a 'First World' and a 'Third World' or a 'North' and a 'South' while ultimately ensuring its longevity. Furthermore, it disregards other contradictory everyday practices, environmental degradation and consumption levels. For instance, the good work of Krochet Kids is entirely dependent upon its continuation of selling piecemeal crocheted accessories, placing the empowerment ultimately in the wallets of affluent consumers and linking any expansion of good work to an expansion of consumerism under global capitalism.

These ideas for an ethical trade regime are certainly not new, emerging from the fair trade movement that originated to oppose unequal trade relations between countries in the post–Second World War Bretton Woods era and with its earliest roots in the 'old moral economy' and boycotts against slave and colonial abuses of production (Jaffee 2007: 17).[4] At the time, fair trade sought to radically rethink trade relations, seeking to make all trade more equitable. Today, however, it exists as a 'fundamental paradox' in that it has slowly given way to the ideological and economic pressures of market liberalization (Jaffee 2007: 1). Instead of dismantling the existing regime of exchange, fair trade functions within the hegemonic trading system of free markets with its niche products existing in tandem with those not designated fair trade. The supervision of what designates 'fair' within fair trade is not monitored by nation-states or supranational organizations, but rather by self-regulatory certification organizations and labelling. Moreover, multinational companies increasingly buy into fair trade as a way to brand themselves good corporate citizens, acquiring smaller ethical companies or starting their own line of fair trade: Coca Cola's acquisition of Honest Tea in 2011, Starbucks' fair trade coffee that is offered along with non-fair trade coffees or Nestlé's limited line of fair trade–certified chocolate.

Crafted goods in particular offer an alternate vision to the mass production of global capitalism with handmade products themselves appearing as a small form of resistance. Localism too rethinks the strategies of the nineteenth- and twentieth-century expansion of capitalism by privileging lived community, small-scale growth and a transparent commodity chain with locally sourced resources and labour. The idea of community – whether real or imagined – is central to these subcultural formations with images and their correlating texts most affectively reproducing these longings for a better world. As Raymond Williams suggests, the commodity 'has passed the frontier of the selling of goods and services and has become involved with the teaching of social and personal values' and is 'rapidly entering the world of politics' ([1980] 2005: 184). The implementation of symbols as commodity occurs through the 'magic' of advertising – a historical development that no longer merely *informs* the public of new products, but convinces them of new 'needs'. Williams understands this as a systemic problem wherein 'the material object being sold is never enough' ([1980] 2005: 185). Rather, the commodity, much in line with Marx's commodity fetishism, takes on mystical qualities, inducing the consumer into seeking material satisfaction for immaterial needs – love, confidence or even a sense of social justice and humanitarian concern.

In a 2013 interview with Henry Jenkins, Sarah Banet-Weiser discussed the implications of commodity activism, which may engender positive effects for social activism when 'not primarily organized around the accumulation of profit or building a corporate brand' because, as she understands it, commodity activism frequently has its goal as 'the identity of the consumer or brand of the corporation, not the activism itself' (Jenkins 2013). Commodity activism is even more nuanced than this, however, with non-profit organizations increasingly turning towards commodification and image-based cause-related marketing. An optics of ethics necessitates visual mediation – typically through social media such as Facebook, Instagram, YouTube and Twitter, but also through websites and physical meetings.

Imagining and the optics of ethics

An optics of ethics as a conceptual framework brings together the divergent characteristics of ethically minded companies and organizations that focus on commodified aid, fair trade or philanthropic endeavours, each featuring the recipient of the organization's will to empower distant others. Fundamental to the characteristics of an optics of ethics is the ways in which image and text work to foster an imaginative longing – a collectivism bound by fixed roles of consumer and producer or saviour and saved.[5] Within fair trade and other organizations that seek to empower those in need through employment, the artisanal producer is central with images demonstrating her happiness to work and supporting text making evident her hardship and how the consumer's purchase will benefit her. Unlike Krochet Kids International, Sudara says nothing of its actual labour practices, other than informing consumers that the products are made 'with hope.' Like most fair trade, however, the organization relies on images of female producers who are gleefully empowered – smiling, sewing or crocheting – and meet the goals of unveiling the commodity fetish by making clear (albeit vaguely) the social relations of production. To 'de-fetishize' a commodity invariably leads to a new type of fetish such that consumers cling to the images, texts and commodities themselves that reveal the lives and needs of the artisan. Sam Binkley and Jo Littler situate this transition in the anti-globalization, anti-sweatshop, anti-consumerism and pro-environmental movements spreading in the 1990s (2008).

The most distinctive quality of a Krochet Kids product – other than its superior craft aesthetic as handmade object – is the Krochet Kids tag with a handwritten name on it, which stands as a signpost alerting potentially oblivious consumers to the dual mission of artisan empowerment and a rejection of the anonymous mass production of industrial capitalism. It stands in stark contrast to other disruptions in the abstract machinery of productive forces such as in 2013 when an Oregon mother found a note from a Chinese forced labourer who made her 'Totally Ghoul' Halloween decoration: 'If you occasionally (sic) buy this product, please kindly resend this letter to the World Human Right Organization. Thousands people here … will thank and remember you forever' (Jiang 2013). Krochet Kids' desire for the female artisan to be known extends beyond a signature on the commodity itself. In 2013, products also featured a tag that asked consumers to scan a QR code so that they could 'find the lady' who made the product and 'write her a thank you note.'[6] Each artisan is searchable on the Krochet Kids website, having her own page where potential consumers may read stories – many quite traumatic, involving the Lord's Resistance Army in Uganda – learn about her dreams for the future, hobbies and a message she may want to share. Akwero Agnes wants Krochet Kids (KKU) to know: 'I send my thanks to KKU and prays that they should be able to continue to help us and other women so that our children can have a future through education' ('Akwero Agnes'). Reading these stories is undeniably compelling, but alongside the text are images that simultaneously reinforce the narrative of empowerment and challenge it. The images appear emancipatory when interpreted through the lens of the text's assertion of empowerment, but when read critically also appear as a particular hierarchical *way of seeing*, reminiscent of an imperialist gaze.[7] On each artisan's page, there is a very clear racial divide between 'producer' and 'consumer,' with the dark-skinned artisan producers (who are in need of empowerment from Western organizations) standing in contrast to the bottom section of each artisan page, 'Products I've Made', which features overwhelmingly light-skinned models who reinforce standard beauty tropes within the United States standing in contrast to the predominately light-skinned models wearing Krochet Kids products. An entire industry perpetuates these images, what Teju Cole refers to as the 'white savior industrial complex' (2012). Cole describes that after watching the Kony 2012 video he tweeted a seven-part assessment, the first of which states: 'From Sachs to Kristof to Invisible Children to TED, the fastest growth industry in the United States is the White Savior Industrial Complex' (2012).

Within fair trade, these tendencies to exocitize, racialize and gender artisan production appear as what Timothy Scrase deems a 'commodification of poverty' in that 'marginalized labor, and people themselves, are exploited for commercial or charitable gain' (Scrase 2011: 54–5). Unlike the traditional images of poverty porn – showcasing the horrors of poverty for philanthropic purposes exemplified in the United States with the 1990s Sally Struthers's Christian Children's Fund images – these new images circulate in the name of 'doing good' and exist to bind consumer-spectators to the positive material action that corresponds with their consumption.[8] Matthias Zick Varul connects this type of consumerist and imperialist gaze to histories of colonialism:

> The fair trade imagination is dominated by agricultural and artisanal producers in Latin America, Sub-Saharan Africa and South Asia – traditional settings for all sorts of daydreaming activities of white Europeans and North Americans, Joseph-Conrad-Land. The dreams hinged onto this imagery can range from radical Left identifications with national liberation movements, which allow the consumer to imagine themself as *guerrillero*, to post-colonial dreams supported by more mainstream products of the culture industry such as the film dramatization of *Out of Africa*, which allow the consumer to imagine themself as a benevolent colonial master or mistress. (2008: 661)

Rather, for Varul the social relations between producers and distributors/consumers only further the colonial orderings of power. Nevertheless, Varul recognizes the contradictory placement of fair trade in a capitalist regime; despite its flaws, fair trade exposes a 'ghost [that] would have remained invisible' (2008: 674). So, on the one hand, artisan bios and Krochet Kids more generally work to expose brutal political, social and economic conditions of women to faraway consumers; on the other hand, such actions simplistically place the solution to conflict, poverty and development within the sphere of consumer culture. Timothy J. Scrase echoes this critical interpretation when writing about artisan communities and globalization:

> Globalization has intensified the precarious existence of artisan communities through increasing global competition, the mass production of craft goods, and shifting trends in fashion, cultural

taste and aesthetics. Both government and non-government efforts at supporting artisans are criticised for providing limited and ineffectual programmes and policies. Moreover, recent consumer trends like 'fair trade' shopping are likewise only piecemeal and limited in terms of the long-term support they can give to struggling artisan communities. When artisans survive, they do so mainly on the periphery of both global and local capitalist economies; this is a situation that has rarely changed over the decades. In various ways, and in specific regional contexts, the globalisation of production exacerbates, rather than diminishes, the marginal status of artisan communities. (2003: 449)

Additionally, a romanticization of craft labour occurs, especially in the minds of postindustrial consumers who understand it as non-alienating and a meaningful skill that brings joy to artisans (tacitly acknowledged by their smiling portraits). Craft as a mode of production stands removed from mass production, but still risks being subjected to the same deskilling conditions wherein artisans merely reproduce designs and colours given to them by someone else. Krochet Kids, for instance, produces the same commodities despite the artisan producing it. Each goes through a mentorship programme to learn the skills (and patterns) to produce the products. The founder of Global Girlfriend relates this need to control design to what she calls the 'Carved Giraffe Theory.' She asks, 'Who wants a carved giraffe? This is not a go-to gift; you can only sell so many carved giraffes' (Edgar 2011: 42). She continues, 'My beef is not with wooden giraffes specifically. My problem is with not teaching artisans in the developing world what mainstream consumers are buying so that the artisans can increase their business and therefore reduce poverty in their lives and communities … artisans need to grow and change with the market' (Ibid.). Hence, empowerment is ultimately subjected to the volatility of markets and the success of campaigns such as Krochet Kids' hashtag movement *#KnowWhoMadeIt*. A compelling video commercial initiated the campaign, which opens with quick-cut frames of artisanal work – a young blonde woman designing a magazine, an ageing Caucasian man hand making a violin, a younger man crafting a surfboard and, finally in the last fifteen seconds, a dark-skinned woman crocheting and a (presumed) Peruvian woman sitting at a sewing machine. Alongside all of these images, a soothing voice narrates:

> What gives an object value? How do you measure its worth? Is it the material? What the product is made of? Is it the construction? The process through which its built? Or is it who made it? The heart, intention, and effort that carried the product from start to finish? Behind every product is a person – a person full of ideas, dreams, and desires. Someone who possesses the inspiration for creation and the potential to break the status quo. Someone whose work is as unique as they are. We believe that this is where the true value of an object lies. Products have worth because people do. ('Know Who Made It')

To return to the idea of imagining and the optics of ethics, Krochet Kids encourages a one-directional gazing that enables consumers to feel good about their purchase by knowing something about its production. Whereas almost all fair trade today relies upon artisan stories to promote goods, Krochet Kids takes this further by individual signatures and the possibility for consumers to write thank-you notes to the woman who crafted the purchased item. Each artisan bio-page collects these thank-you notes – a form of legitimation or online consumer review – and through the commodity and online mediation, consumers give the appearance of feeling a connection.[9] On

Aber Proscovia's page, one consumer writes: 'Aber Proscovia, thank you so much for the care and time you took to make my "Agnes" beanie. I love it so much. I have been spreading the word about my beanie and mentioning your name. I know we are a world away from each other, but I now feel a connection with you and your story. Best wishes in everything! Thank you Aber!' ('Aber Proscovia'). To Akech Santa, someone tells her how they initially almost cut off the tag with her name, but then realized what it was, now feeling inspired and with the 'desire ... for you to see your children through school so they have a fair chance at succeeding' ('Akech Santa'). Some consumers provide details about themselves – where they live, favourite colours, age – but most offer a simple thank you and good luck. And a surprising many 'God Bless.' What is largely absent from the thank-you notes is the acknowledgement of the craft as an explicit form of labour. Instead, the letters read like one friend thanking another for a care-package. Perhaps a recognition of the labour implied in the appreciation of the commodity, but it could also reflect a discomfort on the part of the affluent consumer to think more systematically about consumer habits and the origins of commodities.

Conclusion

In her 1993 ethnographic book *Crafts in the World Market,* anthropologist June Nash argues that crafts are 'a medium of communication between people who live profoundly different lives, but who can respond to the symbols, textures, and forms that express distinct cultural traditions' (1–2). She continues by noting a reversal in flows – no longer from industrial centres of the metropole to the colonial periphery – as 'consumers seek the exotic and unique objects of handicraft production in Third World countries' (Ibid.). In the age of ever-present mass production and capitalist expansion, niche products such as fair trade increasingly find worthy socially conscious consumers. The objects themselves are no longer what appears exotic, however, but rather a 'romantic commodification' or 'commodification of poverty' wherein the act of exotic artisanal labour as a form of empowerment becomes the commodity itself. While the idea of de-fetishization putatively continues with campaigns such as Krochet Kids *#KnowWhoMadeIt,* scanning a QR code to find out the lady who made a particular product and being able to write her a thank-you note, this type of making visible ultimately re-fetishizes, as evidenced in simplistic products like the 'Behind every product is a person' t-shirt or the simple Krochet Kids graphic-tee that reads 'LOVE,' with an image of the African continent substituting the 'o'. Each of these commodities proffers a route to a consumerist fantasy whereby she/he may evoke the imagined bonds of collectivity as a way to feel good as an economic actor, knowing that by buying a hat, a beer or a new pair of underwear, she/he is saving a life, fighting hunger or changing the world.

Notes

1   These slogans come from for-profit and non-profit organizations alike: Krochet Kids International ('buy a hat, save a life'); Toms Shoes trademarked idea of 'One for One,' wherein the consumer buys a pair and a like-product is given to a child in need; FEED Project's goal of providing meals

through the purchase of bags and other products; the Oregon Public House, a non-profit pub; and the Thinx, a company selling 'period-proof' underwear to empower women and dismantle the stigma of menstruation.

2 Krochet Kids International: http://www.krochetkids.org Sudara: http://www.sudara.org; Global Girlfriend: https://www.globalgirlfriend.com (all websites accessed 6 May 2016).

3 This was a 2013 campaign. I am unsure if the campaign still continues with products purchased, but the website still allows for consumers to search for particular artisans and each item made has the female artisan's name written on the tag.

4 For more on the 'old moral economy,' see E. P. Thompson's 'The Moral Economy of the English Crowd in the Eighteenth Century,' 76–136.

5 Roland Barthes describes the relationship between image and text, stating, 'Formerly, the image illustrated the text (made it clearer); today, the text loads the image, burdening it with a culture, a moral, an imagination' (*Image, Music, Text,* 26).

6 From a product personally purchased in 2013.

7 The idea of the imperial gaze comes from Ann E. Kaplan's *Looking for the Other: Feminism, Film and the Imperial Gaze.* Also see Anne McClintock's *Imperial Leather: Race, Gender and Sexuality in the Colonial Contest.*

8 For more on Sally Struther's campaign, see this 1992 infomercial, accessed 6 May 2016: https://www.youtube.com/watch?v=XsxVy7vyyk0. Relatedly, see World Vision's 'Sponsor a Child' program, accessed 6 May 2016. http://www.worldvision.org/sponsor-a-child Lastly, see Swiger 2002.

9 A cynical reading of these actions could be that consumers write thank-you notes as a way to sufficiently brand themselves conscious consumers.

References

'Aber Proscovia,' *Krochet Kids:* http://www.krochetkids.org/beneficiaries/aber-proscovia/ (accessed 28 August 2015).

'Akech Santa,' *Krochet Kids:* http://www.krochetkids.org/beneficiaries/akech-santa/ (accessed 28 August 2015).

'Akwero Agnes,' *Krochet Kids:* http://www.krochetkids.org/beneficiaries/akwero-agnes/ (accessed 28 August 2015).

Barthes, R. (1977), *Image/Music/Text,* Translated by Stephen Heath. New York: Noonday Press.

Binkley, S., and J. Littler. (2008), 'Anti-consumerism and cultural studies', *Cultural Studies,* 22 (5): 519–30.

Brown, W. (2003), 'Neoliberalism and the end of liberal democracy', *Theory & Event,* 7 (1) John Hopkins University Press, https://muse.jhu.edu/article/48659 (accessed November 3, 2017).

Christian Children's Fund. (1992), 'Infomercial'. Available online: https://www.youtube.com/watch?v=XsxVy7vyyk0 (accessed 6 May 2016).

Cole, T. (2012), 'The White Savior industrial complex', *The Atlantic,* 21 March. Available online: http://www.theatlantic.com/international/archive/2012/03/the-white-savior-industrial-complex/254843/ (accessed 29 March 2013).

Duncombe, S. (2007), *Dream: Re-imagining Progressive Politics in an Age of Fantasy.* New York: New Press.

Edgar, S. (2011), *Global Girlfriends: How One Mom Made it Her Business to Help Women in Poverty Worldwide,* New York: St. Martin's Press.

Global Girlfriend Website: https://www.globalgirlfriend.com (accessed 6 May 2016).

Jaffee, D. (2007), *Brewing Justice: Fair Trade Coffee, Sustainability, and Survival*, Berkeley, CA: University of California Press.

Jenkins, H. (2013), 'Thinking critically about brand cultures: An interview with Sarah Banet-Weiser', *Henry Jenkins Blog*, 12 April. Available online: http://henryjenkins.org/2013/04/thinking-critically-about-brand-cultures-an-interview-with-sarah-banet-weiser-part-two.html#sthash.GAnfFWpt.dpuf (accessed 12 May 2015).

Jiang, S. (2013), 'Chinese labor camp inmate tells of true horror of Halloween SOS', *CNN*, 7 November, Available online: http://www.cnn.com/2013/11/06/world/asia/china-labor-camp-halloween-sos/ (accessed 27 July 2015).

Johnston, J. (2002), 'Consuming global justice: Fair trade shopping and alternative development', in J. Goodman (ed.), *Protest and Globalisation*, 38–56, Annandale, New South Wales: Pluto Press Australia.

'Know Who Made It,' Krochet Kids: http://www.krochetkids.org/knowwhomadeit/ (accessed 28 August 2015).

Lyon, S. (2006), 'Evaluating fair trade consumption: Politics, defetishization and producer participation', *International Journal of Consumer Studies*, 30 (5): 452–64.

McClintock, A. (1995), *Imperial Leather: Race, Gender, and Sexuality in the Colonial Conquest*, New York: Routledge.

Mukherjee, R., and S. Banet-Weiser, eds. (2012), *Commodity Activism: Cultural Resistance in Neoliberal Times*, New York: New York University Press.

Nash, J. (1993), *Crafts in the World Market: The Impact of Global Exchange on Middle American Artisans*, Albany, NY: State University of New York Press.

'Our Story,' Sudara: http://sudara.org/pages/our-story (accessed 29 July 2015).

'Punjammies,' Sudara: http://sudara.org/collections/PUNJAMMIES (accessed 29 July 2015).

Scrase, T. J. (2011), 'Fair trade in cyberspace: The commodification of poverty and the marketing of handicrafts on the internet', in T. Lewis and E. Potter (eds.), *Ethical Consumption: A Critical Introduction*, 54–69. New York: Routledge.

Sudara: http://www.sudara.org (accessed 6 May 2016).

Swiger, M. (2002), 'Sally Struthers, christian children's fund, and the construction of whiteness', *Journal of American & Comparative Culture*, 25 (1/2): 199.

Thompson, E. P. (1971), 'The moral economy of the English crowd in the eighteenth century', *Past and Present*, 50 (1): 76–136.

Varul, M. V. (2008), 'Consuming the Campesino', *Cultural Studies*, 22 (5): 654–59.

Williams, R. ([1980] 2005), 'Advertising: The magic system', *Culture and Materialism*, New York: Verso, 2005: 170–95.

World Vision, 'Sponsor a child': http://www.worldvision.org/sponsor-a-child (accessed 6 May 2016).

PART TWO

Craft, the 'handmade' and contested commodification

6

Towards a politics of making

Reframing material work and locating skill in the Anthropocene

Chris Gibson and Chantel Carr

A widespread assumption in advanced economies has been that the decline of manufacturing is inevitable. Within this narrative, making is usurped by a transition to knowledge work, where the value of a product is said to be in its intellectual or design content, not in its material fabrication. In this chapter, we seek to broaden current debates around making in two ways: First, we question the ontological and political premises underpinning the false distinction between making material things and creative labour processes. Second, we argue that a more catastrophic frame, ascendant in the Anthropocene,[1] is necessary to re-evaluate the contributions of making (including, but also beyond, craft and manufacturing) towards survival. Such a catastrophic framing, as urged by climate adaptation scientists, enables a debate in which the broad social or moral dimensions of economic activities are foregrounded, rather than a more narrow focus on manufacturing or craft per se. Put differently, how should we make, and what skills are needed to make, given the looming spectre of economic and environmental crisis? We have argued elsewhere that ensuing carbon-sensitive futures will rely heavily on the abilities of those who can make things and re-purpose materials with minimal energy and resource requirements (Carr and Gibson 2016). Part of the debate needs to be not just how particular skills might support the reinvention of manufacturing or new forms of crafting, but also what capacities and dispositions might exist in 'old' manufacturing regions and cultures, for working with existing physical resources.

The chapter is structured as follows. First, we seek to transcend a historically recurring binary, where small-scale 'craft' traditions (cast as Arts and Crafts-era expertise, or in the mould of pre-Fordist artisanal production) are pitted against large-scale 'manufacturing'. Rather, through a review of research developments across the full spectrum of 'making cultures', we aim to define the contours of a necessary shift to a focus on making (as disposition and practice across and within both scales and modes of production), with materials at the core. Central to many 'making cultures', we argue, are suggestions of sensibilities and dispositions that are centred on a deep and considered relationship with materials. From this perspective we advocate for a renewed focus on making amid ecological volatility. Second, we turn to focus on makers themselves, and what making and material skill might have to offer as we steam headfirst into an era of greater biophysical uncertainty. Those with productive capacity and material skill have seldom featured in debates about ecological crisis thus far, but, we argue, these skills are critically important to a future where extending the life of the stuff around us will be more highly valued. Such makers, skills and dispositions are found in diverse places and industries, and even in the most unlikely of places, in the heart of the carbon-intensive industrial beast.

Manufacture versus craft, or cultures of making?

Making is central to human endeavour – what we make as part of everyday practice forms our identities and place in the world. The mundane experience of making is 'resolutely political, a geographical imperative, and a critical means of operating a meaningful relationship with this material life' (Paton 2013, p. 1084). In an era much abuzz with the prospects of new digital technologies, robotics and 3D printing, it is salient to remember the massive extent to which workers in factories, workshops and homes are still occupied making material things. All manner of deeply profound material knowledge, haptic practices and forms of manual work are still present at the heart of global economies.

In seeking a semantic and ontological shift from manufacturing or craft as separate ontological domains, our intent is to reframe the debate about 'economy' (Massey and Rustin 2014). We need to move onwards from the modern capitalist paradigm of profit-driven, high-throughput production of physical things towards other ways to furnish humans with material comforts. A focus on making as a cultural and economic process is a deliberate attempt to reframe some of the more orthodox thinking about economy and society – where the presumption has been that a broad shift in the character of the contemporary economy has both euthanized manufacture in the Global North and excised material production from tasks of design, intellectual property and marketing (Berger 2013). That shift arguably first emerged with the demise of the guild system, where early industrialists argued that innovation was being constrained by the dominance of carefully guarded oral and haptic methods of skills transfer – and thus separated intellectual functions from material production, socially and spatially (Vercellone 2007). It gathered pace in postwar industrialized countries where capitalists, in efforts to fragment and extract maximum value from labour, reorganized modes of production – and the shop floor – to separate 'mind' tasks (design, finance) from 'body' tasks (assembly, manual fabrication) (Guéry and Deleule 2014). In time the embodied tasks of manual labour were typecast as repetitive and even demeaning, while the mind tasks became associated with higher levels of education, skill, economic value and intellectual satisfaction. Against the mise-en-scène of industrial decline in the Global North, an almost counter-cultural renaissance in small-scale making has emerged, often within industrial cities and regions where manufacturing and urban industrial heritage confers authenticity (Curran 2010). In this world, re-connections are being forged with themes such as quality, providence, craft, ethics, tacit design knowledge, haptic skill and the value of physical labour (see also Adamson 2007; Sennett 2008; Gauntlett 2011; Crawford 2009; Charny 2011).

The respective literatures on craft and manufacturing each have important things to say about making. Research on craft has explored dynamic (new) relationships between individualized and collectivized forms of production and consumption. Crafting often reconnects 'mind' and 'body' in the sites and processes of production, therefore potentially reconstituting the labour process in ways that ascribe agency to workers (cf. Guéry and Deleule 2014; Warren 2014). In multiple spaces of craft making (at home, in collectives, in community maker spaces) researchers have documented possibilities for makers to resist norms of gender and neo-liberal entrepreneurial subjectivities – findings ways and spaces for ethical practice to predominate (Moloy and Larner 2013; Morrow 2014). Across the commercial/non-capitalist divide, maker cultures celebrate forms of proximate sociality (being strongly network-based and emphasizing 'community') and forge closer connections between producers and consumers (Warren and Gibson 2014). Craft makers appreciate the provenance of input materials and emphasize the value of human skill embodied in high-quality things made to last, intended as 'heirlooms' (Rexrode 2014). Greater degrees of material self-sufficiency stemming from craft practice and DIY culture also promote autonomy outside of conventional governance modes (Pickerill and Chatterton 2006), and thus inform localized responses to climate change framed around resource preservation and stewardship. Craft enterprises and contemporary guilds thus play a peculiar role in 'producing' place (Thomas, Harvey and Hawkins 2013).

Nevertheless, where crafting and handmaking cultures grow beyond immediate use value, towards a commercial imperative, 'pleasure and self-fulfilment are often exchanged for what might otherwise be felt to be unstable, precarious, and even exploitive work' (Dawkins 2010, p. 261; see also Luckman 2012; Barnes 2014). Where profit motive reigns, the result is less a radical restructuring of the workplace and more a reconstitution of petite bourgeois modes of production. While crafting cultures provide genuine alternatives to high-throughput commodity production and consumption, associated discourses of 'handmade', 'crafted' and 'bespoke' have all too easily become appropriated as marketing buzzwords by companies selling conventional products (from soft drinks to sneakers), which are made in conventional ways that do nothing to challenge the status quo. Researchers have accordingly made links between craft and the creativity discourse, with accompanying critiques of governmental logics, precarity and the lived experience of work (Banks 2010; Jakob 2013; Luckman 2015; Munro and O'Kane 2017). Meanwhile categories of artisanal expertise are situated in ways that reproduce lingering hierarchical legacies (Herzfeld 2004). Such tensions and contradictions have endured through several cycles of revival since the emergence of the Arts and Crafts Movement over a century ago (Lears 1981). Then a radical emancipatory response to the alienation of factory labour, craft production was deftly relegated to leisure time and its objects rendered a source of elite consumption, when it became clear that the structural conditions that divided the affluent from the poor were insurmountable.

We also acknowledge the importance of parallel critiques of the political economy of manufacturing within the capitalist space economy. In this regard, like Cook (2004), we are inspired by David Harvey's (1990, p. 422) call for radical scholars to 'get behind the veil, the fetishism of the market', to 'make powerful, important, disturbing connections between Western consumers and the distant strangers whose [making] contributions to their lives were invisible, unnoticed, and largely unappreciated' (Cook 2004, p. 642). The things we make and use in life are core to this. Further, making broadens the scope of inquiry beyond the archetypal craft or industrial worker in the Global North, to acknowledge the plethora of extraordinary creative practices being performed by those outside the west, either in waged work or from sheer necessity, without a hint of countercultural aesthetics or nostalgia. For instance, making encompasses the disassembly of things as they flow 'down the value chain' from the affluent to be appropriated elsewhere (Gregson et al. 2010), or making objects of profound use value from otherwise 'worthless' things (Klocker, Mbena and Gibson 2017). Our agenda, then, is to suggest existential reassessment of how we could approach making differently, incorporating anthropological and cultural perspectives on a broader set of material practices amid volatility (Ingold 2010, 2012, 2013), that certainly include craft, but also practices of repair (Bond, DeSilvey and Ryan 2013; Gregson, Metcalfe and Crewe 2009), maintenance (Graham and Thrift 2007; Carr 2017), recycling (Crang et al. 2013; Gregson et al. 2013), and cultures of thrift and scavenging (Lane, Horne and Bicknell 2009). In other words, within a moment of profound material crisis (and emboldened by the notion of Anthropocene), we wish to look beyond existing modes of industrial production, towards opportunities to revisit fundamental questions of how humans manipulate materials, compose objects and construct economies and societies around material things – as well as how this might be done differently.

Makers for the Anthropocene?

Debates about how to reframe 'economy' in light of more catastrophic futures have thus far seldom intersected with questions of makers and their skills, especially within industrial cities and regions. In this second section we seek to broker such a connection and to expand on the locally situated ways in which people acculturated with making are equipped to plan for, adapt to and negotiate the effects of a variable climate. Recent work on global environmental change has shifted its attention from the need to maintain gentle transition to instead comprehend radical transformation (Park et al. 2012). This raises the questions of how to provide alternative means to sustenance and comfort that do not depend on resource abundance, and as to who is best placed to deal with material scarcity, should rationing and shared sacrifice become more widespread necessities (Head 2013). Initiatives such as the Circular Economy (see http://ellenmacarthurfoundation.org/ and Hobson 2015), the field of industrial ecology and investigations into product stewardship offer a range of approaches (Lane and Watson 2012). Here, we are interested in how concepts and critiques of resourcefulness, resilience and everyday practice (e.g. Strengers and Maller 2012; MacKinnon and Derickson 2013) intersect with various scales of making, and what this means for a future where disruption to entrenched patterns of production and consumption appears inevitable.

In a race to narrate a shift to the 'information age', important discussions have been neglected regarding the cultural values that emerge in seemingly imperilled industrial places where physical materials are encountered in everyday work and life, and where things are made (Warren and Gibson 2011). An extended ethnography conducted with skilled steelworkers in Australia, for example, has revealed longheld dispositions of thrift, creativity and care towards discarded industrial materials in the context of homes and neighbourhoods (Carr, 2017). Re-engaging with such workers and practices illuminates an untapped reservoir of skill beyond 'craft' and outside of existing frames of climate change adaptation (which tend to use bald demographic data to model static vulnerability to geophysical risks – see Gibson, Head and Carr 2015). People who are skilled in dealing with the material world in the face of disruption offer a powerful challenge to the idea of the industrial city as terminally ill or lacking resilience, and a place whose whole economic and social structure lies in the path of the 'new' economy.

Normative ideas about how making proceeds tend to focus on bringing skill to bear on material (cf. Sennett 2008). Tim Ingold counters this model with the concept of material 'itineration'. Here space is made for improvisation in the face of changing context, acknowledging that things do not come into being in a physical or temporal vacuum. More simply, 'makers work in a world that does not stand still' (Ingold 2010, p. 93). In such contexts, 'creativity' involves not merely a spark of innovation or the execution of artistic inspiration, but also the capacity to respond to unfolding iterations with materials, to use slowly accrued haptic knowledge to manipulate processes 'on the fly' and to judge how to counteract error and seize opportunities as they evolve. Such conceptions of creativity encompass 'expert' making (as governed within guild and formal apprenticeship systems), but also unheralded acts of adjustment with routine production, and diverse and prosaic forms of material manipulation and repurposing among the poor (for lively examples, see www.mkshft.org).

Yet such resources are clearly endangered. As the literature on craft repeatedly emphasizes, the ability to work with materials in skilled ways is under threat from automation, deskilling and labour precarity (Warren 2016). It has been estimated that as many as forty-seven per cent of all manual jobs are at risk of future computerization (Frey and Osborne 2013). In the face of 'remorseless competition from factory production and its globalization', artisans 'need all the ingenuity they can muster' (Herzfeld 2004, p. 1). And it is concerning that diverse skills with materials are being lost at a time when climate change raises issues of technological and material uncertainty. Further investigation into diverse cultures of making – within Western industrial modernist maker culture; within prosaic collecting/remaking cultures across the Global South; within crafts such as carpentry, luthiery and cabinet-making that are grappling with new conditions of raw materials scarcity and tight regulation – is an important avenue through which manual skills and the reuse of materials can be guided in a productive response to climate change.

Conclusion

Discussions around craft and manufacturing must be more clearly pinned to a range of wider debates: on making, moral economy and ecological crisis (Hudson 2012); progressive policy-making driven by an ethic of care for the long-run viability of neighbourhoods and communities (Clark 2012); the mundane and material ways in which economies are 'made' (Lee 2006); emancipation of both domestic and waged labour (Gibson-Graham, Cameron and Healy 2013; Cornwell 2012; McDowell 2014) and normative critique of the 'rightness'/'wrongness' of forms of production and commoditization (Castree 2004, p. 32). There are existential questions for society and for the state, about a productive basis for society, who makes the things we need, whether via formal industrial organization and specialization or decentralized models of craft, repair and self-sufficiency (cf. Massey and Rustin 2014). As Hudson (2012, p. 374) has argued, 'Knowledge of what it is materially possible to produce is a necessary pre-condition for consideration of alternative conceptions that challenge the hegemony of capitalist material interests and imagine alternative ecologically sustainable and socially just visions of the economy'.

Making is also central to our legacy as a society – economically, ecologically and socially. Generations to follow will be dealing with our made objects, buildings and associated detritus just as we are dealing with the asbestos, lead and concrete cancer from things made in previous generations. A focus on making provides a potential parallel means to connect the urgency of environmental crisis and the spectre of the Anthropocene to critiques of production and consumption (and thence to material aspects of daily life) in ways that make practical sense to people. Ultimately, geographies of making invites debate on what kind of economy we want to become and what kind of social roles we ascribe to manual skill. At stake are paid jobs, but also, individually and collectively, responsibilities to access, use and value material resources ethically.

There is a distinctive role here for craft. Research on craft has focused important attention on the processes, materials and effect of making and the blurring of productive/domestic, sub/urban and private/public binaries (Bain 2013; Luckman 2015). Such contributions also draw attention to the endangered status of particular vernacular or professional skills or ways of working with (and thinking about) materials, in the process offering an important historical framework for contemporary investigations into making (Thomas et al. 2013; Luckman 2012). Like discussions of repair and remake cultures borne out of sheer necessity (Gregson et al. 2010), they are also firmly rooted in context, often evocatively sketching out the relations between material and place.

But our point is not to suggest that craft-based modes of production, through their perceived smallness and localness, provide the preeminent alternative to manufacturing. That, as we argued at the outset, falsely reconstructs the modernist binaries of home and waged production, of artisanal pre-industrial trades against big manufacturing. For even within the industrial behemoth, exemplified in the massive complex of the steelworks, there are small-scale examples of making, repair and non-capitalist provisioning for surrounding households and communities (Carr 2017). Meanwhile in the small-scale culture of domestic craft enterprise, there is a rapidly expanding, fetishized and globally networked economy premised on promoting the entrepreneurial self and continued consumption of stuff (Barnes 2014). Signals for a constructive path forward are indeed present in experimental alternatives opened up by small-scale, non-capitalist and self-provisioning crafting, but – and here is our key point – they are also present in other places, including those deep within the modernist manufacturing enterprise.

Note

1 The Anthropocene is a term that has been proposed across the natural and social sciences to describe a new geological epoch defined by the unprecedented influence of humans on global systems. See Head (2015) for a comprehensive and current review of the term and its politics.

References

Adamson, G. (2007), *Thinking Through Craft*, London and New York: Bloomsbury.
Bain, A. (2013), *Creative Margins: Cultural Production in Canadian Suburbs*, Toronto: University of Toronto Press.

Banks, M. (2010), 'Craft labour and creative industries', *International Journal of Cultural Policy*, 16 (3): 305–21.

Barnes, J. (2014), 'Aspirational Economies of Self and City: The Values and Governance of Independent Crafters in Columbus, Ohio', PhD diss., Ohio State University.

Berger, S. (2013), *Making in America*, Cambridge: MIT Press.

Bond, S., DeSilvey, C. and Ryan, J. (2013), *Visible Mending: Everyday Repairs in the South West*, Axminster: UniformBooks.

Carr, C. (2017), 'Maintenance and repair as "life's work": Linking industrial labour and the home', *Transactions of the Institute of British Geographers,* doi:10.1111/tran.12183.

Carr, C. and Gibson, C. (2016), 'Geographies of making: Rethinking materials and skills for volatile futures', *Progress in Human Geography*, 40 (3), 297–315

Castree, N. (2004), 'The geographical lives of commodities: problems of analysis and critique', *Social & Cultural Geography*, 5: 21–35.

Charny, D. (2011), *The Power of Making*, London: V&A Museum.

Clark, J. (2012), 'Is there a progressive approach to innovation policy?', *Progressive Planning*, 190: 17–22.

Cook, I. (2004), "Follow the thing: Papaya", *Antipode*, 36 (4): 642–64.

Cornwell, J. (2012), 'Worker co-operatives and spaces of possibility', *Antipode*, 44 (3): 725–44.

Crang, M., Hughes, A., Gregson, N., Norris, L. and Ahamed, F. (2013), 'Rethinking governance and value in commodity chains through global recycling networks', *Transactions of the Institute of British Geographers*, 38 (1): 12–24.

Crawford, M. (2009), *Shop Class as Soul Craft: An Enquiry into the Value of Work*, New York: Penguin.

Curran, W. (2010), 'In defense of old industrial spaces: Manufacturing, creativity and innovation in Williamsburg, Brooklyn', *International Journal of Urban and Regional Research*, 34 (4): 871–85.

Dawkins, N. (2010), 'Do-It-Yourself : The precarious work and postfeminist politics of handmaking (in) Detroit', *Utopian Studies*, 22 (2): 261–84.

Frey, C. and Osborne, M. (2013), *The Future of Employment: How Susceptible are Jobs to Computerisation?* University of Oxford, Programme on the Impacts of Future Technology Working Paper, 17 September. Available at: http://www.oxfordmartin.ox.ac.uk/downloads/academic/The_Future_of_Employment.pdf

Gauntlett, D. (2011), *Making is Connecting: The Social Meaning of Creativity, from DIY and Knitting to YouTube and Web 2.0*, Cambridge: Polity Press.

Gibson, C., Head, L. and Carr, C. (2015), 'From incremental change to radical disjuncture: Rethinking household sustainability practices as survival skills', *Annals of the Association of American Geographers*, 105 (2), 416–24.

Gibson-Graham, J.-K., Cameron, J. and Healy, S. (2013), *Take Back the Economy: An Ethical Guide for Transforming our Communities*, Minneapolis: University of Minnesota Press.

Graham, S. and Thrift, N. (2007), 'Out of order: Understanding repair and maintenance', *Theory, Culture and Society*, 24: 1–24.

Gregson, N., Crang, M., Ahamed, F., Akhter, N. and Ferdous, R. (2010), 'Following things of rubbish value: end-of-life ships, "chock-chocky" furniture and the Bangladeshi middle class consumer', *Geoforum*, 41: 846–54.

Gregson, N., Crang, M., Laws, J., Fleetwood, T. and Holmes, H. (2013), 'Moving up the waste hierarchy: Car boot sales, reuse exchange and the challenges of consumer culture to waste prevention', *Resources, Conservation and Recycling*, 77: 97–107.

Gregson, N., Metcalfe, A. and Crewe, L. (2009), 'Practices of object maintenance and repair: How consumers attend to consumer objects within the home', *Journal of Consumer Culture*, 9: 248–72.

Guéry, F. and Deleule, D. (2014) [1972] *The Productive Body*. Zero Books (transl. Barnard, P. and Shapiro, S.).

Harvey, D. (1990), 'Between space and time: reflections on the geographical imagination', *Annals of the Association of American Geographers*, 80 (3): 418–34.

Head, L. (2013), The conversation we need to have about carbon. *The Conversation*. 22 July, http://theconversation.com/the-conversation-we-need-to-have-about-carbon-16142

Head, L. (2015), 'The Anthropoceneans', *Geographical Research*, 53 (3): 313–20.

Herzfeld, M. (2004), *The Body Impolitic: Artisans and Artifice in the Global Hierarchy of Value*. Chicago: University of Chicago Press.

Hobson, K. (2015), 'Closing the loop or squaring the circle: Locating generative spaces for the circular economy', *Progress in Human Geography*, 40: 88–104.

Hudson, R. (2012), 'Critical political economy and material transformation', *New Political Economy*, 17(4): 373–97.

Ingold, T. (2010), 'The textility of making', *Cambridge Journal of Economics*, 34: 91–102.

Ingold, T. (2012), 'Toward an ecology of materials', *Annual Review of Anthropology*, 41: 427–42.

Ingold, T. (2013), *Making: Anthropology, Archaeology, Art and Architecture*, London and New York: Routledge.

Jakob, D. (2013), 'Crafting your way out of the recession? New craft entrepreneurs and the global economic downturn', *Cambridge Journal of Regions, Economy and Society*, 6 (1): 127–40.

Klocker, N., Mbenna, P., Gibson, C. (2017) 'From troublesome materials to fluid technologies: making and playing with plastic bag footballs', *Cultural Geographies*. DOI: 10.1177/1474474017732979.

Lane, R., Horne, R. and Bicknell, J. (2009), 'Routes of reuse of second-hand goods in Melbourne households', *Australian Geographer*, 40: 151–68.

Lane, R. and Watson, M. (2012), 'Stewardship of things: the radical potential of product stewardship for re-framing responsibilities and relationships to products and materials', *Geoforum*, 43 (6): 1254.

Lears, T. J. (1981), *No Place of Grace: Antimodernism and the Transformation of American Culture 1880-1920*, Chicago: University of Chicago Press.

Lee, R. (2006), 'The ordinary economy: tangled up in values and geography', *Transactions of the Institute of British Geographers*, 31: 413–32.

Luckman, S. (2012), *Locating Cultural Work: The Politics and Poetics of Rural, Regional and Remote Creativity*, Basingstoke: Palgrave MacMillan.

Luckman, S. (2015), *Craft and the Creative Economy*, Basingstoke: Palgrave Macmillan.

MacKinnon, D. and Derickson, K. (2013), 'From resilience to resourcefulness: a critique of resilience policy and activism', *Progress in Human Geography*, 37 (2): 253–70.

Massey, D. and Rustin, M. (2014), 'Whose economy? Reframing the debate.' In: S. Hall, D. Massey and M. Rustin (eds.), *After Neoliberalism? The Kilburn Manifesto*, Soundings, http://www.lwbooks.co.uk/journals/soundings/manifesto.html

McDowell, L. (2014), 'The lives of others: Body work, the production of difference, and labor geographies', *Economic Geography*, 91:1–23.

Moloy, M. and Larner, W. (2013), *Fashioning Globalisation: Design, Working Women and the Cultural Economy*, Oxford: Wiley-Blackwell.

Morrow, O. (2014), 'Urban Homesteading: Diverse Economies and Ecologies of Provisioning in Greater Boston'. PhD diss., Graduate School of Geography, Clark University.

Munro, K. and O'Kane, C. (2017) 'Autonomy and creativity in the artisanal economy and *the New Spirit of Capitalism*'. *Review of Radical Political Economics*, https://doi.org/10.1177/0486613417720775

Park, S. E., Marshall, N., Jakku, E., Dowd, A., Howden, S., Mendham, E., Fleming, A. (2012), 'Informing adaptation responses to climate change through theories of transformation', *Global Environmental Change*, 22: 115–26.

Paton, D. A. (2013), 'The quarry as sculpture: the place of making', *Environment and Planning A*, 45: 1070–86.

Pickerill, J. and Chatterton, P. (2006), 'Notes towards autonomous geographies: creation, resistance and self-management as survival tactics', *Progress in Human Geography*, 30 (6): 730–46.

Rexrode, S. B. (2014). 'Studio Craft and the Production of the Heirloom', MFA diss., University of North Carolina at Greensboro.

Sennett, R. (2008), *The Craftsman*, New Haven and London: Yale University Press.

Strengers, Y. and Maller, C. (2012), 'Materialising energy and water resources in everyday practices: Insights for securing supply systems', *Global Environmental Change*, 22 (3): 754–63.

Thomas, N., Harvey, D. C., Hawkins, H. (2013), "Crafting the region: creative industries and practices of regional space", *Regional Studies*, 47: 75–88.

Vercellone, C. (2007), 'From formal subsumption to general intellect: Elements for a Marxist reading of the thesis of cognitive capitalism', *Historical Materialism*, 15: 13–36.

Warren, A. (2014), 'Working culture: The agency and employment experiences of non-unionized workers in the surfboard industry', *Environment and Planning A*, 46: 2300–16.

Warren, A. (2016), 'Crafting masculinities: gender, culture and emotion at work in the surfboard industry', *Gender, Place and Culture*, 23: 36–54.

Warren, A. and Gibson, C. (2011), 'Blue-collar creativity: reframing custom-car culture in the imperilled industrial city', *Environment and Planning A*, 43 (11): 2705–22.

Warren, A. and Gibson, C. (2014), *Surfing Places, Surfboard-Makers: Crafting, Creativity and Cultural Heritage in Hawai'i, California and Australia*. Honolulu: University of Hawai'i Press.

7

Dichotomies in textile making

Employing digital technology and retaining authenticity

Sonja Andrew and Kandy Diamond

Introduction

Artists, designers and craftspeople have been appropriating available technology in their making processes for centuries, but the use of technology as part of the creative process is not without controversy. Hockney's Secret Knowledge (2001) on 'tracing theory' and the use of devices such as the Camera Obscura to aid the development of realism in paintings, particularly the suggestion that optical aids were used in the works of the Old Masters, were vigorously challenged by art historians and scientists involved in the study of optics (see D. G. Stork). In 2001 Steadman published the book *Vermeer's Camera: Uncovering the Truth behind the Masterpieces*, claiming that Vermeer had used a Camera Obscura to create his paintings. The controversy surrounding Hockney's and Steadman's claims in part stems from antipathy towards the idea that artists of the past used available technology within their practice, that technological intervention would detract from the integrity of an artistic work and the skill used in its making, such as the ability to paint a scene only from observation by eye. The implicit question had been raised of artistic skill being 'aided' or 'genuine' if technology was incorporated, even though artists' works are a culmination of practical, intellectual and emotional skills.

However, today contemporary fine artists may choose to employ technology and technologists in the creation of their work, as the concept and their skills in aesthetic vision, planning and judgement to achieve the final realization of the concept are valued above the ability to physically render the work themselves. The authorship of their practice does not have to be rooted in the physicality of making to be considered authentic. Nonetheless, public perception of artistic skill being 'aided' or 'genuine' still persists to some extent in contemporary craft practice. In textiles, as in other areas of artisan making, the hand-skills of the maker are developed through depth of experience to build tacit knowledge of their working processes and this lends authenticity to the craft object. The integration of technology in contemporary textile practice is often perceived as the intervention of a mechanical or digital process that detracts from the hand-skills of the maker, or, alternatively, that the maker is perceived as reliant upon the technology to cover a deficit in hand-skill. In both instances, the perception thus is that the technology 'does the work for them'. In reality, there is much development of tacit knowledge of software and machinery in contemporary textile practice required to incorporate digital technology into the design process in order to successfully realize a textile product.

Therefore, we must consider whether the knowledge that digital technology has been involved in the production of a textile is enough to warrant questioning of its authenticity as craft by the general public. Is it the notion of an object being bespoke or unique that influences perceptions of authenticity in craft? Or is the issue that a craft object should involve labour-intensive hand production by the maker, whereas machines and technology are aligned to industrial production and can easily and perfectly reproduce, meaning that the flaws and discrepancies, the visible signs of the maker at work, are not there? Can craft skill in textile production therefore be identified and verified only through the handmade, when there are routes to incorporate digital technologies as part of the methodology of contemporary textile practice?

Craft is conventionally perceived as using traditional, low-tech processes that involve making by hand, and thus the public perception of authenticity in craft can be impacted when newer technologies are incorporated. Craft is bound by historical antecedents and methodologies, and its perceived value is to some extent defined by the replication of processes that are accepted as traditional and 'keeping history alive'. Understandings of craft are influenced by cultural perceptions of the processes of making at any given time, and textiles particularly are culturally bound to their processes of manufacture; they are described by them and understood through them, and these processes are changing. In the past, block printing was considered a new technology for creating pattern on cloth; screen-printing superseded this, and block printing is now considered a traditional craft process. As digital printing replaces screen-printing, screen-printing is now also becoming increasingly perceived as a traditional process.

As textile practitioners, our – the authors' – working processes embrace new models of making that view digital design and manufacture as an integral component within our creative practice; one which offers not uniformity, but rather the flexibility to explore and create beyond the scope of more traditional textile methods. Therefore, we explore perceptions of authenticity in textile making in this chapter through responses to our own textile practice, examining how our working processes are perceived by the public, and thus whether digital design and manufacture are deemed acceptable within their notion of 'craft' and 'authenticity' in textiles.

Kandy Diamond: Knit and destroy

Within my practice I create both products and art pieces using knitted textiles. Under my label 'Knit and Destroy' I make machine-knitted products that range from brooches to scarves and, for exhibition, larger pieces from 'glow in the dark' trees to 3D posters. I choose to employ machine knitting combined with digital design over hand knitting for a number of reasons. First, the aesthetic – the combination of knit software and machine – allows for graphic imagery to be applied to machine-knitted items. When making products, cost is also an important consideration, and machine knitting allows me to produce designer-made items that are also affordable. Employing this process gives scope for wholesale distribution, as I am still able to make a small profit from selling my items this way. The other advantage of using knit design software is that the design is repeatable; once I have finalized the design, it can be knitted any number of times.

The software that I use most frequently in my practice is Design-a-knit, which was developed for domestic use, the first version being released in 1990. This was developed in the UK by Soft Byte Ltd and within a few years became the world's number one knitting software for domestic use. This software can be used with a number of knitting machines and is used in domestic, educational and designer capacities (Bragg 2016). I use Design-a-knit with a Passap E6000 machine (Figure 7.1). This combination allows for designs of up to four colours to be developed, downloaded and then knitted. Images can be converted by the software from jpeg file to knit design as well as drawing straight into the grid within the programme; I often use a combination of uploading jpegs and drawing into the computer programme using pen and line tools (Figure 7.2). The knitting machine has a console, onto which the pattern is downloaded. Further information such as the number of needles the pattern will be worked across and the type of cast-on required is then manually entered into this console before knitting can commence. Before the pattern is knitted, the machine must be threaded with the correct yarns ensuring there is enough tension on the yarn for it to knit smoothly.

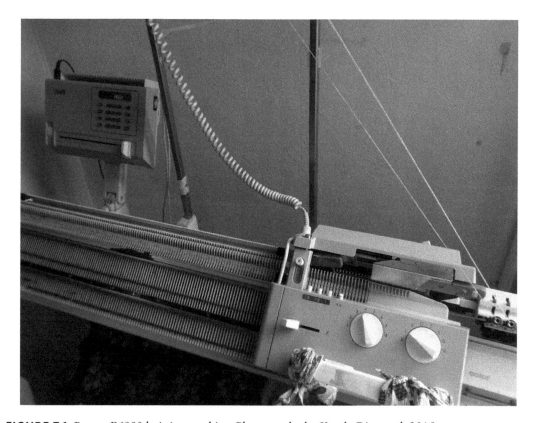

FIGURE 7.1 Passap E6000 knitting machine. Photography by Kandy Diamond, 2015.

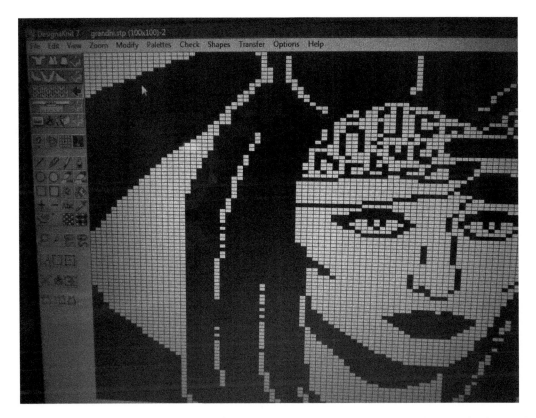

FIGURE 7.2 Stitch pattern created using image conversion and drawing tools. Photography by Kandy Diamond, 2015.

The cleanliness of the machine is also very important; the machine is regularly cleaned to remove any fluff or debris; this is due to the needle selection of the patterning using a sensor. If there is debris on the machine, the sensor will not be able to communicate with the needles effectively, causing problems in the knitting of the pattern. Another consideration is large patterns, as these are downloaded in sections and require attention and accuracy in knitting each section; if one row too few or too many is knitted in any section, the pattern will not match up with the following section.

When the knitting is complete, the products need to be finished; this involves sewing in the ends and sometimes sewing separate knitted parts of one product together. Knitted pieces are then washed or steamed depending on the yarn used. My products are currently sold primarily through my online shops, with a Big Cartel outlet as well as an Etsy shop (Figure 7.3); additional sales are made at contemporary craft fairs, and markets and exhibitions which are carefully chosen to suit my brand and products.

With this knitting taking place in my studio, there is no technical support or design assistance; I perform every role, dealing with all stages of the process from initial sketch to fixing broken machine needles. This means that a full understanding of how both the software and the knitting machine function is essential in order to troubleshoot as things do go wrong. There is a vast amount of tacit knowledge that I have built up over the years of working with this machinery

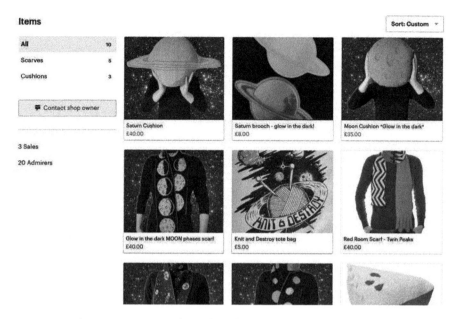

FIGURE 7.3 Knit and Destroy's Etsy online shop https://www.etsy.com/uk/shop/knitdestroy?ref=hdr_shop_menu (accessed 11 September 2015).

and software. However, I feel that if a similar practice were undertaken using hand knitting, the building of tacit knowledge would be more apparent. The hand knitter is clearly using their hands, and with practice comes improved dexterity and speed; their tacit knowledge is built through their experience. An expert hand knitter will be able to fix mistakes, write their own patterns and innovate with stitches and shaping. Within my practice, this kind of accumulated expertise is less apparent and obscured by common misconceptions that 'you program in a pattern and the machine knits away' (Chalmers 2015). I thus feel there is often little understanding of the knowledge and skill needed to create my work.

Within my practice, tacit knowledge has been built up through repeated use of the software and machinery. By using the software on a regular basis, I have worked out things such as the optimum size for images to be imported at, as well as developed increased speed and skill in using the drawing tools. In terms of downloading the software and programming the machine, the processes of multiple-section downloads and sizing have become second nature. In addition to this, the ability to perform minor repairs is essential, and my working knowledge of the knitting machine has been built up over the years, allowing me to assess any machine problems and deal with them effectively. Having worked as a designer/maker using machine knitting for a number of years, I have encountered much ignorance around my processes and sometimes negativity towards them. When selling at craft fairs, comments relating to my working processes have been passed such as: 'It's machine knitted, that's cheating', and 'That's too expensive, it's just machine knitted'. Comments such as these led me to investigate the viewer/consumer's understanding of the process as misconceptions of production due to a lack of understanding of the making process leading to an over-simplification of the skills and time required to make my products.

To begin, in order to gain varied perspectives on my working process, I first looked into customers' understanding of the process, what they knew about machine knitting and what they assume about the making process. In order to achieve this, customers were contacted and a series of questions posed via e-mail in 2015. This process gave a range of responses showing a variety of understandings and assumptions. Regarding machine knitting, some respondents said they knew nothing, others stated that they 'think it's like a mechanical loom' (Chalmers) and 'that it's much easier to make patterns neat. And is presumably much quicker' (Prince), both showing a logical assumption as to what the knitting machine is. Regarding the making process and the functionality of the machine, there were many assumptions around the use of computers and software. There was awareness of the use of software from some respondents: 'It gets fed into a computer which instructs the machine' (Prince) and 'Using … software to translate the design into something you can program into the knitting machine' (Hughes), which showed an understanding of the need for this in order to produce the products that they have purchased. Comment was passed on the physical aspect of the knitting, with one response in particular showing a real understanding of this process: 'Knit the fabric by pulling the carriage backwards and forwards across the needle bed' (Murray-Jones); at the other end of the spectrum, however, we had the response 'Genuinely no idea' (Hale), which demonstrates the range of levels of understanding about the production process, even among buyers. Most of these assume a level of human interaction in the process, as does the response from Griffiths: 'I think that people buying from us would think the same as me which is that machine knitting was still a pretty personal process i.e. it's knitted on a machine by the designer rather than in a large factory'. This is reassuring, as it demonstrates the differentiation between mass production and designer-made despite the employment of machinery.

Retaining the authenticity of my work as handmade craft pieces is extremely important to me as a designer-maker. Having identified that there is a general awareness of the use of machine and software to produce these items, are they still considered by the consumer/viewer as being handmade? From those who had no idea how machine knitting works, 'Yes, 'cause I guess you sit there and make them on your machine even if you don't sit and hand knit them' (Hale), to those with a much more in-depth understanding of the process, all the respondents considered my work to be handmade. Even the respondent who thought that the machine just knits away considers the products to be handmade because 'I know a lot of work and love goes into them' (Chalmers).

In addition to customers, Rachael Matthews was interviewed as my work has been exhibited at her shop/gallery space. This perspective from someone who is within the world of craft and knitting was very valuable, with some interesting comments around the making process such as: 'It doesn't matter how it is made, so long as it is good', as well as comments on skill and authenticity: 'The machine is a tool. Using the tool requires skills, dexterity. Authenticity is in the design, and developing the way the design is put into production – both of these things are done by the author'. A customer (Murray-Jones) also commented on the designer's integrity to the making, saying, 'You're involved in every stage of the production – the knitting machine doesn't just produce it when you press a button.' This shows that there is consideration of the skill required to use the machine and that my work is perceived as handmade despite the use of software and machinery.

With this clear appreciation of my involvement in the process, my next consideration is what holds value in my product for the consumer. Throughout these responses, the words 'unique' and 'unusual' were often used in relation to the products and their design; there was also an indication of the draw of the 'human' element due to my heavy involvement in the process.

Prince stated that 'there's a real sense of love in the process. Also they are so unusual and rare', and Chalmers commented on the production: 'I like the unique design and that's its handmade and not some mass-produced product'. In addition to this, a respondent who had no idea about the process of machine knitting showed a great appreciation for the quality of design and the designer-made element, stating: 'For me it is exceedingly rare to spend that much money on any item of clothing – never mind a scarf! But I just like the design so much and buying from someone who is designing and making items themselves is more special than buying something from Topshop' (Hale).

This really highlights the value to the customer of a product being not only handmade, but also designer-made. Customers have shown a clear appreciation of the technology being an aid to production, rather than something that de-values the craft; my work is still perceived as handmade despite the use of technology. This is positive for the future of craft and demonstrates successful integration of technology with traditional craft methods. It also shows that the stigma around machine knit that I've witnessed is not an overarching view and that people who buy and view my work appreciate the integration of technology to create products that are considered 'unique, well designed, high quality' (Murray-Jones). Regarding viewers of my art within a knitting shop cum gallery environment, Matthews stated that 'customers are not anti-machine – and were fascinated by being able to see both your graphic process and wit. People loved the "posters" in Knit, Knit as poster, the graphic/knitted cross over'. This graphic work could not have been created without the use of software and machinery, and the appreciation of this crossover shows that there is a place for machine knit in knitted art as well as product.

Sonja Andrew: Textile installations

Within my practice I create printed textile installations for public spaces, with work located in hospitals, religious buildings, museums, galleries and corporate spaces. My work focuses on textile semantics and communication, exploring how visual narratives can be constructed within printed textiles, how these narratives are interpreted by audiences and the factors that influence perceptions of the work (Andrew 2008, 2013 and 2014b). My background in textile practice initially started in screen-printing and dyeing. I gradually adopted digital approaches into my working methods, for both design and production, in order to incorporate detailed photographic imagery and experiment with graduated tone and colour overlays that would be difficult to achieve via screen-printing, even if a labour-intensive colour separation process was employed using multiple screens. The digital element of my work forms a background of printed images that are fundamental to the communication of each narrative. This background is then overlaid with screen-printing that enables surface treatments such as flock, opaque pigments and dye effects to be added to the cloth, providing additional images for the narrative, but also bringing visual and tactile contrast to the textile surface. Fragments of digitally printed cloth are then bonded to the surface to optically merge with the background images in some areas, but increase the surface contrast in others, adding to the visual and tactile qualities of the work. Finally, stitch details are incorporated to further enhance the 'signification of textile' (Barthes 1967) and set it apart from imagery produced in other media. This is in part due to my aesthetic decisions as the maker, but also in response to

FIGURE 7.4 Panels 1 and 2 from 'The Ties That Bind (I)' textile installation by Sonja Andrew (2007), in situ at Manchester Museum of Science and Industry. Photograph Sonja Andrew. © Sonja Andrew.

viewer perceptions of the work due to the use of photographic elements on the digitally printed base cloth.

As part of my practice I developed two printed textile installations to communicate a visual narrative on conscientious objection in the First World War (http://www.ahrc.ac.uk/research). The first set of panels (Figure 7.4) were displayed over a two-year period at Walford Mill Craft Gallery in Dorset, Manchester Museum of Science and Industry, Lloyds TSB banking headquarters in Birmingham and Saltaire United Reformed Church in West Yorkshire. To test viewer interpretations of the visual narrative and ascertain their perceptions of the medium of production and processes used, over 300 viewers were surveyed via onsite questionnaires and interviews about their interpretations of the visual narrative. Their perception of the medium of production was also recorded.[1] Responses to the first textile installation demonstrated that many viewers felt the photographic elements that formed the visual narrative could easily be reproduced on other materials. One viewer noted: 'Surface texture did not influence my observation of the images. As most images were photos, surface texture was not important.' Another stated: 'I think that it's the images that stand out, not the media they're on.' A third viewer responded: 'The textiles are more like posters (the set) being more repetitive, similar colours.' Several viewers felt that the intervention of digital technology in the creation of the work meant that multiples of the work could easily be created, with comments such as 'It would work in a poster, photograph or painting form, or as a collage. Computers could be used to create many different works in different media from the "parent".' Some viewers also drew clear distinctions between the labour involved in different production processes, one noting: 'If they were posters I would probably take less notice because I'd think less work had gone into it maybe, but obviously this has taken a while to construct. So I'd say I prefer it like that than in posters.' Others studied the surface of the cloth more closely, observing the overprinting and stitch details:

> I didn't see it at first but sort of looking closer and seeing sort of some of the stitching and different forms of printing that are on it, looking at the layers, that I wouldn't get if it was a website or if it was printed (on a poster). The cross on this first panel, at first glance you see the crown on it, then look closer and it's the cross and then stitch through it and printed on top, and it's the depth that I wouldn't get if it wasn't textiles.

Responses to the first installation effectively became a paradigm from which images, colours and processes could be chosen or rejected for the development of the second triptych. Responses to the use of digitally printed photographic imagery particularly showed some resistance from the general public to accept digital print as an 'authentic' textile process. The digital printing process provided clarity of visual content for communication of the visual narrative, but lacked the tactile qualities associated with textiles and the visibility of the maker's 'hand skills' and their intervention with the cloth, so the use of additional textile processes had to be increased in the second installation.

The second textile installation (Figure 7.5) was displayed at Bankfield Museum and Art Gallery, West Yorkshire, and Manchester Museum of Science and Industry. One hundred and forty viewers were surveyed about the textile panels (70 at each site). This work achieved greater acknowledgement of it being 'textile' when evidence of elements incorporated by the maker by hand, such as stitch, flock, applique and screen-printing, were more extensively and more clearly evident on the surface. One viewer noted: 'I think it works better in textiles because of the overlapping of fabric and techniques used – example – the way the wire comes out of

FIGURE 7.5 Final textile triptych panels for 'The Ties That Bind (II)' textile installation by Sonja Andrew (2008), in situ at the Bankfield Museum and Art Gallery. Photograph Chris Harper. © Sonja Andrew.

the fabric'. Others particularly noted the layering on the surface, with one viewer commenting: 'Textile enables varied surface, texture, and is therefore of greater visual interest: in layering, printing, stitch, fringe. Bare information would be imparted via a photo or web but additional experience of surface would be lost.' Another viewer stated: 'Textiles have an added meaning to me – the history of cloth – everyday use and the fading/rotting qualities that evoke memories of

FIGURE 7.6 Additions to the digitally printed textile surface via heat transfer, bonded frayed fabrics, stitch, screen printing and flocking. Details from 'The Ties That Bind (II)' textile installation by Sonja Andrew (2008). Photograph Chris Harper. © Sonja Andrew.

their own. The images would still be strong in the other media but would lack the added layers of textile.' A third viewer responded: 'The process used here would appear to allow layers with links to time passing by – repeated printing over.'

The additional surface treatments also led more viewers to comment on the 3D qualities of the textiles. One viewer noted: 'The panels are 3D and very tactile. Other methods would have been flat and not "emotional".' Another stated: 'Wouldn't have the 3D interaction a textile can give.' A third viewer commented: 'Textile has helped with the image. The fact that the textile does not lie flat also enhances the view.' However, there were still responses that expected more evidence of the hand-skills of the maker within the work. One viewer noted: 'Fabrics needed working on in a different way – more interaction with the maker.' Other responses showed that viewers had greater engagement with the work due to the textile medium, such as 'Feeling of past wars through aged textiles and photographs. Lack of support from country and church subtly shown. We would not have spent as much time interpreting the works in other mediums.' The issue of the labour-intensive nature of some of the textile processes was also raised by several viewers, one noting: 'I relate to all visual work but prefer the tactile qualities of fabrics/textiles. I love the way colour can be absorbed and also can "sit" on the surface. The stitching is also a time consuming activity that engages you with the work. The "make do and mend" connection also.' What became clear from the range of responses was the publics' expectation that the processes of textile making should be explicit in the object, particularly those rendered by hand by the maker, and in doing so provide some assurance that the labour and time of the maker had been invested in the production of the work.

Transitions between hand and digital processes are now embedded in my working methodology. Progress with creating the textiles takes place when working with digital layers in software such as Adobe Photoshop or making additions by hand to the textile surface, neither having greater or lesser value in my practice, but rather both playing an equal part in my working process. Tacit knowledge of making processes – both digital and hand rendered – has been built over time. One of the issues in using digital production methods for textile printing is that the technology is available via specialist print bureau to anyone who wishes to access it. For printed textile practitioners, the digital design software is a necessary tool to format their work for digital production methods, but the intrinsic quality of work created using digital design software comes from the elements imported (such as images) and the practitioner's ability to realize their ideas with these elements using the software, with hand-generated work scanned in that retains the practitioner's personal aesthetic, which is not lost through digital manipulation.

Conclusion

Plurality of process now informs the development of many contemporary textile artefacts. As multiple streams of technical knowledge in both digital and hand-rendered processes are combined in textile making, the crafted object becomes more than the application of one specific skill. The labour-intensive nature of textile practice has not really changed, the introduction of digital technology has just rebalanced where time is applied to the design problem, shifting time from the physical creation of the artefact to its planning and development. The tacit knowledge gradually built by using the technology parallels the tacit knowledge built through mastering a skill by hand. Technology and hand creation are no longer in opposition, but interwoven to enable more personalized approaches to textile production. Practitioners are exploiting technology to push their practice forward and evolve their field, and cultural perceptions of what constitutes craft, fine art and design change over time; their boundaries often merge, so the craft paradigm is always shifting. But in recent years this paradigm has undergone a major change due to the introduction of digital technology. Traditionally craft reveals process and mass manufacture hides it; therefore, uncertainty is introduced when digital technology and methods associated with mass manufacture are incorporated into craft, and the viewer is forced to reassess the paradigm that craft is in. To the public, digital technology is not part of the craft paradigm, as craft is historically aligned to the handmade. While practitioners are embracing the experimental opportunities of digital technologies within their working processes, and the concept of combining digital and handmade is no longer a dichotomy, the final artefacts are open to scrutiny beyond the art and design community. Dormer (1994, pp. 17–18) notes that 'every craft has a technical language' and that we 'test the language against the practice' with the craft outcome assessed by peers against what is considered current good practice. While makers may accept the 'new authenticity' of artefacts incorporating digital technology, public acceptance of the use of digital processes in textiles will shape if, and how, they are received as crafted objects. It is clear from perceptions of the knit and print artefacts discussed in this chapter that the idea that technology 'does the work for them' and the separation between digital and hand produced still persists to some extent among the general public. But public understanding and acceptance of digital technology within textile artefacts is starting to change as more craft objects become available that incorporate digital design and manufacture as all, or part, of the making process. A new form of authenticity in textile craft is emerging; as public awareness of the challenges of working creatively with digital technology increases, this new authenticity should become more accepted. Contemporary craft is in a new age where digital technology should enable, not dictate, the maker's ability to realize their vision, and the integrity of the object – its authenticity as craft – should be secured through the maker's tacit understanding of the digital technology they employ and their ability to manipulate this technology to create the desired outcomes.

Note

1 The viewers in the survey by S. Andrew for both textile installations remained anonymous; age, gender and occupation were recorded in order to review the data and examine any correlations between these factors and viewer responses.

References

Andrew, S. (2008), 'Textile Semantics: Considering a Communication-based Reading of Textiles', *Textile: The Journal of Cloth and Culture*, 6 (1): 32–65.
Andrew, S. (2013), 'The Medium Carries the Message? Perspectives on Making and Viewing Textiles', *Journal of Visual Arts Practice*, 12 (2): 195–221.

Andrew, S. (2014a), 'Image and Interpretation: Encoding and Decoding a Narrative Textile Installation', *Journal of Textile Design Research and Practice*, 2 (2): 153–86.

Andrew, S. (2014b), 'A textile narrative of John Edgar Bell, conscientious objector', http://www.ahrc.ac.uk/research/readwatchlisten/ imagegallery/2014galleries/atextilenarrativeof johnedgarbellconscientiousobjector/ (accessed 10 September 2015).

Barthes, R. (1967), '*Systeme de la Mode*', Paris: Editions du Seuil. Reprint in English (1990) *The Fashion System*. Berkeley: University of California Press.

Bragg, M. (2016), Interviewed by Kandy Diamond, *phone interview*, 19 May 2016

Chalmers, P. (2015) Interviewed by Kandy Diamond, e-mail interview, 02 August 2015.

Dormer, P. (1994), *The Art of the Maker, Skill and its Meaning in Art, Craft and Design*, London: Thames and Hudson.

Hockney, D. (2001), *Secret Knowledge: Rediscovering the Lost Techniques of the Old Masters*, London: Thames & Hudson.

Steadman, P. (2001), *Vermeer's Camera: Uncovering the Truth behind the Masterpieces*, Oxford: Oxford University Press.

Stork, D. G. (2003) 'Colour and Illumination in the Hockney Theory: A Critical Evaluation', 11th Colour and Imaging Conference Proceedings, Society for Imaging and Science Technology: 11–15.

8

People have the power

Appropriate technology and the implications of labour-intensive making

Gabriele Oropallo

Within sustainable development discourse, the issue of energy is particularly powerful – no pun intended. Reliance on fossil fuels has a multiple impact on the ecosystem, from the blight often inflicted on natural landscapes when oil and gas are extracted and shipped around the planet up to the quantity of carbon released in the atmosphere when they are burnt. When fossil fuels are turned into other forms of energy, they power machines that easily outdo humans in productivity, just as the Luddite conservatives lamented in the age of the Industrial Revolution. Appropriate technology (AT) is an approach proposed to escape both energy-intensive lifestyles and unemployment-yielding mechanization. First formally articulated by the economist E. F. Schumacher, AT favoured labour-intensive approaches to production as opposed to capital-intensive ones, and labour-intensive modes of use as opposed to energy-intensive ones. Less mechanization, and more muscle power. Less state-level planning, and more decentralized management of production. This decentralization would happen, thanks to the creation of smaller units that relied on self-sufficiency and identification with one's local community (Schumacher [1973] 2011).

E. F. Schumacher was a German-born exile who took refuge in the UK during the Second World War. In the 1930s and 1940s, while a research fellow in economics at the University of Cambridge, he worked with John Maynard Keynes and became acquainted with the Aston family, the owners of the *Observer* newspaper. After the conflict, he naturalized as a British citizen and worked for the National Coal Board for two decades. In 1947, he started regularly contributing to the *Observer* on planning and economic matters. AT's vision was originally suggested as a means to support a gentle, considerate industrialization of former colonies with the formal dismantlement of the British empire after the Second World War. Schumacher perceived the introduction of manufacturing models borrowed from Europe and North America as a danger for the social structures of countries where labour was abundant and inexpensive. Energy-intensive machinery needed fewer workers to produce large amount of goods, leaving many unemployed. His first-person analysis and his personal opinions were translated into the proposal for an intermediate application of technology in the form of small-scale manufacturing tools and techniques. Schumacher did not find surprising that this would cause a decrease in the pace of production, but he considered achieving an increase in employability much more desirable (Schumacher 1975).

In the first part, this chapter looks at the genealogy of AT and the Intermediate Technology Development Group (ITDG), the organization Schumacher founded in 1966 as an instrument to implement the theory in actual projects. It will then examine some examples of AT artefacts and pieces of machinery designed for the so-called developing world. This review will also allow us to come to a set of conclusions about the implications of this centre-periphery – or more precisely North-South – approach to design for labour-intensive use. Schumacher's own reading of historical processes such as modernization and industrialization raises the question as to what extent his labour-intensive model can be said to empower the individual, as opposed to confirming the preexisting social, political and economic structures. If social forces shape artefacts and technology (Bijker and Law 1992), and communities are built around shared technical knowledges (Leroi-Gourhan 1945), then the material environment a society builds around itself is ultimately a projection of its aspirations.

Appropriate technology in the context of decolonization

In April 1976, the chair of the UK's Royal Commission on Environmental Pollution, the physicist Brian Flowers, was invited to pronounce the opening address to a symposium on 'Design for Need: The Social Contribution of Design', held at the Royal College of Art, London. The symposium was promoted by the International Council of Societies of Industrial Design (ICSID), an international organization that unites a series of national design agencies and institutions, and aims to represent the voice of the design profession worldwide. Flowers started his intervention by expressing his disappointment around the absence from the event of his colleagues of the Imperial College, London – engineers and scientists who were at that very moment working on technologies aimed to solve the very issues listed by ICSID as topics of discussion during the symposium: environmental technology, prosthetics, conservation of energy resources, even technology literacy in India. He proceeded to lament the fact that technology was seen by his contemporaries more as a threat than as an opportunity, admittedly because the most recent advances in technology had been intimately associated with warfare. He then appealed to designers for helping to bridge this gap: 'You use your privilege of being artists to question the established rightness of things, you subvert the industrial society, you propose alternatives' (Flowers 1977, p. 12). The remark might have sounded quite unfortunate to the audience in a moment in which design education and design theory were intensively absorbing methods and concepts from disciplines such as anthropology, semiotics, cybernetics and ecology. Also, Buckminster Fuller preferred to speak about 'design science'.

What were the alternatives Flowers was championing? Most of the technologies he mentioned in his talk, he admitted, are energy-intensive, and the 'world is burning up its resources fast' (1977, p. 11). Those technologies implied a way to progress based on labour-saving, energy-consuming, capital-intensive modes of production. 'Could there be something wrong with economic theories that require massive unemployment to solve our problems?' asked Flowers to his audience. 'High technology seems at present to demand such a course. Might it not be better to choose a technological path based instead on full employment and human dignity?' (1977, p. 10). Yet, he added later, 'We shall need more technology, not less. But it will have to change its direction, towards something the world can better sustain. Is this what this Symposium is about?' (1977, p. 11). Flower's questions tap into the intellectual milieu of the age, with design undergoing an 'anthropological turn': a realignment of strategies and intents in which the overarching rationalist worldview of modernist design was replaced with a social agenda articulated as interventionist vernaculars (Clarke 2016).

AT was one of the theories discussed at the Design for Need symposium, and it offers the opportunity to look exactly into the question of energy within this new intellectual environment. The theory was first articulated by Schumacher as 'intermediate technology' in an article called 'How to Help Them Help Themselves' that appeared in the *Observer* on 29 August 1965, in which he took stock of his experience as visiting planner overseas. In 1955, Schumacher had taken a three-month sabbatical from his position as civil servant at the National Coal Board. He used this period to visit Myanmar, which had then been the independent republic of Burma for only eight years, and since that first trip he had taken an interest in the economic planning of the newly decolonized countries that were then one by one departing from the British Empire. The issue of their industrialization was central, especially at a time when the two main world powers were competing to recruit countries into their blocs and prepared to transfer technology to obtain this goal. In his 1965 *Observer* article, Schumacher's concept of intermediate technology was a response to what he perceived as a problem, namely the implementation of mechanized production in developing countries. In Schumacher's 'us-and-them' narration, the version of the history of technology he adopted was one of a linear progress from less complex machinery and techniques to more complex ones. It also alas implies a moral duty on the part of the most 'advanced' societies to look after the less developed ones.

Schumacher's opinions had been anticipated during the debate on technology choice that had taken place in other former parts of the empire during its dismantlement. Among decolonized countries, the example of India is illustrative, for it saw in the very early years of its existence as an independent democracy the direct confrontation of two contrasting visions on technology and industrial culture. These visions were embodied in the two early political leaders of the state. Mahatma Gandhi favoured a labour-intensive, low-technological approach. This was iconically represented by the charkha, which became the symbol of his political movement and that today figures at the centre of the national flag. The charkha is a light and portable spinning wheel that really allows for mass production only if used by a large number of workers. This vision relied less on government-led planning and allocation of resources and more on the responsibility of the individual to contribute to the national domestic product through the immediate reward of hand-assembled produce – the specular contrary of the Marxian alienation of the labourer on the assembly line (Cotgrove 1972).

On the other hand, Jawaharlal Nehru, the first prime minister of the country, supported big technology and large-scale design interventions on the environment. These interventions included the large-scale dam projects he considered to be the new temples of the country, or the construction of Chandigarh, the new capital of Punjab that was planned and mostly designed by Le Corbusier during Nehru's term of office (1947–64). The founding of a school such as the National Institute of Design in Ahmedabad in 1961 was largely the result of a report on design training commissioned by the government and written by the American designers Charles and Ray Eames (1957). According to the STS scholar Roli Varma, Schumacher also offered his advice to the young democracy, but his recommendations to rely on intermediate technology were ignored by the government (Varma 2003).

Schumacher's proposal could rely on a remarkable amount of social capital. The same year as his article appeared, a formal organization called Working Group on Intermediate Technology was established in London to explore the implementation of intermediate technology in former colonies. The organization was founded by officials from a heterogeneous collection of interest groups made up of philanthropic organizations, government bodies and private corporations. The former included the Freedom from Hunger Campaign, the Society of Friends and the Ariel Foundation. The state was represented by the UK Ministry of Overseas Development, the Commonwealth Development Corporation and the Overseas Development Trust. The industrial partners included the engineering firm Rubery Owen, the oil consultants Walter J. Levy and the Bowater Corporation, among others. The Shell oil corporation was also an early supporter, in what in hindsight could be seen as either an early attempt for a major corporation to polish their public image or a genuine investment opportunity ('Action on Intermediate Technology' 1965). During its inception stage, the group was headquartered in the offices of an organization known as African Development Trust, itself administered by the African Bureau, a non-governmental institution founded and directed by anti-apartheid activist Rev. Michael Scott (Jack 1960).

In 1966 the Working Group on Intermediate Technology was renamed Intermediate Technology Development Group. In 1967 it relocated to new offices near Covent Garden, London. The ITDG at that point was led by Schumacher and two assistants of his, George McRobie and Julia Porter. The former was a Canadian researcher who immediately before the founding of ITDG had studied traditional folk technology in the Canadian Arctic regions, the Scottish Highlands and India. Julia Porter was largely responsible for fund-raising (Porter 1969). Another two members who were notable during the first decade of the ITDG existence were Marilyn N. Carr, who was also a civil servant at the United Nations, and was interested in gender issues, and Peter Stern, an engineer who mostly worked on the development of water and sanitation systems.

We shape our machines: Making and empowerment

Where not only colonial powers but also their companies were being identified as part of the machinery of colonization, their leaving could be called for as part of the decolonization process. Within this landscape, intermediate technology potentially provided an opportunity for former colonial ties to be maintained under a different name. This could happen both at governmental level with the involvement of official bodies and in terms of the personal network commonwealth officers had previously built and could continue to rely on as consultants for the ITDG. Most importantly, it was also an occasion for British industry to supply developing markets with basic, simple pieces of machinery and tools. A review of the titles of the articles the press in Britain and beyond dedicated to the new sensation paints a picture of the expectations placed upon the whole enterprise.

In 1966 the *Financial Times* published two articles about intermediate technology. The first, on 28 July, was unequivocally entitled 'Old Technology – A Possible Boon to the Emerging Nations' and went under the section heading 'U.K. Machinery':

A recent British export mission to Nigeria took with it a booklet listing hand-operated machinery being made in Britain … Dr. E. F. Schumacher, the National Coal Board economist who was formerly a consultant to the Indian government, argues that the setting up of modern factories in these countries can even harm their backward populations by ruining their traditional craft trades and discouraging them from progress ... [The] encouragement of intermediate technology could do more than anything else to raise demand for all kinds of goods in the countries where it operates, and this can only benefit the British export drive. ('Old Technology' 1966)

The booklet mentioned in the *Financial Times* article was then gradually expanded and eventually printed for sale in 1967 with the title 'Tools for Progress'. The publication was a catalogue of products and designs that could be mail ordered from British companies. The other article was published four months later, on 14 November 1966. It was titled '"Simplified" inventions for the developing world' and featured a photograph of a hand-operated washing machine designed and manufactured by Colgate-Palmolive for the Mexican market. The US corporation was one of the early funders of the ITDG. The article also made a first connection between the work done by George McRobie in Scotland, implying that the potential of intermediate technology could be put at use also in less developed areas of Europe and North America.

Other stories featured in magazines or newspapers occasionally had even more crude titles, which reflect views that were common currency at the time. A feature entitled 'Inexpensive Technology' appeared in the December 1966 issue of the science magazine *Nature*. Another one entitled 'Simple Equipment for Simple People' was published in *The Statist* on 16 December 1966. Another early supporter of Schumacher's ideas was the Catholic Church. A conference on intermediate technology and development was held in Rome at the Vatican City in October 1968. The official newspaper of the Vatican City, *L'Osservatore Romano,* ran several stories on the event. In these news items it routinely reminded the reader that the rationale behind all the contributions to the conference was to focus on human well-being as the main objective for development.

Between 1968 and 1970, *Tools for Progress* managed to be enthusiastically reviewed in outlets as diverse as the July 1969 edition of the *Whole Earth Catalog*, the *Standard Bank Review* in 1969 and the Shell oil corporation's magazine *Span* in 1970. The hat-trick is particularly remarkable because the *Whole Earth Catalog*, edited by countercultural superstar Stewart Brand, was an extremely respected publication within the North American countercultural movement for its dedication to self-sufficiency, do-it-yourself, holism and ecological design. Any form of liaison with big corporations was, by them, categorically ostracized. Like *Tools for Progress*, the *Catalog* was also a mail order catalogue that featured information and product reviews. Remarkably, its subtitle was 'Access to Tools'. The common investment in this phrase is a marker that they bought a shared affinity with a humanistic milieu that aimed to reappropriate the machine to man, and make the alienating industrial means of production a means of individual self-development. This is how the *Catalog* praised *Tools for Progress*:

Great Britain does it again (I'm beginning to feel like a Loyalist) way ahead of the let-General-Motors-do-it U.S. Here in one tasty catalog are all the 'equipment and materials for *small-*scale development available in The United Kingdom'. Pictures, description, prices, and detailed access information on all manner of do-it-ourself tools, from hand ploughs to air houses. (Whole Earth Catalog, 1969, p. 91)

The photograph that accompanies the review features what seems to be the cover of a provisional print proof of *Tools for Progress*, with a series of black squares where the images would then actually be printed. Thus, it might be the case that the *Whole Earth Catalog* review was actually informed more by enthusiasm for a project only superficially known and less by an actual familiarity with it.

In 1971 ITDG commissioned a study to Bridge, a consultancy based on Sloane Street, London. Bridge submitted a report with recommendations for future administration, promotion and funding of the group. The document was extremely matter-of-fact and included a detailed vision for the group, which up to that point had been run by Schumacher, McRobie and Porter in a casual fashion. Bridge's vision for the ITDG featured a formal organization chart and dedicated a remarkable amount of attention to the issue of the name. The group did not change name immediately, even though internally the wording 'intermediate technology' indeed kept being considered confusing. It seemed to refer exclusively to developing countries, and thus restrict the organization's horizons. During the early 1970s, the expression 'appropriate technology' started to be used in its stead. It was perceived to be more universal in tone, and more inclusive.

In October 1974, George McRobie was invited to open a series of lectures on environmental issues held at Imperial College, London, under the auspices of the Institute of Cultural Research (1975). His paper was titled 'Toward a Non-violent Technology' and developed on a theme that Schumacher had already touched upon in his essay 'Technology with a Human Face', in which he argued that modern technology had become 'inhuman' because its benefits have not been distributed equally across society. Technological advance, in Schumacher's reading of the history of technology, is used by the elites as a means of capital extraction, rather than a way to achieve better living conditions for the masses (Schumacher [1973], 2011, pp. 120–34). In his talk, McRobie pointed out that technology is a field to be negotiated through individual choice (1975, p. 2). Instead of merely accepting technology as something imposed upon us, individuals can appropriate it as a means of personal development. McRobie mentioned a series of allied experiences, which signalled that AT and ITDG were not isolated realities. Among these examples were the dire forecasts of the 1972 book *Limits to Growth*, and the work of organizations such as Friends of the Earth, the Soil Association (also led by Schumacher) and the Conservation Society, and magazines like *The Ecologist*, *Undercurrents* and the *New Scientist* (McRobie 1975, p. 5). Participation within design and manufacturing was in fact a professed core aim of the AT movement throughout its history (Day and Croxton 1993, pp. 179–83). Technology, argued McRobie, did not proceed along a linear path. Individuals were not forced to follow a single line of technological determinism:

> If, as many of us now believe, the structures based on large-scale 'robber economy' technology are increasingly unacceptable on social and human grounds; threatening to our survival on ecological grounds; and increasingly insupportable on economic (energy) grounds; then the economy we must envisage must be less city-centred, with manufacturing ... much more evenly spread throughout the country, and families, communities and society as a whole much more self-sufficient in food and the basic necessities of life. (McRobie 1975, pp. 6–7)

During the second half of the 1970s, McRobie kept writing about technology choice in 'rich countries' (McRobie 1981) and submitted at least one proposal for governmental funding on the establishment of an AT programme for the UK (McRobie s.d.). However, the only outcome of the programme was a series of studies commissioned by ITDG to Loughborough Consultants Ltd. Among the papers the Loughborough University–owned consultancy firm produced for ITDG, one proposed to implement AT as a means to prolong cars' lifespan. A few pages into the report, the idea that design can contribute to overcome quick obsolescence is quickly abandoned by the authors. Car buyers, they argue, would not be prepared to purchase vehicles that are more durable and expensive than the current ones on the market. Neither would they accept settling for vehicles with a lower technological content. In its stead, they propose a marketing strategy. Cars would be leased to consumers with servicing included, in order to maintain economies of scale for the manufacturers and create jobs in the sector of repair and maintenance. In effect, less than on environmental sustainability, the focus of the proposal was more on reaching a compromise between the needs of industrial development and maintaining constant employment through technocratic planning (Loughborough Consultants s.d.). For all intents and purposes, this programme would have effectively been state-run car leasing.

Our machines shape us: Making and subjectivization

During the 1970s and 1980s, ITDG published a series of Project Bulletins (Intermediate Technology Development Group 1979–86). These profiled completed projects mainly for fund-raising purposes. They provide a number of details on the way the group operated in that period (ITDG 1979–86). At the time there were three offices in the UK: one in London, one in Rugby and a workshop hosted by the University of Reading. The group was staffed predominantly by designers and engineers who would look for problems to solve in the developing world and conceive solutions. The Reading and Rugby offices developed and tested prototypes. Many of these designs were, however, actually then commissioned to British manufacturers and then shipped to Africa, South Asia or Latin America.

The 'small farm transport vehicle' provides an example of the limitations this UK-centric approach suffered. The vehicle, a sturdy hybrid between a wheelbarrow and a forklift, was designed and built by ITDG before 1985. After the early prototypes were sent to the southern Indian state of Tamil Nadu, the local ITDG staff realized that the ergonomics of the vehicle did not suit the most common body proportions among the intended users. The bulletin dryly reports the episode in these terms: '[The] prototype demonstrated that minor changes were required to the handle geometry to suit local people. These changes were incorporated on later prototypes.'

Thomas Kuby was a German designer who, after studying at the HfG Ulm, the Institute of Design in Chicago and Royal College of Art in London, worked for ITDG until 1973. In April 1976 he presented a paper at a symposium held at the RCA on 'Design for Need: The Social Contribution of Design' (Kuby 1977, pp. 33–8). In his presentation, Kuby gave an account of a particular piece of equipment designed by ITDG, the egg-tray machine. This was a project that Schumacher himself had initiated and that was routinely quoted as a successful example of AT (Marsh 1978, p. 851; Matlock 1981, pp. 129–41). The problem the machine sought to solve was the lack of suitable forms to transport the eggs to market in Zambia. Paperboard trays like those in use in Europe or North America would have improved transportability and enlarged the potential market for the goods. However, the smallest machine on the market in the early 1970s had a capacity of 1.3 million trays per year and cost roughly GBP 120,000. The machine was fully automatic and required only one operator. Pace and volume of production were beyond the needs of the users the machine was meant for. ITDG, writes Kuby, 'set out to develop an intermediate alternative and in technical terms it succeeded'. The first prototype exceeded all expectations and cost merely GBP 6,000, one twentieth of the original price (Kuby 1977, p. 37).

The issue with the machine, however, was that ITDG was using the existing social, economic and political structures to develop and deliver its machine, and in so doing, they were only confirming them. Design and technology are shaped by social forces, they reflect the aspirations of a community. But the intervention of ITDG in Zambia was actually providing more of an obstacle to the process than facilitating it. The machine was manufactured in the British Midlands and then shipped to Africa. A short informational video was also released by Thomas Kuby himself to show how the machine worked. In the five-minute film, allegedly shot in Limuru, Kenya, an ITDG engineer is shown demonstrating how the device works to a surprised local. The machine is fed water and old newspapers, which are rendered into a pulp and then pressed into shape by a moulded hand press. At the end of the film, the learner is made to stand on a pile of egg trays to show their resilience. The film closes on the smiling, surprised face of the supposedly future operator of the labour-intensive machine. Once in Africa, the governmental authorities and the entrepreneurs who had ordered it started requesting amendments and modifications to its design. Distribution channels departed from main urban areas, and so a small volume of production was less than desirable. The fact that ITDG designed labour-intensive machinery suddenly became an opportunity for the machine owners to increase profit margins:

Step by step ... the 'alternative' character of the new technology has been eroded. Today a Mark III version of the egg-tray machine is being built which is said to produce more than two million trays per year and to cost £100,000. Scale, output and price being about the same, the intermediate technology concept shrinks to a cynical proposition to offer the poor countries of the world a primitive, labour-intensive technology which has most of the disadvantages of large scale while lacking all the positive sides of modern technology and automation. The story seems to have gone full circle but it isn't even back where it started. (Kuby 1977, p. 37)

In fact, as early as 1975, the Swedish economist Claes Croner had expressed scepticism at the World Bank's decision to fund a number of intermediate technology projects in an article in which he reviewed the conceptual premises of intermediate technology. Croner warned in particular against the dangers associated with the naive reasoning that low wages were a good ground for adopting labour-intensive production. Labour seemed cheap only when thought about in Western standards. But in fact what is low is not the price of labour, but the workers' wages; as Robert Solo argued in a 1969 review of labour-intensive technology in developing countries:

The low level of wages of labor in developing countries has been put forward naively as the reason for adopting labor-intensive technologies ... . certainly wages in these countries are extremely low – but this does not mean that labor is cheap. The laborer may be cheap, but his labor, understood as an input in production, can be very expensive compared to the labor inputs purchased for a much higher wage rate in advanced countries. (Solo 1969, p. 98)

When technologies like those provided by ITDG were delivered to a developing country without changing any of the existing political, economic and social structures, the effect was paradoxical:

Only in a development strategy that aims at transforming the basic structure of underdeveloped countries, i.e. the foreign dependency, ownership and power relations and income distribution, will the development of massive labour-intensive methods in certain sectors become a meaningful and viable means for creating productive employment. The application of large-scale labour intensive methods ... presupposes that the low rate of wages – which is one of the most dramatic manifestations of underdevelopment–will be maintained, reduced further or, alternatively, that wages grow at a significantly lower rate than labour productivity. While this may be a realistic assumption in fascist-type military dictatorships like Chile or Brazil (which, incidentally, are also supported by the World Bank), it is not likely to be acceptable to Indian construction workers. (Croner 1975, p. 1777)

AT machines and tools were purportedly designed as a means to bridge the technological gap between industrialized and industrializing societies. Their proponents recruited support on the basis of an apparently reasonable argument: that labour is more abundant in developing countries and that it is reasonable to tap into this resource instead of relying on mechanization, or building the necessary infrastructure to reach remote areas. This assumption is technically plausible, but it is also the limit of AT. The tools and the machines might be ingenious and functional, but they mostly fall short of representing the aspirations of supporting individual or social development. The labour that powers their gears is imagined to be inexpensive, and it winds up being forced to stay in that state of inexpensiveness: 'The problem with employing object-centred methodologies to work that is based in the social is that the latter remains an immaterial space; it consists of intangibles, such as Michel Foucault's "always-ready" pervasive power structures' (Janzer and Weinstein 2014, p. 330). Machines function as moulds that shape their subjects, but, at the same time, one also continuously struggles to change that mould and readapt it. The passive subject wants to be an active subject.

Conclusion

The decolonization process provided an occasion for AT to receive attention, attract resources and actually be implemented in South Asia, Africa and Latin America. Its proponents were then quick and keen to emphasize its universal scope. Small-scale, miniaturized, fragmented social and industrial structures were celebrated for being more advanced than the mammoth-like structures of the past. AT received governmental funding in Britain to test and experiment viable approaches to industrial design and production even at the national level. This all happened within less than a decade after Schumacher's original manifesto had first been launched from the pages of a British newspaper (Schumacher 1965). Opportunity, vision and translation were initially crucial in establishing its credibility. AT remains popular with design education and development aid (Mulberg 1993; Nieusma 2004). As a programme, however, over the decades it lost ground in the developing regions of the world it had originally been conceived for because of its inability to generate economies of scale, and function in a competitive environment.

Its principles have in fact found a more fertile ground in Europe and North America (McRum 2011). Recently, the repair and the maker movements have also situated themselves along similar lines, being small scale, slow approaches that ultimately rely on the (self)enrolment of the users as source of labour. Labour-intensive, small-scale fabrication and a vague notion of 'enoughness' also imbued Radical Technology and other DIY movements of the 1970s. If the infusion of labour in the life cycle of an artefact is stretched beyond the phase of manufacturing, it can be ultimately assimilated into the moment of use or consumption. During the past decade, several authors and researchers have studied the implications of this overlapping of roles (Mugge et al. 2009), or the effects this form of participation has on product lifetimes through emotional attachment (Chapman 2005). When the distance between makers and users is reduced, they often end up being the same person (Knott 2013; Ritzer and Jurgenson 2010).

References

Action on intermediate technology. (1965), *The Times*, 1 September

Bijker, Wiebe E. and Law, John (1992), *Shaping Technology / Building Society: Studies in Sociotechnical Change*, Boston, MA: MIT Press.

Bridge. (1971), *The Intermediate Technology Development Group: An Analysis and Recommendations For Future Administration, Promotion and Funding of the Group*[report], Practical Action Archive, UK: Rugby.

Chapman, Jonathan. (2009), 'Design for (Emotional) Durability', *Design Issues*, 25 (4): 29–35.

Clarke, Alison J. (2016), 'Design for Development, ICSID and UNIDO: The Anthropological Turn in 1970s Design', *Journal of Design History*, 29 (1): 43–57.

Croner, Claes. (1975), 'Labour-Intensive Construction Methods and Unemployment: World Bank Study on Substitution of Labour and Equipment in Civil Construction', *Economic and Political Weekly*, 10 (46): 1775–79.

Day, George and Croxton, Simon. (1993), 'Appropriate Technology, Participatory Technology Design, and the Environment', *Journal of Design History*, 6 (3): 179–83.

Eames, Charles and Ray. [1994 (1957)], *The India Report*, Ahmedabad: National Institute of Design.

Flowers, Brian. (1972), 'Opening Address', in *Design for Need: The Social Contribution of Design*, edited by Julian Bicknell and Liz McQuiston, 10–14. Oxford: Pergamon Press.

Hardin, Garrett. (1970), 'Everybody's Guilty: The Ecological Dilemma', *California Medicine*, 113 (5): 40–147.

Intermediate Technology Development Group. (1967), *Tools for Progress: Guide to Equipment and Materials for Small-Scale Development*, London: Intermediate Technology Development Group.

Intermediate Technology Development Group. (1979–1986), *Project Bulletins* [loose papers]. Practical Action Archive, Rugby, UK.

Jack, Homer A. (1960), 'A Guide to African Organizations', *Africa Today*, 7 (1): 11–2.

Janzer, Cinnamon L. and Weinstein, Lauren S. (2014), 'Social Design and Neocolonialism', *Design and Culture*, 6 (3): 327–43.

Knott, Stephen. (2013), 'Design in the Age of Prosumption: The Craft of Design after the Object', *Design and Culture*, 5 (1): 45–67.

Kuby, Thomas. (1977), 'Social Forces Determine the Shape of Technology', in *Design for Need: The Social Contribution of Design*, edited by Julian Bicknell and Liz McQuiston, 33–8. Oxford: Pergamon Press.

Leroi-Gourhan, André. (1945), *Milieau et technique*. Paris: Albin Michel.

Loughborough Consultants Ltd. N.d. 'A birds eye view of prolonged car life' [report]. Practical Action Archive, Rugby, UK.

Marsh, Peter. (1978), 'Commercial Egg Trays Vindicate Schumacher', *New Scientist*, 80 (1133): 851.

Matlock, W. Gerald. (1981), 'Technology for Today', in *Realistic Planning for Arid Lands: Natural Resource Limitations to Agricultural Development*, 129–41. Chur: Harwood Academic Publishers.

McRobie, George. (1975), 'Towards a Non-Violent Technology' [unpublished paper]. Practical Action Archive, UK: Rugby.

McRobie, George. (1981), *Small is Possible*, New York: Harper and Row.

McRobie, George. N.d. "Creating an Alternative Economic Framework for the U.K.: A Proposal" [unpublished paper]. Practical Action Archive, UK: Rugby.

McRum, Robert. (2011), 'How EF Schumacher, author of the global bestseller Small Is Beautiful, came back into fashion', *The Observer* 27 March: *The New Review*, 8–11.

Mugge, Ruth, Schifferstein, Hendrik N. J. and Schoormans, Jan P. L.. (2010), 'Product Attachment and Satisfaction: Understanding Consumers' Post-Purchase Behavior', *Journal of Consumer Marketing*, 27 (3): 271–82.

Mulberg, Colin. (1993), 'Confronting Real Problems: Cross-Cultural Design and Intermediate Technology Projects in Schools', *Journal of Design History*, 6 (3): 209–13.

Nieusma, Dean. (2004), 'Alternative Design Scholarship: Working Toward Appropriate Design', *Design Issues*, 20 (3): 13–24.

Old technology—a possible boon to the emerging nations', (1966), *The Financial Times*, 28 July

Porter, Julia. (1969), 'Simple Tools for Progress', *Standard Bank Review*, September.

Ritzer, George. (2013), 'Prosumption: Evolution, Revolution, or Eternal Return of the Same?', *Journal of Consumer Culture*, 14 (1): 3–24.

Schumacher, E. F. (1965), 'How to Help Them Help Themselves', *The Observer*, 29 August

Schumacher, E. F. [2011 (1973)], *Small is Beautiful: A Study of Economics as if People Mattered*, London: Vintage.

Schumacher, E. F. (1975), *People's Power: Address at the Annual General Meeting of the National Council of Social Service*, December 1974. London: NCSS.

Solo, Robert. (1969), 'Capital and Labor Intensive Technology in Developing Countries', *Journal of Economic Issues*, 3 (4): 96–103.

Varma, Roli. (2003), 'E.F. Schumacher: Changing the Paradigm of Bigger Is Better', *Bulletin of Science, Technology and Society*, 23 (2): 114–24.

Whole Earth Catalog. (1969), July. Menlo Park, CA: Portola Institute.

9

The ghost potter

Vital forms and spectral marks of skilled craftsmen in contemporary tableware

Ezra Shales

It sounds absurdly romantic to claim two country potters who make prototypes on the potter's wheel have fundamental roles in the production chain in two lines of tableware produced by the few remaining large-scale British twenty-first-century ceramic manufacturers, namely the Portmeirion Group and the Royal Doulton. Especially as the phenomenon contradicts the much-heralded dissemination of 3D computer design, rapid prototype printing and the transition to global outsourcing. One firm projects the image of a humble rural potter to market its product as a historical English tradition, while the other suppresses this contribution entirely and sells the maker's hand under the guise of a celebrity author. The anomaly is strangely disruptive of contemporary expectations concerning large-scale corporations' methods and techniques. Who could guess that a potter's wheel was more expedient and affordable to produce prototypes than the leading-edge technologies of the day? This chapter looks at the marks of handicraft and the marketing of pottery to explore two key issues this situation give rise to. First, it will define the labour of the potter's wheel when nostalgia for 'handicraft' creates an increasing lack of clarity concerning what it might entail. Secondly, it will explore the value these two potters place on their skills and usefulness when universities and art schools are spurning their knowledge as passé training that is overly technical, and the wheel is also increasingly uncommon in factories due to outsourcing and a tendency to invest in managerial methods instead of skill retention.

'Today there exists a radical division between the factories on the one hand, and artist-potters on the other', wrote George Savage in 1954, and this generalization of a massive divergence separating twentieth-century mass-manufacturing firms and individual artists and academic-artists holds true still today (Savage 1954, p. 25). Savage was a foremost pottery expert and enthusiast who published lively surveys and accessible encyclopaedias in the mid-twentieth century. In the era he wrote, studio potters like Bernard Leach and Michael Cardew publicly decried the 'soulless mechanical' quality of British industrially manufactured ceramic tableware, both in lectures and in publications (Harrod 1999, p. 35). Today, contemporary scholars such as Tanya Harrod still repeat this, more as a shorthand truism about middling commodities than a mean-spirited slur.[1] To alert us to the larger historical context when factory work is expected to be unimaginative, reflect on a fictitious confession of upward mobility: 'After graduating from art school with a Masters degree, the offer to join a factory was too good to refuse.' Eyeing factories as fabulous career solutions was a nineteenth-century fable. However, more recently it has been regarded as a nightmarish demotion in expectations, not an upwardly mobile pathway. Especially in art and studio craft circles, there is a prevailing fear that when the individual is subsumed and production becomes impersonal, anonymous, a degradation of genius is likely. Skilled hands are supposed to make unique marks, to be tools that confer individualization upon artefacts and reaffirm the individual maker. But an artisan who labours in large-scale manufacturing is expected to accommodate by adulterating their artistry. To identify a specific hand in contemporary tableware production is often impossible, usually because of a deadening effect of culture-by-committee. Some services might bear the traces of carefully calibrated references to the labour of potting, but most of the surface ornament is designed and moulded to achieve uniformity, not eccentricity.[2]

However, today at least two potters produce elegant 'casual china' that features the contemporary fad for showing 'the marks of throwing' as a primary texture – they are ghostpotters, authoring the semblance of individuality within corporate anonymity. Using their skills, pottery-manufacturing plants are mass-producing intentionally cultivated idiosyncrasy, not their traditional refined wares (that historically aimed to erase signs of handmaking). The consumer is thus buying the stylized semblance of wheelwork, not something actually formed on the wheel but slipcast in a plaster mould. In this instance, therefore, the job of the ghostpotter is to exaggerate signs of craftsmanship – to make 'soulful' mechanical pottery. One, John Webber, makes forms for Royal Doulton, a subsidiary of WWRD Holdings Ltd, which was acquired by Fiskars Corporation in July 2015. Webber is celebrated as an auteur by the firm in their publicity. The other, Kevin Millward, makes works for the Portmeirion Group, but he remains anonymous as the line is advertised as designed by Sophie Conran.

Kevin Millward is a potter of numerous speeds – not one who champions the hand, the wheel or the mould so as to put any method of production as superior to another. He is a fascinating study as a labourer because of his eloquence and self-awareness that his obsolete skill set has never been more applied to tangible goods and yet never garnered less respect than in his stints in academia. Today, his prototypes for mugs and plates have been reproduced in the hundreds of thousands. When I first met him in 2013, he was keen to walk through the Portmeirion outlet shop in Stoke-on-Trent and identify each piece he had made – or is it designed? Or is the right term 'potted'? To dispel my disbelief, he showed me his iPhone, which was loaded with images of unfired greenware in his studio that matched the Sophie Conran ware on display – the same rippling wobble was in all the pottery. The reason for my shock was not that I had imagined Portmeirion's work was actually made by Sophie Conran, daughter of Sir Terence of Habitat and Conran shop fame. I had not envisioned her at the wheel centring five pounds of clay as the muck splattered about. As a jaded consumer, I had incorrectly assumed that behind the Conran branding effort was a committee of marketing specialists and focus groups that imagineered these well-branded commodities by sending a digital file overseas to outsource production, and that the potter's marks were probably simulated. As a historian of design, I was mistaken to think the potter's wheel to be obsolete. Twenty-first-century technology and mass production have not yet buried the potter's wheel or the individual potter as a resource. Millward lives in a bucolic hamlet

FIGURE 9.1 Kevin Millward in his studio holding a prototype. Courtesy Ezra Shales.

outside of Leek, England, and his wheel-thrown pots are sent across the world to China to be copied – slip cast in moulds with all of its texture and imperfections intact – and then shipped back to Europe, North America, Australia and New Zealand as well as Korea, Japan and China. Bed, Bath and Beyond describes Portmeirion's Sophie Conran tableware as a charming 'nod to Japanese serenity and a wink to English eccentricity'.[3]

Millward's workshop confounds because his artisanal skill is devoted to resolving a myriad of other peoples' artistic identities. He produces ware for corporate ceramic firms and also batches in the dozens for studio potters who advertise their pottery as being made with a 'personal touch'. Exactly whose expression or self-expression is visible in the clay is difficult to sort out. Apart from the wobbly ware marketed under the Sophie Conran label, Millward supplies sleek teapots if Portmeirion needs a more elegant and urbane option, trays for a robotic system to feed paraplegics, bespoke mortar and pestle sets for gourmets (sold under the name John Julian), rustic French jardinières and, perhaps, most strikingly, mugs that are retailed at the Covent Garden market and online by Gemma Wightman.

Whether the mugs are imbued with an individual's personality or a committee's is another visual enigma. If uniqueness is being subcontracted out to Millward and he works as an alternate artisanal hand, he doesn't mind remaining anonymous so long as the customer pays. As he sees it, he is lucky to make a living as a potter, and his success lies in his manual skills, his eye trained in figure drawing classes and, most importantly, his ability to 'put any genre on'. His sublimation of his own ego might not seem to be a skill to many, but it is – and was once a constituent feature and traditional aspect of academic and non-university handicraft – as well as older modes of apprenticeship. Upscale kitchen accessories like 'artisanal mortar and pestles' are marketed as expressing Julian Sainsbury's 'instinctive sculptural understanding of form' but emerge from Millward's handiwork. Another client with less regal name recognition, Wightman, dosed her sales pitch with patriotism: 'Hand thrown in the finest porcelain in the Gemma Wightman Ceramics studio in Surrey this beautiful mug embodies beauty and function in equal parts. A super stylish contemporary design and handmade individually right here in Britain!'[3] Wightman's website suggests that individuation can be taken one step further by the consumer: 'For a personal touch why not add an inscription to the inside rim of one or more of the pieces?'[4] Which touch is personal, which one is individual and which is self-expressive? Reception suggests a variety of interpretation is possible.

Kevin Millward showed me that he copied Gemma Wightman's work for her – he could throw fifty of her mugs in one hour, far superior to her own speed and ability to be consistent. When Wightman gave Millward a set of loose metal type to impress and 'personalize' her mugs with the saying 'KEEP FULL WITH TEA PLEASE', Millward moulded these into a plaster unit – making the task one impression instead of twenty-one distinct actions for each letter. Wightman was peeved that Millward's type was very consistent – the potter intent on selling herself as artisanal was disconcerted that Millward's type was uniform, an adjective that did not suit her image. Moreover, she said her customers noticed the difference between her unstamped work and his, an outcome that is unavoidable in Millward's eyes, as his thicker fingers leave coarser ribs in the mugs, and Wightman is 'a wisp of a woman, while I am a man of fourteen and a half stone'. What makes artisanal labour personal, unique or individuated surely is complex – and so is thinking about which technological markers cultivate such associations. Is it the hand size or the body weight, the wheel or the plaster mould? If Millward understands he can't physically throw precisely like another potter because their physiques differ, he knows that he is still more proficient at being his clients than they are. Inhabiting other aesthetic sensibilities and being efficient at the potter's wheel are virtues that were once common in Stoke-on-Trent and elsewhere, but which are now rare, at least in commercial production. Millward's virtuosity at potting is such that in 1980, when Emanuel Cooper, one of the most outspoken champions of handicraft, was asked to pose in an advertisement for a wheel, he asked that Millward be called down to throw an enormous bowl on that wheel – Cooper's own skill not lending sufficient hyperbole to the advertisement.

Walter Gropius's charge to his students that Bauhausler 'give up the old romantic way of working' in order to produce 'rational' products whereby 'art and technology' are unified is an easy narrative when kept abstract, but harder to transmute into material production and human labour. In the Bauhaus potshop, Otto Lindig moulded thrown ware to preserve the marks of human hands on the potter's wheel and alternately trimmed moulded pieces with deep incisions in order to add the appearance of wheel-made work to moulded ware. He also applied this ornament of labour to moulded stoneware production at the State Majolika Manufactory of Karlsruhe. Did Lindig's pots give up romantic ways of working but lay claim to the need to artificially maintain the mark of human sentience? Were his intentions sentimental, and earnestly so? Lindig's ware can be read as a striving to maintain humanism amid mass production or as a student disregarding his teacher, and in so doing understanding human desires more acutely. While scholarship on Bauhaus art has been prone to over-intellectualize the work, there is merit to pondering whether Lindig was trying to juggle an abstraction of labour. Was his interweaving of self-referential indexical signs of labour an intentional subtext of the pottery? Whereas tablewares of the 1930s, most notably such as Fiestaware, met consumers' desires for overt signs of handicraft and human idiosyncrasy in an age of expanding mechanical production, Lindig's work is usually considered in a pre-commercial context. Lindig might not have been the first ever to encode the potter's hand in large-scale ceramic production, but his work is indicative of a romanticism that developed in the twentieth century. Nineteenth-century romantics dabbled in historicism. Potters revived salt-glazed textures and theatrically robust visibly thumb-printed handles, but that surface ornament tended to be about refinement and adding heritage rather than the indexical mark of an artistic hand.

However, to return to Gropius, just what might have been meant by 'the old romantic way of working' in regard to the potter's wheel? The wheel has a long history in industry and also in vernacular cultures. The treadle powered momentum wheel that many studio craft practitioners revere as traditional has its origins, Millward notes, not in folk labour but in manufacturing. The idea of consistent mechanical motion first utilized child labour, and Josiah Spode's great wheel has been preserved from 1800 as a tangible evidence of this divided labour that preyed on indentured families. It was in the nineteenth century that the treadle was incorporated as a labour-saving device; child labour laws necessitated the change as well as a managerial pay scale that tracked salaries in relation to pots that were 'good from the kiln'. Quantity began to be more profitable than careful production, but that wasn't the potters' innovation. The mechanical device of the wheel became obsolete in production only after the First World War; photographic evidence locates wheels in factories in the first decade of the twentieth century in both Staffordshire and Denver, Colorado, among other places. Many tools gained a belt-driven shaft that was steam powered. The tool was mechanical for certain, requiring balance and consistent rotation. So the wheel is a technology that should not necessarily be read in opposition to industry, even though it has in recent years since M. C. Richards described it as a Zen-like practice to achieve individual contemplation (Richards 1964, pp. 34–5).[5] 'Tell your local potter that their treadle wheel is not descended from vernacular or folk handicraft but a cast off from the factory', says Millward, winking. The Bauhaus injunction to unify art and technology sounds easy until you look at Millward's wheel and realize it is not romantic and yet still does not seem to be what we talk about when we generalize about 'technology'.

Despite the fact that the wheel is, in most cases in Europe and the Americas, technologically advanced, it has come to represent an artisanal tool, seen and considered in opposition to both steam and electric power and the computer era. This is ironic because, as Kevin Millward's labour proves, wheel throwing remains economically viable. When Portmeirion's designers generate 3D designs in a computer program such as Rhino, it takes a day and nearly a thousand dollars to print out a pattern mimicking the eighteenth century – such as a complex rouletting or engine turned surface, a textural checkerboard. Prototypes made by contemporary digital artistry often cannot be put into production because the corners have too sharp a radius to be translated into plaster moulds. Moreover, the marketing department might reject the proportions or the shape. In this way it is more efficient and economical to employ Millward to make a hundred variations by hand than use the latest digital technologies. He has moulded an impression of a computer-generated ornament, an eighteenth-century pattern once made on a lathe, and then transferred the decoration onto his own wheel-thrown mugs. In this way he is not working in opposition to computer-aided design; he is simply working faster than most designers and their machines possibly can.

FIGURE 9.2 3D-printed mug in the foreground; mugs with plaster impressions in the background. Courtesy Ezra Shales.

Millward still makes his own work too, and looking at it one can see why Portmeirion's head of design selected him to realize Sophie Conran's tableware. He describes his own fluid forms as 'wibbly wobbly'. Portmeirion knew the textural surface that Sophie Conran desired and asked the Gladstone Museum, a living history site in an old Stoke-on-Trent pottery, for its recommendation of a skilled thrower. Millward's own wares have more emphatic hand marks – such as vertical indentations on the sides of his bowls that he makes with wooden dowel when the clay is still wet. To compare his own mugs to his designs for Sophie Conran reproduced overseas, both have a conical body. However, his own studio ware is a bit squat with a wider foot. Portmeirion's Sophie tapers so much it is tippy (see Figure 9.3). In Millward's view, the Sophie mug 'looks right but functions poorly'. The handles differ more, as his is an extrusion – an eighteenth-century method of producing standardized tubes of clay – which he imprecisely and visibly tears open, just at the thumb rest. On Portmeirion's Sophie, the strap handle resembles an adolescent teen queen's ponytail. An improbably statuesque handle, it leaves little room for Millward's thick fingers (and my own). Millward is supplying Portmeirion with what it wants – what he calls 'a diluted version of bad 1960s pottery' – the skilled potter knows he is dumbing down his handicraft. He made several variations and finds Portmeirion's a poor choice – but knows it wasn't his to make – and admits his selection might not have fared as well in online shopping or the shop window. His handle is a more

FIGURE 9.3 Portmeirion/Sophie Conran cast mug (left), Kevin Millward wheel-thrown mug (right). Courtesy Ezra Shales.

sophisticated subtlety, a detail for connoisseurs and historians to savour but one that is generally lost on the public and a form that is impossible to slip cast.

The Sophie teapots are crowned with wiggly lids, an idiosyncrasy to give the novice buyer a sense of tactile engagement. Millward remembers Portmeirion's instructions: 'Add a bit more wobble to the knob.' The plates stack and fit our industrial lifestyle of dishwashers, but have eccentric lips that droop like wet cardboard more than anything organic. It is noteworthy that when the line debuted in 2006, the work stream was outside of the factory's comfort zone. At the garden party to announce the new line of manufacturing, marketing was ahead of production. On his potter's wheel, Millward himself threw a dozen sets of each luncheon service, comprising mugs, a range of three jugs and also plates in three sizes, and – when the tableware was met with intense interest and an award – Portmeirion expedited the shipment of these prototypes overseas. Actual handicraft was responsible for the critical reception, and then mass production ensued. Yet no critic described it as handicraft; it was novel industrial design. Sophie Conran graciously accepted an award for the design. Millward graciously recognizes he is a 'bottom feeder' and is content with the arrangement.

Proud of his work with Portmeirion on the Sophie line, Millward is most possessive of his ability to 'put his business hat on': 'No one would buy it if it had my name on it', he resolves, adding that the product still carries in it three essential components: his skill and sense of form, the art director of Portmeirion's savvy in terms of marketing, Sophie's own sense of style and, most importantly of these three, the Conran name, an English regal provenance that is the contemporary version of the eighteenth-century approval of the Duchess of Devonshire or Madame Pompadour. Wedgwood and many other companies since have long advertised in this manner of celebrity associations. The involvement of Sophie Conran is not specious; she is an active tastemaker even if she is not potting.

Irreverent to studio potters who speak of the 'handmade' with moral superiority and self-assurance, Millard exhibits a sense of humour in his own work. The cipher of English potter Edmund de Waal is indecipherable and stamped on the side of each of the austere cylinders he exhibits in massive shelving arrangements. Such art-gallery-bound pottery bears stamps that are visible but not legible. Millward's blue ink stamp, 'Handmade in England', is on the underside and crisp. Stamping with ink instead of embossing is a nod to early industrial patriotic-histrionics. Moreover, Millward's rubber stamp was a self-conscious attempt to thumb his nose at studio pottery's chic conventions that veer towards austerity and *wabi-sabi* Japonisme (see Figure 9.4). Yet Millward's satirical wit could easily be overlooked, as it, like his role-playing in aesthetic genres, is repartee understood most often by connoisseurs. Few craftspeople are now trained to inhabit another artist's aesthetic sensibilities.

FIGURE 9.4 Kevin Millward wheel-thrown mug, stamped 'Handmade in England'. Courtesy Ezra Shales.

To note a parallel example to the Sophie line, in 2012 Wedgwood-Royal Doulton began to plan an '1815' line that also emphasized manual throwing. Again this iconic manufacturer also skirted high-tech 3D printing to ask a skilled artisan, in this case John Webber, to collaborate on short-term contractual project. Webber is a retired university professor, and a former student was working in the industry who identified Webber as a potential collaborator. Royal Doulton's '1815' line is similarly manufactured in China, and the appearance of variety is actively cultivated in that each mug in a set of four has a slightly distinct handle. Mix-and-match colour is also pre-planned to cultivate the appearance of idiosyncratic handicraft. Whereas virtuosic potters 200 years ago aimed for standardization and deliberate visual coherence, the small differences in Webber's thrown work were sometimes too subtle and required the block and mould shop and corporate design team to etch deeper ripples into the wares. However, unlike Millward, Webber is featured on the Royal Doulton website and cast as a 'country potter', apt if the ware commemorates 1815 as a lost moment of 'Merrie Olde Englande'. But to sidestep nostalgia, it is good to remember that Doulton began in Lambeth serving greater London and that Webber might enjoy the country life but taught ceramics as studio art at Staffordshire University at a time when the industry was in decline and slowly backing off from a long relationship with the school. Webber enjoys the collaboration with Royal Doulton, but it is an entirely new chapter in his career and one that he had never previously valued as an ambition. What is perhaps most significant to me about Webber is the joy he takes in shaping the 1815 service: he feels like his work is finally reaching a broad audience and that large-scale reception is exciting in a rewarding manner that his previous work never achieved when he was exhibiting in small galleries or teaching in an art school. Maybe the idea of art schools graduates who aspire to factory mass production are not so ridiculous after all. Webber and Millward are absolutely of one mind on this sentiment: they feel that consumers are indeed touching their handiwork, communing with their hands, however mediated the labour and production might be.

So what does such tableware tell us? Does the pottery materialize David Pye's warning that 'the danger is not that the workmanship of risk will die out altogether but rather that, from want of theory, and thence of standards, its possibilities will be neglected and inferior forms of it will be taken for granted and accepted'? (Pye 1968, p. 28). Pye, generally sage, here sounds a bit like a crank of the Bernard Leach variety. Certainly no *theory* ever produced one of the previous golden ages of handicraft; patronage has more often been the deciding factor, not artistic intention or genius. Attempts to cultivate sentience and pseudo-risk in tableware are now part of predictable cycles of marketing strategies, on the one hand, and yet Pye's fears are somewhat warranted by the public's lack of attention to workmanship. However, proclaiming imminent degradation is too easy a jeremiad for a critic to deliver, even if it seems likely that there will be ever fewer connoisseurs able to differentiate throwing. Is it standards we need or a fresh conception of labour in craft, craft as design and the wheel as a machine?

It is a strange story with no moral to add balm to our desire for soulful lives: in our so-called postindustrial economy, two highly educated and skilled manual craftsmen remain ready and cheerful to invert their virtuosity at the potter's wheel. The general public enjoys fingering dumbed-down thumbprints. The potters themselves are pleased to re-enter the factory reclassified as freelance consultants where once they were mere 'mechanics'. Meanwhile schools have systematically dismantled the programmes that these potters emerged from; they are rare in Stoke-on-Trent for the first time in 200 years.[6] I have been fortunate to be able to discuss such questions with the ghostpotters Kevin Millward and John Webber, but in all likelihood, anonymous labour like theirs will no longer be in Stoke-on-Trent in future decades but will migrate to farther shores. Skill is easily lost in a generation but can be assembled only incrementally, over several lifetimes of labour.

Notes

1 Tanya Harrod has used the shorthand description 'soulless quantity of British ceramic industry' several times, both in a lecture at Westminster University, 18 July 2014, and in one delivered at Alfred University on 5 November 2009, Available online: http://ceramicsmuseum.alfred.edu/perkins_lect_series/harrod/index.html (accessed 10 May 2016).

2 See Bernard Leach's 1927 critique that 'after 100 years, the [British] trade offers us crockery which is cheap, standardized, thin, white, hard, and waterproof – good qualities all – but the shapes are wretched, the colours, sharp and harsh, the decoration banal, and the quality absent' only endures among those unwilling to recognize the rich variety within manufacturing of that era, which ranged from Clarice Cliff's *Bizarre* line to Cornish kitchen ware to Heal's merchandizing of 'Beauty in Utility.' Bernard Leach, Potter's Outlook (Sussex: Handworkers' Pamphlets, St. Dominic's Press, 1928), 27–8. Years later, Michael Cardew wrote self-aware of his inability to work at Spode and his greater comfort in a 'studio' setting: 'The main difference between the way of working at Copelands [Spode] and that of our little group in Winchcombe was not, essentially the difference between mechanization and handwork; it was rather the difference between a very large, sophisticated organisation and a very small primitive one.' Michael Cardew, *A Pioneer Potter, An Autobiography* (London: Collins, 1988), 98. Available online: http://www.bedbathandbeyond.com/store/product/sophie-conran-for-portmeirion-reg-dinnerware-in-white/114351 (accessed 10 May 2016).

3 Wightman refreshed her personal website in Spring 2016 and no longer uses this copy, but it still can be found on other sites. Available online: http://www.notonthehighstreet.com/gemmawight-manceramics/product/hand-thrown-porcelain-straight-sided-mug (accessed 23 May 2016).

4 Wightman changed the wording on her new site but she still offers 'For a personal touch add an impressed inscription of your choice.' Ibid.

5 'What I care about, it is the person', wrote M. C. Richards. 'This is the living vessel: person. This is what matters.'

6 When David Queensbury ran the ceramics department at the Royal College of Art in London in the 1970s and actively designed for industry, he was remarkable and unusual. Generally, voices in academia and ceramic manufacturing have expressed contempt for the other.

References

Cardew, M. (1988), *A Pioneer Potter, An Autobiography*, London: Collins.
Harrod, T. (1999), *Crafts in Britain*, New Haven: Yale University Press.
Leach, B. (1928), *Potter's Outlook*, Sussex: Handworkers' Pamphlets, St. Dominic's Press.
Pye, D. (1968), *The Nature and Art of Workmanship*, Cambridge: Cambridge University Press.
Richards, M. (1964), *Centering in Pottery, Poetry and the Person*, Middletown: Wesleyan University Press.
Savage, G. (1954), *Porcelain Through the Ages*, London: Penguin.

PART THREE

The work of craft

10

Our future is in the making

Trends in craft education, practice and policy

Julia Bennett

With the growth in the interest and value (both economic and emotional) attached to the notions of 'crafted', 'handmade' and 'authentic', the contemporary cultural and creative economies are experiencing a period of significant growth. In craft itself, this trend is manifesting itself at a time of increasing diversification of practice and approaches to making, which, in turn, is posing new challenges and proposing fresh understanding of concepts such as discipline, materials, curation, audience and locality. At the same time, this curiosity and excitement about craft is raising new questions about how we learn, and the value we attach to education and training designed to support making.

Drawing on recent data on the contribution of craft skills to the UK economy in craft industries, the creative industries and other sectors, this chapter considers the role of innovation in driving a growing craft economy and how it is shaping new developments in materials, making and tools. The implications of these changes, and their relationship to trends in craft education and training, are explored. Questions are posed on craft's future economic and social contribution, exploring how makers and educationalists might together address challenges in craft and what role government policy might play in reversing recent years' declines in provision of, and participation in, craft education.

Craft today

Craft enjoys a huge diversity of expression, embracing internationally recognized artists and cutting-edge innovators, alongside increasing engagement in making by amateurs pursuing personal education and artistic pleasure or seeking an additional income stream. Craft businesses are a strong component of the UK's thriving creative industries, contributing £746 million gross valued added (GVA) to the UK economy, rising to £3.4 billion when including GVA generated by craft occupations outside craft industries[1] (TBR 2014). Taking into account the economic contribution of those in associated supply chains, Deloitte (Monitor Deloitte 2015) estimates the GVA of making to be worth between £15.5 and £18 billion to the UK annually. In addition to its economic value, craft is also a vital aspect of our social and cultural life, with surging popular interest in both buying and making craft.[2] 5.6 million craft pieces are purchased each year; 16.9 million (40 per cent of adults) have purchased a craft object; a further 9.6 million (23 per cent) would consider buying one in the future. A conservative estimate of the total value of these annual sales was £913 million in 2010 (Yair 2010). Advances in materials science and craft processes, together with more affordable digital fabrication technologies, are disrupting and transforming how craft is practiced. Makers are now contributing to scalable innovation in many other sectors including science, engineering, manufacturing, technology and medicine (Yair 2011a).[3]

Craft remains connected to materials, processes and techniques from its past, yet makers are constantly rethinking their practice in response to a changing world. Makers are exploding previous notions of making, calling into question the permanence of objects that we normally associate with traditional craft. In contrast to the tangible craft objects that can be easily valued in monetary and cultural terms and preserved for the future, UNESCO has raised the profile and value of ephemeral work through its 2003 *Convention for the Safeguarding of the Intangible Cultural Heritage*.[4] Thus, the process of making becomes as important as the objects that are produced, and the emphasis of the word 'craft' moves from that of a noun to a verb. In this context of rapid and exciting change, craft education and training are essential to produce makers of the

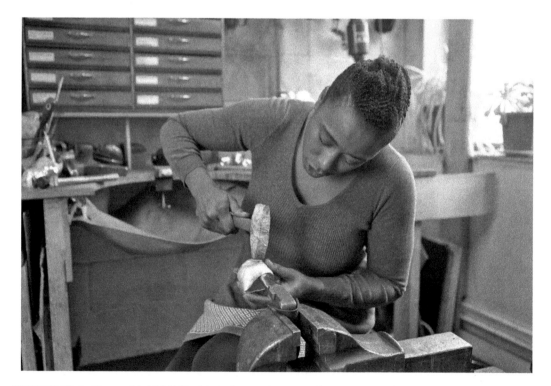

FIGURE 10.1 Silversmith Ndidi Ekubia in her studio at Cockpit Arts, London, December 2013 ©Sophie Mutevelian.

future, to realize the potential of evolving skills and to harness the innovative capability of making. They prepare those with craft skills for the wider creative economy and beyond. Indeed, the UK government's Creative Industries Council (2014) identifies education and skills as fundamental to the future success of the creative industries.

All good news?

The conditions for the continued growth of interest in craft appear to be strong, which would suggest that opportunities for existing and future makers to learn new skills are healthy. In generating and collating evidence about trends in making, the Crafts Council found, however, that anecdotal evidence of problems was increasing. We were hearing of a number of course closures, not just in higher education (HE), but also in further education (FE) and schools. The Cultural Learning Alliance[5] and the National Society for Education in Art and Design[6] were gathering data in their respective fields, and members of the All-Party Parliamentary Groups on Design and Innovation and on Art, Craft and Design in Education were reporting similar concerns from staff in schools and HE.

Against this background, the craft sector lacked a robust evidence base on the state of education and training; we therefore decided in 2013 to examine recent trends in these areas. We commissioned an investigation into patterns of provision and participation in all stages of formal education and training from Key Stage 4 to postgraduate study[7] over a five-year period, using case studies to illuminate the findings (TBR and Pomegranate 2014c, d and e). We issued an update with a further year's data in 2014 (TBR and Pomegranate 2014a and b), and the latest findings were published in *Studying Craft 16* (TBR 2016). Our objective was not only to increase our understanding of the trends in craft education and training, but also to contribute to the debate about how best to secure creative education in general, and craft education in particular, through all levels of our education system. We are keen to build a strong evidence base and actively to advocate for the importance and protection of craft education and training in a climate of rapid and continual reform.

The evidence on craft education and training

So what did our research findings tell us? Participation in craft-related subjects at school and in FE is falling at an alarming rate. Between 2007/09 and 2012/13, participation in craft-related design and technology GCSEs fell by 25 per cent.[8] Participation in craft-related subjects in adult general FE[9] fell 41 per cent between 2007/08 and 2012/13. However, it is in HE where the main loss is felt. Against heavy investment in art and design education elsewhere around the globe,[10] the number of craft-related HE courses available in England fell 46 per cent in the five years from 2007/08 to 2012/13. Almost half the courses available in 2007/08 have disappeared. There was a particularly sharp decline between 2009/10 and 2010/11, when courses (mainly first degrees) reduced in number from 826 to 523 (37 per cent). Regionally, there was a sharper rate of decline in HE courses in the North East, North West and West Midlands than in the rest of England. Specific disciplines were found to be at particular risk. There has been a reduction of more than 50 per cent over five years in the number of courses available across England as a whole in glass, furniture, ceramics and product design (83 per cent, 65 per cent, 61 per cent and 85 per cent, respectively). The cost of such craft courses is often high compared with other art and design provision, not least because of the equipment and space needed.

In spite of this significant reduction in provision, it was welcome to find that participation in craft-related HE was rising. This pattern in HE contrasts with most other stages in education where available provision is delivered increasingly in smaller units, but learner numbers are falling. Overall participation in HE (taking postgraduate and undergraduate student numbers together) increased by 11 per cent over the five-year study period, although learner numbers fell slightly in the most recent year by around 3 per cent between 2011/12 and 2012/13. Postgraduate numbers increased by 40 per cent (rising from 1,180 in 2007/08 to 1,970 in 2012/13). Student numbers on all first degrees remain 9 per cent higher than in 2007/08, but numbers on other undergraduate programmes (including foundation degrees, HNCs and HNDs[11]) have fallen below 2007/08 levels (by 3 per cent). This is of concern as evidence shows that these 'other' HE routes attract more black and minority ethnic entrants to careers in craft than do bachelor's degrees.[12] (However,

FIGURE 10.2 Glassmaker Michael Ruh in his studio, London, December 2013 ©Sophie Mutevelian.

provisional, unconfirmed findings for 2014/15 suggest that undergraduate participation has now fallen back to 2007/08 levels and includes a higher proportion of non-UK domiciled students.)

Looking at other routes into craft careers, there is a longstanding culture of 'informal'[13] apprenticeships in the sector, but data for these routes are unavailable. Figures for government-funded craft apprenticeships remain tiny. Apprenticeship starts on the jewellery and silversmithing framework, for example, were 50 in 2011/12 and 40 in 2012/13. We anticipate that numbers are now likely to increase, with a craft apprenticeship framework approved and a new apprenticeship standard emerging following government apprenticeship reforms developed through the Craft Apprenticeship Trailblazer and the Furniture Manufacturer Standard. The most significant increase in craft training participation has taken place in employer-related FE (89 per cent), with a large relative increase in the availability of craft provision in the last two years covered by the study. However, numbers are dramatically different: 890 adults in employer FE in 2012/13, compared to 12,000 learners in general FE.

Overall, the data continue to imply a lack of opportunities for coherent progression between education stages. Provisional, unconfirmed findings from the next iteration of our analysis of longitudinal data suggest that this situation is continuing and, in some cases, worsening. Early indications are that the number of students starting entry-level courses in craft in FE are holding up, but this may be at the expense of higher level opportunities and the number of guided learning hours.[14] At the same time, the number of HE foundation courses (the one-year transitional preparatory courses for HE or employment that enable students to explore a wide range of art and design areas) appear to be declining significantly. Learner numbers in our earlier, published findings clearly demonstrate an appetite for engaging with craft and taking courses. However, the declining participation figures suggest both that there may be a reducing engagement with craft in schools in Key Stages 1–3 and gaps in progression routes from Key Stage 4[15] to higher stages. Across education stages, there is concern among educationalists that advice and guidance on progression routes and careers in and through craft is weak.

It is useful to consider these findings in the context of official data about the qualification levels of the established workforce. The Department for Culture, Media and Sport (DCMS) regularly produces data on the creative economy[16] and employment trends (DCMS 2015a and b). Following the publication of Crafts Council evidence on the craft economy (TBR 2014) and constructive dialogue with officials, the DCMS included partial estimates for craft for the first time in 2015. While a welcome step forward in government recognition of craft's contribution to the economy, the figures do not reflect the full breadth of workers with craft skills.[17] It is interesting, as a result, to compare these figures with the Crafts Council's data. The official statistics show a relatively low qualification level of people working in craft compared to those in other creative industries or the wider economy. As compared both with the creative industries and in the wider creative economy, craft is shown to have the lowest number of people who have a degree or equivalent (25.2 per cent of craft jobs), and the highest number of people for whom A Levels, GSCEs (or other equivalent qualifications) are the highest qualification achieved. These figures posit that those people working in craft are over five times more likely to have no qualifications than those working in the rest of the creative industries. At GSCE, A Level and in other qualifications, craft workers' highest qualifications are only slightly above the UK national average (with one exception). This contrasts with Crafts Council figures (Burns Owen Partnership 2012, p. 6) which show that those with a craft-related degree (including those who chose craft as a first career as well as returners) account for 61 per cent of makers. With an estimated average maker age of 48 (ibid., p. 7), those working in craft were also, in some cases, pursuing HE qualifications at a time when student numbers in HE were far lower than today. The same official statistics also show that craft has the highest number of people from less advantaged backgrounds compared to other creative industries.

The Crafts Council continues to advocate for more comprehensive government data, drawing on the contribution of craft skills in a considerably broader set of craft disciplines and employment settings than are currently represented. Positive dialogue with government departments is vital to the improvement of such data. Indeed, it is welcome that the Office for National Statistics, the UK government's official statistics body, has recently recognized the importance of including the contribution of microbusinesses[18] to the economy and, in particular, those not appearing in national figures as the businesses generate a turnover below the income threshold required to pay value added tax (VAT).[19] For craft businesses, of which nearly 90 per cent are sole traders (Burns Owen Partnership 2012, p. 21), such a move is very welcome. However, the point here is that irrespective of the numbers of makers obtaining HE qualifications, or succeeding in business, they are all dependent on participation in craft-related education and training in their earlier education, in particular at GSCE, A Level and other equivalent Level 2 and Level 3 qualifications. These remain vital routes into craft in the UK, both for those going onto FE and HE and in particular for those who may gain no further qualifications at a higher level. Without this educational foundation, the risk to the pipeline of future makers is concerning.

Policy drivers

To understand the drivers for these changes in participation and provision we need to examine the trend of significant policy change by successive governments. In the UK, the craft sector is shaped by policy in three government departments: Department for Education; Department for Culture, Media and Sport; and Department for Business, Innovation and Skills (and is indirectly affected by local policy in a fourth department – Department of Communities and Local Government). Craft benefits from the rising profile of the creative industries in these departments, yet there can be tensions between differing departmental priorities. The negative impact of recent UK government policies on craft education provision and participation, outlined below, places at risk the drive to build on the economic contribution of the creative industries.

In government policy terms, the purpose of craft education is as an instrumental tool, preparing learners for employment. While the economic contribution of craft needs greater recognition and support, it is important also to acknowledge its role in developing the haptic and creative skills so important for all young people and their learning. Craft has an intrinsic value as an activity for individual personal development, well-being and artistic pleasure. Gardner's theory (1991) of multiple intelligences describes the different kinds of minds learners possess and the different ways in which they learn, remember, perform and understand, all as vehicles for solving problems or making things, as well as developing our understanding of ourselves and those around us. Gardner's work builds on understandings of learning advanced earlier by, for example, Dewey (in particular his advocacy of practical education 1938), Kolb (1984) and Hein (1996). Gardner opposes the uniformity and universality of some approaches to learning, asserting that educators should not follow one specific model and the perceived current bias towards linguistic and numerical-logical modes of instruction.

The bias towards instrumental learning is reflected in the increasing focus on performance management of education under recent governments. The 2010 coalition government introduced the English Baccalaureate (EBacc), a school performance measure designed to measure how many pupils achieve a grade C or above in the core academic subjects[20] at Key Stage 4 in any government-funded school. The EBacc risks crowding out the study of other important subjects, particularly the creative arts, while acting as a disincentive for schools to offer or promote craft-related courses and for young people to choose them. There is a growing consensus among interested organizations, including NESTA (Bakhshi and Windsor 2015), the Creative Industries Federation (2015) and, indeed, the government's own select committee on culture media and sport (2013), either that arts subjects should be included in the EBacc or that the performance framework should be amended so as not to disincentivize schools offering the creative arts.

The 2015 UK government has rightly identified that there is a skills gap in STEM (science, technology, engineering and maths) subjects that it is now working to address. However, the government's own Creative Industries Council (2014) is echoing employers' calls for the need to embrace creativity by turning the focus on STEM into STEAM (science, technology, engineering, *arts* and maths), thus including arts subjects as central knowledge alongside scientific understanding. This point has also been reinforced by the House of Commons Culture, Media and Sport Committee (2013) and the Creative Industries Federation (2015). Yet in speeches some government ministers have questioned this approach, seeking to cast doubt on the validity of the connection.[21] As schools implement the new National Curriculum,[22] the government must ensure that students up to Key Stage 3 receive a solid grounding in the arts and design. Students aged 14–16 (Key Stage 4) should be able to access the widest possible programme of creative subjects to prepare them to play a full part in the knowledge economy. The school performance framework itself creates a downward pressure on young people to pick those so-called facilitating subjects that students are advised to choose to keep their university options open. NESTA (Bakhshi and Windsor 2015) calls on the government to challenge The Russell Group[23] of universities to include the arts in their list of 'facilitating subjects'. In the context of concerns about the quality of careers advice and guidance in relation to craft, The Russell Group's approach is likely to inhibit further students' willingness to entertain the pursuit of creative subjects in HE.

Ways forward?

How do we address the challenges facing craft education and training in the current climate and what are the conditions that would help to facilitate improvement?

Following the publication of our first report series (TBR and Pomegranate 2014c, d, and e), the Crafts Council held a series of meetings across the country to hear the ideas, responses and experiences of the making community, with a view to producing an education manifesto for craft and making. We set up focus groups, sent out consultation questionnaires and built on everyone's evidence and experience to generate momentum and inform the manifesto. With wide crafts sector support, the Shadow Secretary of State for Education, Tristram Hunt MP, launched *Our Future Is in the Making: An Education Manifesto for Craft and Making* (Crafts Council 2014) at a cross-party event at the House of Commons in November 2014.

Responding to our data and to views expressed during consultation, the manifesto set out five calls for change, which together form a unified plan of action:

1 Put craft and making at the heart of education. Offer opportunities to make throughout education. Revitalize learning with hands-on experience and stimulate take-up of GCSEs in art, craft, design and technology.

2 Build more routes into craft careers. Make visible the diverse career opportunities available through craft education. Create equality of access to training through apprenticeships.

3 Bring craft enterprise into education. Promote enterprise at every stage of learning. Make more opportunities for craft businesses and educators to work together.

4 Invest in skills throughout careers. Invest in teachers' training in craft skills. Create more opportunities for makers to develop their skills throughout their careers.

5 Promote world-class higher education and research in craft. Support the UK's internationally renowned higher education craft courses. Invest in cutting-edge artistic and scientific research in craft and making. (Crafts Council 2014, p. 3)

Crucially, the plan of action is both an advocacy document pointing to policy change and a plan of action. It addresses not only government and partners' priorities, but also those of makers and the craft sector, as we work together to find solutions.

One of the ways in which we can increase the capacity of the sector is to diversify further the routes into craft. Apprenticeships offer job opportunities and training routes, including into HE, thereby increasing social mobility. Craft businesses are willing to employ apprentices and pass on their skills, and yet employer-related learning remains small scale due to barriers facing microbusinesses, such as limited time to train and undertake the administration and accreditation requirements associated with apprenticeships. Colleges by contrast are incentivized to pursue bigger businesses with large numbers of apprentices. One solution to this may be to enable business clusters to support apprentices and to access greater government support. Deloitte (Monitor Deloitte 2015), for example, identifies a package of potential business support for those microbusinesses displaying high growth characteristics, based on six themes where interventions could be targeted to support scaling up: talent, mentoring, market stimulation, access to finance, infrastructure and culture. Improved entrepreneurship education both at school and beyond would encourage more young adults to feel confident in pursuing and setting up their own business ideas. Too many students today are still anticipating that they will find a job with an employer, rather than through setting up their own businesses.[24]

We need to continue investment in the evidence base about participation and provision of craft education and training, in order to inform effective advocacy. The Crafts Council will continue to commission and publish biennial analyses of longitudinal data. The development of new types of school – not just academies, but the more specialist university technical colleges, free schools and studio schools – offers an opportunity to explore what can be achieved with a stronger and more holistic emphasis on creative education, where those schools choose to explore imaginatively their exemption from the National Curriculum. The challenge will be to ensure that the lessons of rigorous evaluation of the enhanced creative education offered by such schools are used to shape national policy and to scale up positive outcomes across all schools. It also vital that makers are seen as career role models, not only for young people in schools, but also for those who shape their life choices, as parents, friends and careers advisers. This is particularly important amid concerns about the quality of advice and guidance on craft careers. At the same time, the notion that we are educating young people for jobs as yet unnamed[25] is very relevant to the diversity of careers pursued by makers working in a world of fast evolving material capabilities. The Crafts Council is working with makers and Inspiring the Future,[26] an organization that connects schools with volunteers from the world of work, who in turn commit an hour a year to speak about their job.

For existing craft business, continuing professional development remains vital. The Crafts Council hosts its own programme of professional and business development for makers throughout their careers, delivered in partnership with higher education institutions and other national and regional organizations. The programme is underpinned by a long tradition of developing talent, with iconic makers Tom Dixon[27] and Thomas Heatherwick[28] among those supported early in their careers. The aim of our talent development programme is to support artistic and entrepreneurial excellence at every career stage. Portfolio working and multiple roles, diversification into other sectors and the balancing of opportunities for commercialization with personal practice are factors influencing the nature of craft and makers, as well as the design of the programme. Findings from the evaluation of earlier programmes (Burns Owen Partnership 2009) informed this programme, such as the need to respond to wider agendas around entrepreneurship and innovation. Make Your Future is a new three-year nationwide initiative to ignite a passion for craft among 6,000 young people in schools and enable them to discover their craft and making talents. The programme is a response to *Our Future Is in the Making: An Education Manifesto for Craft and Making* (Crafts Council 2014), delivering a practical pupil-focused intervention and developing sustainable working models for bringing making skills back into secondary schools.

Lastly, we need to be passionate about increasing the understanding of how public investment in arts contributes to growth in the creative industries. Both the Arts Council England (CEBR 2015) and the Creative Industries Federation (2015) have published evidence showing how UK support is falling behind other countries in Europe[29] and demonstrating how public investment provides vital training, research and development and ideas which underpin the broader growth in the arts and creative industries. Only through partnership working between makers, educationalists and the wider creative economy will we be able to create a rounded package of intervention and support to foster and develop the potential of making and its vital contribution to our economy and society.

The Crafts Council

The Crafts Council is the UK's national development agency for craft. Our goals are to build a strong economy and infrastructure for craft, to grow and diversify craft audiences, and to champion high-quality contemporary craft practice nationally and internationally. We attract over 2.8 million visitors each year to our exhibitions, fairs and online showcases; curate the Crafts Council Collection; support makers' professional development; and stimulate the British contemporary craft market, carrying out research and promote craft. At the national level we work closely with the Creative Industries Council, aligning our priorities with those of Create UK, while at an individual level we help makers to promote their work and develop their professional skills and help communities to access craft as participants and audiences.

Notes

1 Such occupations include the application of, for example, textiles skills and knowledge in the automotive, health and synthetic biology sectors. See note 16 below for an explanation of the UK government's approach to counting craft's contribution to the economy.

2 In England, 2013/14, 19.8 per cent of the population participated in craft activities and attended exhibitions Department for Culture, Media and Sport Taking Part Statistical Releases, 2013/14.

3 See also Make:Shift 2014, which cast a spotlight on makers accelerating the pace of innovation in process, material, tools and techniques. (http://www.craftscouncil.org.uk/what-we-do/ms-2014) Make:Shift 2016 focused on innovation in robotics, smart materials, bio design and wearables (http://www.craftscouncil.org.uk/what-we-do/makeshift-2016/)

4 UNESCO 2003

5 The Cultural Learning Alliance. (http://www.culturallearningalliance.org.uk/evidence)

6 National Society for Education in Art and Design. (http://www.nsead.org/home/index.aspx)

7 The decision to focus on formal education and training was driven by the availability of data. A number of museums, galleries and community organizations host courses in craft and making, but data are not nationally available for comparison. We hope to address ways of gathering data on provision and participation in the informal sector in future research.

8 This compares with a 3 per cent fall in the total number of GCSE students in the same period.

9 Adult general FE is used here to refer to education (in addition to that received at secondary school) that is distinct from the HE offered in universities.

10 Andrew Marr quotes: 'China, where more than a thousand art and design colleges are operating' in the Magazine section of the BBC website, 21 November 2012. (http://www.bbc.co.uk/news/magazine-20391905) (accessed 27 July 2015).

11 A Higher National Diploma (HND) or a Higher National Certificate (HNC) is a work-related HE or FE course in the UK. The former is usually the equivalent of two years full-time at university, the latter of one year.

12 Our first study (TBR and Pomegranate 2014d), analysing data from the years 2007/08 to 2011/12, revealed a 14 per cent increase in participation in HE craft courses, driven in the main by a substantial increase in non-UK-domiciled students, suggesting a commensurate decline in participation by UK-domiciled students. Our subsequent study (TBR and Pomegranate 2014a) did not break down these data, but we plan to include this again in our 2016 study.

13 Here 'informal' is used to denote non-government apprenticeships, but in fact, in ordinary language terms, they may be highly formal, for example, livery company apprenticeships.

14 The term 'guided learning hours' refers to the tutor-led contact hours required to support learner achievement of a module or qualification.

15 The National Curriculum for schools in England is divided into five key stages: Key Stage 1 corresponds to primary school years 1 and 2 (ages 5–7), Key Stage 2 to years 3–6 (ages 7–11),

Key Stage 3 to secondary school years 7–8/9 or (ages 11–13/14), Key Stage 4 to years 9/10 to 11 (ages 13/14 to 16) and Key Stage 5 to years 11 and 12 (ages 16–18) – also, confusingly, known as sixth form from earlier systems.

16 The DCMS definition of the creative economy includes all those employed in the creative industries and the contribution of those who are in creative occupations outside the creative industries.

The creative industries are a subset of the creative economy that includes just those working in creative industries irrespective of their occupation (they may be either in creative occupations or in other roles, e.g. finance).

Creative occupations are a subset of the creative economy which includes all those working in creative occupations, irrespective of the industry that they work in.

17 DCMS uses the following Standard Occupational Codes (SOC codes):

5211 Smiths and forge workers

5411 Weavers and knitters

5441 Glass and ceramics makers, decorators and finishers

5442 Furniture makers and other craft woodworkers

5449 Other skilled trades not elsewhere classified

These sit alongside the Standard Industry Classification (SIC codes) 32.12 Manufacture of jewellery and related articles

The Crafts Council is in discussion with DCMS about evidence (TBR 2014) for the use of a broader basket of SOC codes in the economic estimates.

18 Microbusinesses are business with 0–9 employees. (Ward and Rhodes 2014, p. 3)

19 VAT must be paid when VAT taxable turnover is more than £83,000 in a 12-month period (Her Majesty's Revenue and Customs. (https://www.gov.uk/vat-registration/when-to-register) (accessed 09 May 2016)

20 Core subjects are English, mathematics, history or geography, the sciences and a language.

21 Rt. Hon Nicky Morgan MP, secretary of state for education in a speech on 10 November 2014, and Nick Gibb, MP, in a speech on 11 June 2015.

22 See Department for Education. (https://www.gov.uk/government/publications/national-curriculum-in-england-secondary-curriculum)

23 The Russell Group is a self-selected group of twenty-four UK universities, established to represent its members' interests.

24 See Young 2013, 2014; Dellot 2015; O'Leary 2014

25 Tristram Hunt in a speech on 20 March 15 to the Association of School and College Lecturers, quoting Andreas Schleicher of the OECD.

26 http://www.inspiringthefuture.org/

27 http://www.tomdixon.net/uk/

28 http://www.heatherwick.com/

29 CEBR (2015) shows that Britain invests a smaller percentage, 0.3 per cent, of its total GDP on arts and culture than other countries. Germany invests 0.4 per cent, the EU as a whole 0.5 per cent, Denmark 0.7 per cent and France 0.8 per cent.

References

Bahkshi, H., Windsor, G. (2015), *The Creative Economy and the Future of Employment*, London: NESTA.

Burns Owen Partnership. (2012), *Craft in an Age of Change*, London: Crafts Council, Creative Scotland, Arts Council of Wales and Craft Northern Ireland.

Burns Owen Partnership. (2009), *Crafts Council: Next Move Evaluation Final Report*, London: Crafts Council.

CEBR. (2015), *Contribution of Culture Industry to the National Economy*, Arts Council England.

Crafts Council. (2014), *Our Future is in the Making – An Education Manifesto for Craft and Making*, London: Crafts Council.

Creative Industries Council. (2014), *Create UK, UK Creative Industries Strategy*, Creative Industries Council.

Creative Industries Federation. (2015), *Creative Education Agenda*, Creative Industries Federation.

Dellot, B. (2015), *The Second Age of Small: Understanding the Economic Impact of Micro Businesses*, RSA.

Department for Culture, Media and Sport. 2013/14, Taking Part Statistical Releases.

Department for Culture, Media and Sport. (2015a), *Creative Industries Economic Estimates, January 2015*, DCMS.

Department for Culture, Media and Sport. (2015b), *Creative Industries 2015: Focus on Employment, June 2015*, DCMS.

Dewey, J. (1938), *Experience and Education*, Kappa Delta Pi.

Gardner, H. (1991), *The Unschooled Mind: How Children Think and Schools Should Teach*, New York: Basic Books.

Hein, G. (1996), "Constructivist Learning Theory", in G. Durban (ed.), *Developing Museums for Lifelong Learning, Group for Education in Museums (GEM)*. London: The Stationary Office.

House of Commons Culture, Media and Sport Committee. 2013, *Supporting the Creative Economy, Third Report of Session 2013–14*. London: The Stationery Office Limited.

Kolb, D. (1984), *Experiential Learning: Experience as the Source of Learning and Development*, Englewood, Cliffs, NJ: Prentice-Hall.

Monitor Deloitte. (2015), *Making in an Industry 4.0 World*, Here East.

O'Leary, D. (2014), *Going it Alone*, London: Demos.

TBR. (2014), *Measuring the Craft Economy*, London: Crafts Council.

TBR. (2016), *Studying Craft 16*. London: Crafts Council.

TBR and Pomegranate. (2014a), *Studying Craft 2: Update on Trends in Craft Education and Training*. London: Crafts Council.

TBR and Pomegranate. (2014b), *Studying Craft 2: Data workbook 2*, London: Crafts Council.

TBR and Pomegranate. (2014c), *Executive Summary of Studying Craft Report 1*, London: Crafts Council.

TBR and Pomegranate. (2014d), *Studying Craft: Trends in Craft Education and Training Full Report 1*, London: Crafts Council.

TBR and Pomegranate. (2014e), *Studying Craft 1: Data Workbook 1– February 2014*, London: Crafts Council.

UNESCO. (2003), *The Convention for the Safeguarding of Intangible Cultural Heritage*.

Ward, M. and Rhodes, C. (2014), *Small Businesses and the UK Economy*, London: House of Commons Library.

Yair, K. (2010), *Consuming Craft*. London: Crafts Council.

Yair, K. (2011a), *Crafting Capital: New Technologies, New Economies*, London: Crafts Council.

Young, L. (2013), *Growing Your Business: A Report on Growing Micro Businesses*, London: Crown.

Young, L. (2014), *Enterprise for All: The relevance of Enterprise in Education*, London: Crown.

11

Establishing the crafting self in the contemporary creative economy

Susan Luckman and Jane Andrew

Alongside more traditional selling options such as shop-based retail and commission sales, online craft retail sites are attractive to many creative sole traders and SMEs and have catalysed an explosive expansion in the international creative marketplace. A creative micro-economy that provides a rich international online marketplace enabling buying 'directly' from the maker offers both creative graduates and more established designer-makers micro-entrepreneurial pathways not previously open to them. However, the ease of establishing online shopfronts hides the complex work required to start and run a small business, especially one in an increasingly globally competitive space with isolated producers and narrow profit margins. This raises new challenges for craftspeople and designer-makers, who require not only practice-based skills but also new entrepreneurial skill-sets – both technical and personal – to operate successfully as a micro-enterprise in this emerging global market. To maximize the potential of these opportunities at a practical level, skills in professional practice need to be complemented by other capacities. Notably, these include the skills to successfully negotiate the use of social media as a marketing tool that requires the promotion of maker self-identity as part of the whole package of value being sold. Drawing upon initial data from a large three-year empirical investigation into the experiences of both recent graduate and established Australian craftspeople and designer-makers, this chapter explores the question: What are the self-making skills required to succeed in this competitive, social media–fuelled environment?

The evolving market for craft and the handmade

The past two decades have more broadly witnessed increasingly globalized and competitive markets in all sectors of the economy. Technology has not only enabled advances in the means of production, but also facilitated innovations to traditional distribution models in which physical shopfronts and product shelf-space are being usurped or coupled with online shopfronts. As Anderson observes:

> Our culture and economy are increasingly shifting away from a focus on a relatively small number of hits (mainstream products and markets) at the head of the demand curve, and moving toward a huge number of niches in the tail. In an era without the constraints of limited shelf space and other bottlenecks of distribution, narrowly targeted goods and services can be as economically viable as mainstream fare. (Anderson 2007, p. 52)

Within the market for craft and handmade goods, such long tail distribution is perhaps best illustrated by online shopfronts such as Big Cartel and County Culture, Makers Lane and, most famously, Etsy, who in 2015 saw over US$2.39 billion worth of merchandise sold globally (https://www.etsy.com/au/about?ref=ftr). Launched in 2005, Etsy currently (2017) boasts over twenty-eight million active buyers and 1.7 million active sellers (https://www.etsy.com/au/about?ref=ftr). But Etsy.com and other international brand creative marketplaces are just the highest-profile tip of a much larger iceberg that includes a plethora of online retail sites specializing in handmade small-scale creative production, as well as increasing numbers of sites curated by traditional craft gatekeepers such as guilds and professional associations. Thus, a recurrent theme in the research is how 'easy' it is to establish an identity, an online retail presence and market oneself:

Q: Yep. What about updating your online shop or profile?
A: I would say that's easy.
Q: Yep why would you say that's easy?
A: Because the website just kind of structures it, and so you just, you do this, you do this, you do this, and it's listed as opposed to – now you can sort of talk the description to your phone -

Textile Artist, Sydney

A: Yeah. I, so we used Weebly which is a website, and it's very easy. I find it so unnecessary to go in and to HTML code and everything like that when you have the ability to actually just drag and pull wherever you want to have a photo and everything. So it's a very easy set-up and I've done everything myself.

Woodworker/Designer, Brisbane and Stockholm

However, to compete successfully in the rapidly changing online distribution marketplace, makers need to be more active in the way they engage existing and potential customers. Social media marketing and networking, alongside the growth of global online distribution networks, have enabled the contemporary design craft maker to extend their market exposure and sales distribution boundaries beyond traditional business models. Within such a marketplace, just having a well-designed website to promote your work is 'so last century', and despite, or indeed because of, the lower barriers to entry into this marketplace, the risks associated with establishing and running a small craft-based business remain.

Our research participants are all too aware of the 'pros and cons' of engaging in sales sites such as Etsy. For some, the sheer number of sellers was seen as an impediment to the visibility of their products. For others, sales volumes didn't warrant the effort, especially when the costs of postage from Australia to elsewhere in the world are factored into the buying decision. For others still, online sale sites lacked the personal touch and the ability for potential customers to 'try on' the highly tactile, handmade product.

Q: Have you tried Etsy at all?

A: Yeah.

Q: No luck?

A: At first we didn't want to go near there because there's so many people doing it, it's so hard to be known. I mean, I feel like I'm just, we're just a small fish in this big ocean and then I look at it and I'm like 'is it worth doing?' But we did consider it an option. We created an account. We haven't uploaded anything yet. … We kind of always want to do things differently; when people are doing this, we like to do something else. … That's why, that was our last resort. … Is online really the way to go?

Textile Artist, Melbourne

I explored Etsy at one stage and couldn't be bothered. You'd look up jewellery on Etsy and there's 7,500 whatever pages … you'd get lost on something like that. … I look at Etsy a little bit the same way as I look at markets and think that people, when they're buying from those sorts of places, they don't want to pay big bickies. And I think that that's actually a bit of an issue with online selling. People actually want to be able to pick up the goods and try them on and see that they really like this bracelet or it suits them or whatever. And I've found that my website, a lot of people will go – friends and people who want me to make for them go – to the website and have a look and then come and make the arrangement off the website. Because they want to be able to consult and they want to be able to, as I say, pick it up, feel it, look at it, whatever.

Gold and Silversmith, Melbourne

Well Etsy was never my main focus anyway. I used Etsy as a way of creating an online portfolio for actual brick and mortar stockists. So if they wanted to see what my products were I said, 'Go on to my Etsy shop, you can see all the prices, you can see everything photographed, you can see the whole range, then you can come to me again and tell me what you want and we can put a wholesale order together.' But because I then have this Etsy shop set up of course sales came through that as well. But my ideal way of selling is wholesale, big orders, sending them off and being done with. Etsy has me running back and forth to the post office for one greeting card in my lunch break, and I just think, 'This is not worth $6.' Unless it's a big order.

Illustrator, Adelaide

Social media 'busy-work': Low barriers to entry, high to success

So, while for most within the Australian making community, setting up one's own website and perhaps professional social media presence is relatively easy, in this new and increasingly crowded market what is clearly starting to emerge is the challenge and time commitment needed

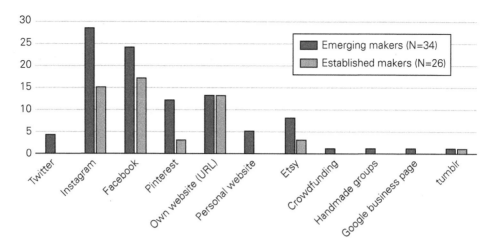

FIGURE 11.1 Interviewees' Professional Social Media Profile.

to develop and maintain an online presence that helps them stand out from the crowd. Some are succeeding, such as the above-mentioned woodworker/designer who focuses on Instagram. They work hard to constantly refresh the beautiful images of their products and their brand world, extending the networks these are popular in, leading to steady sales generated largely via this one social media tool. Indeed the popularity of Instagram over websites such as Etsy, at least for Australian makers, is one of the stand-out findings of the research thus far (see Figure 11.1). With its focus on a curated photographic aesthetic in a design-oriented marketplace, Instagram is proving successful for those whose work lends itself to stylized presentation in aspirational interior settings. For those makers with a skillset that incorporates styling and photography skills alongside making, this in many ways forms part of the product. But as another of our research participants acknowledges, labouring on one's social media presence may generate followers, but it doesn't necessarily translate into sales of the objects you make:

I have quite a presence on Instagram because it's such a visual medium, and a little bit on Facebook. I have a lot of friends within the creative industries, so we help promote one another, and obviously we complement each other. My website which I launched towards the end of last year obviously is a great first impression for people, and I have had a few people approach me who've seen my work on Instagram who've then said 'Oh I'd like to stock your work'. But aside from that, it's so funny, you think that once you've created something that people love that it's just going to just flow, but it doesn't work like that, you still have the persistence and the perseverance and the approaching people, because no one's going to buy your product until they know that it's been road tested. Regardless of online shops, they won't work until you've got a presence, and that will probably take me quite a few years … some people are very active on Instagram and it's a great medium, but to be honest it's very visual and I think people like what you do but it doesn't necessarily mean they're going to follow through and buy it. I think that's what people have to understand is when someone likes you and they follow you they may just enjoy looking at your work, that in itself to a lot of younger people is ownership, so they don't feel they need to then go and buy it. A lot will try and create a similar feel within their home or in their workspace, so really you're just trying to carve out a market within a market almost.

Designer/Metalworker, Adelaide

This maker offers a nuanced understanding of the situation, one informed by her own expertise and experience not just in design and making, but as a well-connected individual within the cultural and creative industries more broadly.

But a concerning tendency evolving, especially among the emerging makers we are interviewing and tracking the progress of across the three years of the research project, is the false security that having an online business identity *ipso facto* brings with it. One trend we will continue to track is the greater emphasis emerging graduates place on the ease and importance of social media marketing. While emerging makers were far more likely to report finding marketing 'easy' as compared with established makers, despite this 'ease' they clearly did not have the Web traffic, sales or profile of those who found this aspect of their practice 'harder'. The maintenance of social media profiles can take up much of the time makers have to give to their business each week. The simplicity, especially for so-called digital natives, of creating profiles appears to be masking the real challenges of building a reputation or brand – particularly across multiple social media, own website and retail website platforms – one that converts to sales and not just 'likes'. So, on the plus side, the boom in online sales opportunities and methods has democratized access to the marketplace, bypassing traditional professional gatekeepers and market intermediaries including guilds or professional associations[1], and retailers who all traditionally provided market access, as well as business and professional development advice. However, on the down side, the 'busy work' of maintaining a social media profile and building networks can provide the sense of working at marketing growth, while in reality delivering little return for effort:

I'm getting responses so then they go to the market really, they don't really [buy online], I've had lots of people view my website but only three people buy from my website.

Fabric Artist, Melbourne

Successful creative self-employment is clearly more than a case of 'build it (online) and they will come'. Indeed, rather than being a licence for instant success and profile, having an online professional identity, not just for makers but more widely for workers across many creative professions, is now simply a taken for granted as a starting, not end, point. It is something you need to have as a default; it will not necessarily build your reputation or sales, but existing online in a professional website proves simply that you exist, are contactable. Being 'Google-able' professionally is a new baseline, offering evidence of the reality and legitimacy of your professional identity. Operating in tandem with, but not effectively in addition to, your offline presence:

And I also need to have a good website because I remember even when I was looking at artists for research if they didn't have a nice website, I kind of didn't really pay attention. It was that design aspect almost, I want to look at something nice and then I'm more invested. So I'm probably not going to design my own website but I need one.

Glass Maker, Adelaide

Many current makers still recall the pre-internet craft marketplace, where professional practice-based associations (not commercial operators) ran 'professional' craft fairs where stalls were run by, among others, potters, glass artists, jewellers, instrument makers and textile artists, all of whom handed their goods over to the purchaser wrapped in newspaper. In this recent past, branding was a business card and, if you had a computer, a rudimentary website. Today image is everything, as is cultivating 'Brand You' (Tom Peters 1999 cited in Brouillette 2014, p. 41). Now the norm is to have multiple social media presences, thus adding a layer of complexity and increased demand upon the time creative entrepreneurs need to spend working on their business, above and beyond the actual work of making. It is not surprising therefore that the vast majority of our interviewees report significant hours are spent creating and maintaining a professional and engaging online presence, not to mention building and maintaining the networks which make these sites useful and viable as promotional tools.

Q: Experience with the online world. Now you've got an Etsy shop, how long have you had that?
A: Oh long time I think, since 2008 or something.
Q: How have you found it?
A: Patchy, very patchy it's like anything online, you really have to work at it. I find that the more you list [the better] and apparently you're meant to list one a day.
Q: Really?
A: To keep your head above everybody else, then you will get return, but who's got time or the discipline to do it I guess?
Q: How much time a week do you spend updating all those websites?
A: I spent yesterday updating my website, it depends on what I've got. ... I try at least to be on there once a week, and they've got a new thing where you can promote your shop – I'm doing that every couple of days but, but I've got it down to a fine art using an iPad and the app, the app's so much easier.

Milliner, regional South Australia

I've got my website, plus eBay, my Facebook page which is highly important actually, I'm getting more response there than I ever do on my website, and my Instagram, so managing all that takes a lot of time. So I worked for three hours today, but really that was two hours weaving and then I had an hour on the internet organising all that. And I've [also] got new products I haven't actually put on my website yet, I've got to take photos of them, so, secretly, I would like to employ someone to do all that, but then I kind of want to take them, so that's why it's a slow business.

Fabric Artist, Melbourne

In this retail environment, social media (including Etsy's own support group), and new pop-up artist-run initiatives (including retail spaces), are seen as very collegial, sharing, 'lift all boats' cultures where information can be freely sought and shared.

It takes more than making skills to make a successful craft enterprise

Despite the changes in the distribution models for handcrafted products, developing and sustaining a profitable creative enterprise that can replace other forms of paid employment is dependent not only on creative talent but also on business acumen. With the rise of social media as a central element of the marketing and promotion of any enterprise, the ease of establishing an online shopfront hides the complex work required to start and run a creative small business practice. One of our emerging makers, a former public servant with high-level IT skills summed up the skills needed to develop and run a successful craft enterprise:

> You just need to be everything and it's a bloody big ask for one person. Like you can't do it all at once. You need to be marketing savvy; you need to identify your market. Like doing the NEIS [New Enterprise Incentive Scheme] program was very helpful for that because you either do a Certificate III or IV – like I did a Cert IV in Small Business Management – and in doing that you actually write a business plan. So instead of just sitting there and working through textbooks it's actually very relevant. …
>
> You've just got to do it all. You've got to market; you've got to make; you've got to design; you've got to sleep; you need a really broad skill set.

Shoemaker, Adelaide Hills

For many of the makers we have so far interviewed, exposure to business skills development through their undergraduate degrees was minimal, if not non-existent:

> Q: And you were saying before that you've found in some aspects your professional practice development through the uni wasn't quite enough.
> A: Yeah exactly. I think for me it's something that needs to be addressed earlier in the degree. Because you're coming into your third year and they're pushing you to go and seek out to do exhibitions and all of that on your own, and by that point myself, I'd already kind of developed that skill, I'd already been pushed to do that and I'd had an exhibition in my second year. But a lot of people need that person to tell them to do it. But once you've finished your third year, if you've not had, like if you've only just recently had that kind of experience, there's not that ability for you to have that, and the group of people to support you in getting on with that. … We had a lot of people come in and talk about how they, like it was pretty much, like professional practice is just about grants writing. We had people come and talk about their success stories, but never about running a business. I think that's something that's kind of completely overlooked in that sense. I'm trying to remember what the syllabus was, but it was mostly around grants and writing essays and things like that.

Glass Artist, Adelaide

To help facilitate building their creative micro-entrepreneurial business skills, many of our research participants have joined relevant peak bodies, notably including their local ACDC (Australian Craft and Design Centres)-affiliated organization, with the professional, especially business, skills development and affordable insurance packages they offer being particular attractors. However, alternative online peer-based networks are perhaps used more actively and frequently by emerging makers in search of practical business information.

Quite a number of our participants have undertaken the New Enterprise Incentive Scheme (NEIS) business course referred to above.[2] But to be eligible for NEIS training the applicant must be at the time registered for Newstart unemployment allowance. During the thirteen-week training programme, participants develop a NEIS Business Plan, on completion of which they earn a nationally recognized qualification (Certificate III in Micro-business Operations or Certificate IV in Small Business Management) and receive business mentoring during the first year of the operation of the business. On completion and approval of the business plan, participants receive NEIS Allowance for thirty-nine weeks of business operation. The NEIS Allowance is equivalent to the single, twenty-two years of age or over, no children rate of Newstart Allowance. But while a notable proportion of our research participants have undertaken or are undertaking the NEIS scheme, a surprisingly large number of them have never heard of it. Two of our established makers in particular acknowledge the positive impact that NEIS had on the development of their enterprise:

> Because I didn't have an interior or an architecture degree and industry was low at that time – the housing industry – … . I felt I don't have any choice but to start my own business, there's no other way to do it. I did a NEIS course and that was fantastic because they do this thing where they make you figure out what your competitive advantage is which took me weeks and a lot of tears and going 'no, I'm no different to any furniture designer, how am I ever going to make a successful business?', but what I figured out from that was there was lots of woody cabinet makers and people who did benches and tables and none of that has changed, but there wasn't many people doing upholstery. So that's where I went, I'm focussing on the upholstery side of things and going from there and I still keep that upholstery focus and it's interesting when I do collaborate with architects [which I do] all the time now. The fact that I do the upholstery side of it they really appreciate that because they can knock up joinery designs and stuff no problem, but they all feel a bit lost on that upholstery side of that because it is a bit specialist. So it was a good choice 15 years ago.
>
> Furniture Designer, Adelaide
>
> I did a course run by Australian Government. It was called NEIS Scheme. … And that was amazing I have to tell you. That actually set me up. That started me to think properly about every step and this is how they showed me that you have to choose one day for your administration and that's normal. You have to have a day like that to deal with all the issues. So now I don't have to complain 'oh I hate paperwork and everything', I just do it in between and I just call it my administration time. But NEIS helped me to plan and to get all the ideas together.
>
> Ceramic Artist, Canberra

Either by choice or by necessity, many working in the cultural and creative industries (stemming either from their tertiary studies or via a different route) develop what Hall refers to as Protean Career, in which the individual constructs their vocational identity through the recurrent acquisition or creation of work (likely to occur on a freelance or self-employment basis), and strong intrinsic motivations for, and personal identification with, a particular career (Hall 2004). This often non-linear career path is in stark contrast to historical notions of career development in which pathways are explicitly and implicitly defined by tertiary study, industry and organizational cultures. With thirty-two emerging makers interviewed, it is clear that the challenges of the DIY entrepreneurial career paths now afforded them are being embraced as offering valuable new possibilities, especially for creative graduates not content to wait for employment or sales opportunities to find them. This precarity of employment and income generation is highlighted by Throsby and Zednik's (2010) research that found within their principal artistic occupations, only just over one-quarter of all artists' work as employees within the arts and cultural sector on a permanent or casual basis and are paid a salary or wages. The remaining three-quarters operate as freelance or self-employed individuals (Throsby and Zednik 2010, p. 53). Despite this fact, many leave art or design school with limited skills to develop and run a sustainable enterprise to support their creative practice, let alone generate enough income from their practice to provide them with a minimum wage.

In an era where city planners and regional economic development agencies use the arts and creative sectors as flagships to attract investment and signify a lively and buoyant economy, and governments across OECD nations emphasize the importance of supporting small businesses to create job growth, it is surprising that entrepreneurship and enterprise development remains at the periphery of the visual and applied arts curriculum. Within our participant interviews thus far there has been minimal reference to their participation or recollection of the content of formal business or enterprise development within formal study. Importantly too for those educators who do include such content, early data are showing that those that did indeed encounter some form of business or professional development learning while at design/art school did not necessarily realize the significance of the information being conveyed at the time. However, once they became self-employed they found they were on a steep learning curve and had to be resourceful to replicate the kinds of informational and advice access they had previously taken for granted while studying. Therefore, the kind of guidance provided institutionally is probably not best focused upon the everyday minutiae of running a business. Aspects of commercial practice, such as setting up a payment system on your website or processing a sales transaction, really become 'take on board' relevant only when you need to action them yourself, and peer networks and internet searches quickly become key up-to-date sources of information around possible options. What is probably best focused upon within training curricula is a broader emphasis upon building up students' entrepreneurial subjectivities and attitudes. This needs to sit alongside the provision of exemplar models of some of the various design craft career pathways potentially open to them, and advice on how to best place yourself along a continuum of practice which can encompass gallery pieces through to outsourced production.

Acknowledgements

This research was supported under the Australian Research Council's Discovery Project funding scheme (project number DP150100485). We thank Belinda Powles for her ongoing invaluable input and assistance with the research project and, as always, the makers generous enough to share their stories with us.

Notes

1 Though it does need to be acknowledged here that these are increasingly finding a new role in this saturated marketplace as curators of quality, that is, as ironically being revalued in the new online economy precisely for their gatekeeping function in a saturated market.

2 https://www.employment.gov.au/neis-training-support-and-payments

References

Anderson, C. (2007), *The Long Tail: How Endless Choice is Creating Unlimited Demand*, London: Random House.

Brouillette, S. (2014), *Literature and the Creative Economy*, Stanford: Stanford University Press.

Hall, D. T. (2004), 'The protean career: A quarter-century journey', *Journal of Vocational Behaviour*, 65 (1): 1–13.

Throsby, D., and A. Zednik. (2010), *Do you Really Expect to Get Paid? An Economic Study of Professional Artists in Australia*, Sydney: Australia Council for the Arts.

12

Handmaking your way out of poverty?

Craftwork's potential and peril as a strategy for poverty alleviation in Rockford, Illinois

Jessica R. Barnes

'Can you make your own job?' the mayor of Rockford, Illinois, asked of unemployed people in his city (Ludwig 2013). Mayor Larry Morrissey has partnered with the online craft marketplace Etsy to retrain people in the city to make their own jobs as craft entrepreneurs. As entrepreneurial 'makers' engaged in small-scale production of handmade arts and crafts, these unemployed workers are the creative human capital who are hoped to transform Rockford into a 'maker city'. Numerous media outlets, such as Bloomberg Business (Tozzi 2013) and CNN Money (O'Brien 2015), have taken up the narrative of an 'Etsy economy' offering a development alternative in areas suffering from postindustrial economic woes such as high unemployment rates due to the loss of manufacturing jobs. Academics and regional planners have long regarded entrepreneurship and the arts as the future of employment and economic growth in many postindustrial countries. However, producing and selling handmade crafts shares little in common with the generally more highly paid occupations Florida (2002) has lumped together as the creative class whose human capital can revitalize cities. Although many crafters are extremely creative and skilled in their work, they often earn little or no money for the sale of their pieces. Such efforts reflect neo-liberal tendencies for encouraging entrepreneurship and transferring the responsibility for poverty to individuals. The arts labour market is often discussed as a prominent site of neo-liberal tendencies of self-employment, risk and poor pay (Ellmeier 2003; Dawkins 2010; Bain and McLean 2013; Loacker 2013). In this context, the recent resurgence of interest in crafting as a strategy for market-based development and poverty alleviation highlights the potential of craftwork as a way to make a living, particularly for women balancing childcare and paid work. However, in terms of monetary value, craft entrepreneurship's potential as an economic development tool may be fairly limited. In this chapter, I use content analysis of media reports, programme documents and the Etsy website itself to critically examine Etsy's Craft Entrepreneurship Program (CEP) in Rockford as a strategy for craftworking as poverty alleviation.

Etsy's The Craft Entrepreneurship Program

> Since we need an 'Etsy Economy' has Etsy begun any partnerships with high schools or job training? We'd love to explore.
> —*Tweet from the Mayor of Rockford, Illinois, to the CEO of Etsy (Morrissey 2012)*

In response to this tweet by Mayor Morrissey the online craft marketplace Etsy developed pilot endeavours for poverty alleviation through crafting micro-businesses (Mauriello 2013). An 'Etsy economy' as described by Dana Mauriello, the director of Human Scale Labs at Etsy, involves people 'building businesses and *defining success on their own terms*, by selling handmade goods, vintage items and craft supplies directly to buyers on the Etsy Marketplace' (Mauriello 2014). The Craft Entrepreneurship Program (CEP) used in-person classes to teach low-income people how to utilize their craft skills to earn income by selling their work on the Etsy online marketplace. The curriculum, which was designed by Etsy, consists of fourteen hours of training over four weeks and instructs students in multiple topics such as marketing, search engine optimization, photography, pricing and business growth strategies. In practice, it is community partners, non-profit organizations or public institutions that provide the education and resources to programme participants. They provide the facilities, recruit participants and hire a local Etsy seller as a teacher. Only students with existing craft skills can enroll. Pilot programmes began in Rockford and the Bronx, New York, in 2013. In Rockford the programme is provided by the Rockford Housing Authority (RHA), a municipal corporation that manages the nearly 2,000 public housing units in the city.

Situating The Craft Entrepreneurship Program

An intensification of individualization and competition exemplary of neo-liberalism encourages people to become entrepreneurs of themselves (Foucault 2008), using their own human capital to become producers and sources of earnings and to apply economic analysis to multiple spheres of life (Ellmeier 2003). Such neo-liberal mentalities, or taken-for-granted societal understandings, organize society and people's relationships to work (Foucault 2008; Lazzarato 2009), particularly for cultural workers (McRobbie 2002; Ellmeier 2003; Gill and Pratt 2008; Dawkins 2010). Social norms, corporate actors, markets and the state govern individual entrepreneurs, but not through strategies of constraint; rather, governance *mobilizes* subjects to become entrepreneurs. The CEP is an example of these tedencies, as crafters living in poverty are encouraged to become entrepreneurs by their city government and the Etsy corporation.

For Foucault (2008), the enterprise form is generalized throughout society as a way to use one's abilities, as opposed to signifying a business or a firm specifically. For example, a crafter invests her knowledge of making and design, time and labor to create her craft and hopefully realizes profit in terms of monetary income if the craft sells, and in terms of psychological profit or 'psychic income' from personal satisfaction gleaned from the making process (Foucault 2008, p. 244). For Foucault, human capital is understood in terms of abilities or skills that can be deployed in any one of a number of activities or enterprises, a machine that can produce an income or earning stream, and workers appearing as a 'sort of enterprise for himself' (Foucault 2008, p. 225). The working person uses their abilities in multiple enterprises, crucially, towards multiple ends, including earning not only a monetary income but also satisfaction. Foucault understands the neo-liberal social fabric as constructed of generalized forms of enterprise, which allows competition to organize and regulate society. *Homo œconomicus* (the classical economic man) in neo-liberal society invests human capital in various enterprises as an 'entrepreneur of himself, being for himself his own capital, being for himself his own producer, being for himself the source of [his] earnings' (Foucault 2008, p. 226). Crafters leverage their human capital in the hopes of earning monetary and psychic incomes (Barnes 2014).

Cities are also trying to leverage human capital to spur economic development. Creative index approaches have received particular attention in development schemes as popularized through Florida's (2002) notion of the 'creative class', which understands 'creative' people as the key resource through which places can grow and compete economically. For Florida (2002) a wide range of occupations from engineers to artists make up the creative class. However, the fuzziness of this concept based on occupations and educational attainment as indicators of creativity in practice is problematic because it homogenizes diverse actors with different work trajectories, incomes and politics (Markusen 2006). Despite this relatively under-tested relationship, artist-based revitalization strategies are popular for regional development because they require fairly small investments. The presence of artists is thought to contribute to regional economies by drawing creative workers in through local cultural amenities (Florida 2002; Currid 2009), branding places as cultural milieus, and creating arts jobs and revenues (Currid 2009).

City officials in Rockford embraced the CEP as a strategy for both leveraging the creative class for redevelopment of the city and alleviating poverty. It could be understood as asset-based community development because it utilizes existing resources within a community for economic and social development (Breitbart 2013). Mayor Morrissey and other city officials saw value in place rather than understanding Rockford as a blank slate in terms of cultural value. The CEP is meant to teach Etsy selling to people who already know how to craft. One of the goals of the CEP was to create a new narrative for the city and its residents and the city's efforts were internationally recognized through and at the 2014 Place Marketing Forum, where it won the award for Best Territorial Marketing; the White House Maker Faire and 'Strong Cities, Strong Communities'; and the Clinton Global Initiative. These alternate subjectivities show agency at the scale of the community and individuals (Gibson-Graham 2003).

Online marketplaces have created possibilities of connecting crafters with consumers in distant locations and opened access so their ranks have swelled as craft sellers bypass the gatekeepers of the traditional cultural economy (e.g. craft fair organizers, art galleries) (Shultz 2011). Etsy accounts tend to cluster in midsized cities such as Rockford due to a lack of local physical intermediaries, though this has forced crafters themselves to take on roles as intermediaries (Shultz 2011). Women have historically dominated participation in handicrafts, and this demographic also makes up the majority of sellers on Etsy. Having children and assuming the responsibility of primary caregiver for those children often led female crafters out of waged work outside the home to craft entrepreneurship where they can control the spaces and times of work to (ideally) fit with responsibilities for the care of young children (Oberhauser 1995; Bachrach and Main 1998; Barnes 2014). Bachrach and Main (1998) find that women often take up microenterprise as a strategy to 'have it all', even though women's businesses largely remain precarious and marginal. Women's involvement in homework, such as craft making, serves as an effective economic strategy for coping with downturns in the formal economy (Oberhauser 1995; Jakob 2012). However, Bachrach and Main (1998) also note how microenterprise is often problematic and at times detrimental to women's livelihoods due to them choosing unprofitable businesses (such as crafting). A renewed interest in craft is revaluing women's domestic work (Luckman 2013; Bratich 2010) and continuing the debate on whether such work is empowering for women or simply creating wealth for the craft support industry, including Etsy (Jakob 2012; Barnes 2014).

Nascent craft entrepreneurs can be understood through the concept of *aspirational economies* (Barnes 2014), systems of production and consumption of resources that include multiple notions of value and are practiced by people who focus more on experience and hope for future successes than on immediate material gains. Aspirational economies blur the boundaries between professional occupations and amateur avocations and consider the ongoing processes of becoming (or not), in that aspirants' eventual success is not inevitable and often fleeting if achieved at all. The hope that drives aspirational economies can bind aspirants to precarious work in many industries, but art-related industries in particular are thought to be at the vanguard of such tendencies (Gill and Pratt 2008; Luckman 2012). Can aspirational economies be sustained and should they be encouraged for the poor and marginalized crafters participating in the CEP?

Programme results

Twelve people participated in the pilot CEP in Rockford in 2013 and five of those participants ultimately opened online shops. There was some publicity associated with the programme, which highlighted a few of the crafters and their work (Etsy blog articles and videos; the *Rockford Register Star*; CNN Money; Bloomberg News). Even with this publicity, however, only one of the shops had any sales. Over the next two years that one shop had four sales. By 2015, two years after the pilot programme, none of the participants' shops had any items listed for sale. However, materials provided by the RHA showed that these crafters were still active locally offline by selling at the Rockford City Market and attending other business development workshops. Although it is early in the programme, based on the results thus far the potential for poverty alleviation through craft entrepreneurship seems to be very limited for most participants.

But this is hardly surprising; most craft sellers on Etsy receive similarly low returns (Etsy 2013). Just 26 per cent of US-based Etsy sellers are full-time employees, while 48 per cent are independent, part-time or temporary workers (Etsy 2013). With a median household income of $44,900, 10.2 per cent lower than the national average, Etsy sellers are combining income from both salaried jobs and entrepreneurial efforts to make a living (Etsy 2013). Although there are a few success stories, most incomes are skewed towards low values. But these relatively low earnings were part of the narrative about the CEP from the start. In reference to creating full-time jobs, Dana Mauriello, who oversaw development of the CEP for Etsy, explained, 'We're not telling that story, because we don't think that's a practical goal in the short term. If you can sell an item this week, that's great. And if that goes toward your savings, that goes toward paying your utility bill, that's amazing' (Small Business.com 2014). However, although the CEP was not generating much in terms of monetary values, the city and participants were gaining other types of value from their efforts.

Craftwork can be work on the self and crafters reported gaining non-monetary values from their experiences as aspiring entrepreneurial crafters (Etsy 2014). As neo-liberal subjects crafters invest their human capital in entrepreneurial enterprises, hoping to earn monetary income and often, in the process, gaining what Foucault (2008, p. 244), as we saw above, called 'psychic income'. In aspirational economies such as crafting, monetary incomes are often relatively small and psychic incomes serve as a major motivator to sustain people's efforts (Barnes 2014). In this way for many practitioners the crafting process creates personal value for the maker in terms of pleasure and the 'transformative value of making things yourself' (Dawkins 2010, p. 263). Often these personal pleasures are a precursor to decisions to try to earn income. CEP participants like many arts aspirants draw on numerous benefits thought to arise from the arts experience: intrinsic benefits such as captivation, spiritual awakening and aesthetic growth, and personal development benefits such as critical thinking and creative-problem solving (Mccarthy et al. 2005; Luckman 2012). There may also be values related to people's quality of life such as undertaking craft work to fulfil a desire to work from home to facilitate care of dependents (e.g. children, elderly parents) or as part of retirement. Caregiver is a subject position that CEP participants embody, whether as care for others or the self. Personal values are interwoven with the notion of care. For example, crafters who gain therapeutic value from their work are performing care of the self through their practice. In an Etsy-produced video on the project, CEP participants described craft making as therapeutic and used crafting as a technique to help build their self-respect (Etsy 2014).

Implications

But despite the positive outcomes identified above, injustices emerge from crafters taking up a *new production of subjectivity* as described by Read (2009), a neo-liberal mode of subjection in which market logic and individualization permeate one's understanding of themselves and all spheres of life. Crafters' sense of individualization leaves sellers with no one to blame but themselves when their businesses are unsuccessful and they are alienated from their fellow sellers who are the 'competition' rather than potential allies in collective action. These injustices might be compounded for poor people with limited resources. Crafters enact hidden injustices on themselves through self-exploitation as they work unpaid and underpaid hours unregulated by formal labour laws trying to realize unrequited dreams of starting and sustaining their own microbusinesses.

Corporate and market-oriented governance on Etsy can foist numerous injustices on craft sellers. Etsy is far and away the largest marketplace for handmade goods with substantial daily buyer traffic. Crafters establish their online stores and try to build a customer base on Etsy because of its market dominance and ease of access. The Etsy marketplace is a private space where rights of access and speech are tenuous and can be stripped from sellers at any time. Also, the rules of the selling space may shift at the discretion of the company, as they did in 2013 when Etsy changed its policy to allow manufactured items designed by sellers to be offered in the handmade marketplace. Although this policy change allows sellers to scale up their businesses by outsourcing aspects of production, it also makes it difficult for sellers who exclusively hand-make their products to compete with the price points of manufactured goods, and for many it undermines the handmade ethic on which Etsy has been built.

Crafters often pursue and continue their entrepreneurial attempts while accepting little monetary compensation due to earning psychic incomes (Barnes 2014). This practice underpins aspirational economies and is problematic due to self-exploitation. Middle-class crafters who do not earn adequate money to sustain their businesses are often able to continue their pursuits by self-subsidizing their craft selling through other income sources (e.g. waged work and/or a partner's income) (Barnes 2014). However, low-income people employing crafting as a strategy for poverty alleviation might not have the additional incomes needed to sustain a business. CEP participants having no active Etsy shops two years later may illustrate how aspirational economies are less accessible to poor people because they lack the resources to work through an immediate lack of material gain. Although the CEP participants have disengaged with the Etsy online marketplace as a point of sale, they are still active locally, participating in continuing education courses and selling in booths at the Rockford City Market.

Even with the accessibility promised through a global online marketplace like Etsy, many crafters still build their businesses based on a loyal consumer market, which commonly is localized (Barnes 2014). Craft fairs in particular allow face-to-face interactions between crafters and customers, which provide psychological motivation for sales and facilitate socialization (Storper and Venables 2004). Also, Shultz (2011) found it was easier for crafters to become established in smaller craft communities such as midsized cities because there is less competition. The social proximity many crafters experience through interactions in the local community reduces direct competition and could in turn create more opportunities for collaboration and collective action. Geographic proximity does not guarantee such relationships because trust is often required to form social proximity (Ettlinger 2003) and social proximity can occur at a distance via online interactions (Jones, Spigel and Malecki 2010).

Conclusion

A survey of 5,500 US Etsy sellers found most sellers earned only a few thousand dollars a year, yet the dream of craft entrepreneurship is selling as the Etsy marketplace has grown to more than one million active shops (Etsy 2013). But how can city and regional development authorities promote selling online crafts as poverty alleviation when the chances of earning significant incomes are limited? As of 2015, CEP was active in seventeen US cities and two British cities.[1]

Craft entrepreneurship is an *aspirational economy* based on multiple conceptualizations of value – it is mostly sustained through rich psychic incomes, hope for monetary incomes and subsidization from other sources. However, Leyshon, Lee and Williams (2003) note that spaces of hope can be diminished by material inadequacies or incorporation into the mainstream. In most contexts, aspirational economies can persist even if artists exit frequently due to constraints on their livelihoods, because there tends to be an oversupply of aspirants entering the field (Menger 1999), but there may be detrimental effects to individuals and communities in relation to these exits. In the process, these aspirants may amass large financial debt, tax their social capital and experience intense emotional stress and a sense of grief with the loss of their entrepreneurial pursuit

(Cardon et al. 2012). According to a 2012 report on US entrepreneurs, 82 per cent of start-up funding came from personal, family and friend sources and two-thirds of businesses failures were the result of difficulties obtaining financing (Kelley et al. 2012). Such negative experiences may deter further entrepreneurship. Few scholars have examined how exit may occur though the notion of precarious work related to the culture industries has a large place in the literature (Ellmeier 2003; Gill and Pratt 2008; Ross 2008). Understanding the widespread pursuit of entrepreneurship as a process, whether it is sustainable for individuals or not, can offer a greater sense of the values that are produced and consumed by artists' work. Becker (2009) discusses how the process itself, including failures that may be associated with it, has value in the art field and argues, 'Embracing failure is actually *essential* to all unique achievements and should not be feared any more than the accidental or the unexpected, all of which might turn everything around and open up possibilities not recognized or understood at the outset of the project.' Many craft entrepreneurs build their human capital through the process of aspiring to create a sustainable business on Etsy and retain these gains whether or not the business is a conventional success.

Craft entrepreneurship helps crafters to justify using their human capital towards a desire for creative arts-based work, but it does not offer sustainable livelihoods for the poor. Prevalent neo-liberal tendencies in society make market logics common sense, so even if the promise of a lucrative craft business is a chimera, chasing that dream of trying to earn monetary value *seems* more logical than doing something simply because you love it. Crafters also take up entrepreneurship in a context of precarious work where the demands of a flexible labour market create an absence of steady jobs – meaningful and not (Standing 2011). The CEP will likely continue and grow even though the individual monetary gains will be too limited for widespread poverty alleviation precisely because of the alternative types of value fostered through participation: psychic income earned by participants, the presence of a few success stories in terms of city rebranding and huge growth opportunities for the craft-related business services who peddle the craft entrepreneurship dream.

Note

1 In 2015 Etsy's Craft Entrepreneurship Program was operating in Watsonville, CA; Albuquerque, NM; Dallas, TX; Chattanooga, TN; St Petersburg, FL; Newark, NJ; Albany, NY; Santa Fe, NM; Madison, WI; Cleveland, OH; Poole, UK; and Oldham, UK.

References

Bachrach Ehlers, T., and K. Main. (1998), 'Women and the false promise of microenterprise', *Gender & Society*, 12 (4): 424–40.

Bain, A., and H. McLean. (2013), 'The artistic precariat', *Cambridge Journal of Regions, Economy and Society*, 6 (October): 93–111.

Barnes, J. R. (2014), 'Aspirational Economies of Self and City : The Values and Governance of Independent Crafters in Columbus, Ohio', PhD diss., The Ohio State University, Columbus, OH.

Becker, C. (2009), *Thinking in place: Art, Action, and Cultural Production*, New York: Paradigm.

Bratich, J. (2010), 'The Digital Touch: Craft-work as immaterial labour and ontological accumulation', *Ephemera: Theory and Politics in Organization*, 10 (3/4): 303–18.

Breitbart, M. M. ed (2013), *Creative Economies in Post-Industrial Cities: Manufacturing a (different) Scene*, Farnham, Surrey: Ashgate.

Cardon, M. S., M. D. Foo, D. Shepherd, and J. Wiklund. (2012), 'Exploring the heart: Entrepreneurial emotion is a hot topic', *Entrepreneurship Theory and Practice*, 36 (1): 1–10.

Currid, E. (2009), 'Bohemia as subculture; 'Bohemia' as industry: Art, culture, and economic development', *Journal of Planning Literature*, 23 (4): 368–82.

Dawkins, N. (2010), 'Do-It-Yourself : The precarious work and postfeminist politics of handmaking (in) Detroit', *Utopian Studies*, 22 (2): 261–84.

Ellmeier, A. (2003), 'Cultural Entrepreneurialism: On the changing relationship between the arts, culture and employment', *The International Journal of Cultural Policy*, 9 (1): 3–16.

Etsy. (2013), 'Redefining Entrepreneurship : Etsy Sellers ' Economic Impact', Etsy.com. Available online: http://extfiles.etsy.com/Press/reports/Etsy_RedefiningEntrepreneurshipReport_2013.pdf (accessed 13 January 2014).

Etsy. (2014), [web video] 'Etsy's Craft Entrepreneurship Program in Rockford', Available online: https://youtu.be/JtoNjFNszaU (accessed 10 January 2015).

Ettlinger, N. (2003), Cultural economic geography and a relational and microspace approach to trusts, rationalities, networks, and change in collaborative workplaces, *Journal of Economic Geography*, 3 (2): 145–71.

Florida, R. (2002), *The Rise of the Creative Class and How It's Transforming Work, Leisure, Community and Everyday Life*, New York: Basic Books.

Foucault, M. (2008), *The Birth of Biopolitics: Lectures at the Collège de France, 1978-1979*, trans. G. Burchell, New York: Palgrave.

Gibson-Graham, J. K. (2003), 'An ethics of the local', *Rethinking Marxism*, 15 (1): 49–74.

Gill, R., and A. Pratt (2008), 'In the social factory?: Immaterial labour, precariousness and cultural work', *Theory, Culture & Society*, 25 (7–8): 1–30.

Jakob, D. (2012), 'Crafting your way out of the recession? New craft entrepreneurs and the global economic downturn', *Cambridge Journal of Regions, Economy and Society*, 6 (1): 127–40.

Jones, B. W., B. Spigel, and E. J. Malecki. (2010), 'Blog links as pipelines to buzz elsewhere: The case of New York theater blogs', *Environment and Planning B: Planning and Design*, 37 (1): 99–111.

Kelley, D. J., A. Ali, C. Brush, A. C. Corbett, M. Majbouri, and E. G. Rogoff. (2012), *Global Entrepreneurship Monitor 2012 United States Report*, Wellesley, MA: Babson College.

Lazzarato, M. (2009), 'Neoliberalism in action: Inequality, insecurity and the reconstitution of the social', *Theory, Culture & Society*, 26 (6): 109–33.

Leyshon, A., R. Lee, and C. C. Williams, eds. (2003), *Alternative Economic Spaces*, Thousand Oaks, CA: Sage.

Loacker, B. (2013), 'Becoming 'culturpreneur': How the 'neoliberal regime of truth' affects and redefines artistic subject positions', *Culture and Organization*, 19 (2): 124–45.

Luckman, S. (2012), *Locating Cultural Work: The Politics and Poetics of Rural, Regional and Remote Creativity*, New York: Palgrave Macmillan.

Luckman, S. (2013), 'The Aura of the analogue in a digital age women's crafts, creative markets and home-based labour after Etsy', *Cultural Studies Review*, 19 (1): 249–70.

Ludwig, A. (2013), 'With help from Etsy, a small-city mayor brings the maker movement to the classroom', Forbes, 16 September. Available online: http://www.forbes.com/sites/techonomy/2013/09/16/3056/ (accessed 4 April 2015).

Markusen, A. (2006), 'Urban development and the politics of a creative class: evidence from a study of artists', *Environment and Planning A*, 38 (10): 1921–40.

Mauriello, D. (2013), 'Craft entrepreneurship: Year in review', Etsy News Blog, 20 December. Available online: https://blog.etsy.com/news/2013/craft-entrepreneurship-year-in-review/ (accessed 16 July 2014).

Mauriello, D. (2014), 'Scaling an Etsy Economy for a changing workforce', Knight Blog, 7 May. Available online: http://www.knightfoundation.org/blogs/knightblog/2014/5/7/scaling-etsy-economy-changing-workforce/ (accessed 15 May).

Mccarthy, K. F., E. H. Ondaatje, L. Zakaras, and A. Brooks. (2005), *Gifts of the Muse: Reframing the Debate About the Benefits of the Arts*, Santa Monica, CA: Rand Corporation.

McRobbie, A. (2002), 'Fashion culture: Creative work, female individualization', *Feminist Review*, 71: 52–62.

Menger, P.M. (1999), 'Artistic labor markets and careers', *Annual Review of Sociology*, 25 (1): 541–74.

Morrissey, L. (MayorMorrissey) (2012), '@chaddickerson Since we need an 'Etsy Economy' has Etsy begun any partnerships with high schools or job training? We'd love to explore.' 30 Aug. 2012, 9:14 p.m. Tweet. Available online: https://twitter.com/mayormorrissey/status/241388490108047360 (accessed 4 January 2014).

Oberhauser, A. M. (1995), 'Gender and household economic strategies in rural Appalachia', *Gender, Place & Culture*, 2 (1): 51–70.

O'Brien, S.A. (2015), 'How Etsy's IPO could save cities.' CNN|Money, 11 March. Available online: http://money.cnn.com/2015/03/11/smallbusiness/etsy-b-corporation-ipo/index.html (accessed 4 April 2015).

Read, J. (2009), 'A genealogy of homo-economicus: Neoliberalism and the production of subjectivity', *Foucault Studies*, 6 (February): 25–36.

Ross, A. (2008), 'The new geography of work: Power to the precarious?', *Theory, Culture & Society*, 25 (7–8): 31–49.

Shultz, B. J. (2011), 'Handmade and DIY : The Cultural Economy in the Digital Age', PhD diss., University of Tenessee, Knoxville, TN USA.

SmallBusiness.com Staff. (2014), 'The Etsy Craft Entrepreneurship Program Helping Create an 'Etsy Economy', SmallBusiness.com, 10 April. Available online: http://smallbusiness.com/news/trends/etsy-craft-entrepreneurship-program (accessed 23 April 2014).

Standing, G. (2011), *The Precariat: The New Dangerous Class*, New York: Bloomsbury Academic.

Storper, M., and A. J. Venables. (2004), 'Buzz: Face-to-face contact and the urban economy', *Journal of Economic Geography*, 4 (4): 351–70.

Tozzi, J. (2013), 'Etsy Wants to Be the Rust Belt's New Factory', Bloomberg News, 25 September. Available online: http://www.bloomberg.com/bw/articles/2013-09-25/etsy-wants-to-be-the-rust-belts-new-factory (accessed 8 April 2015).

PART FOUR

Craft-driven place-making and transnational circuits of craft practice

13

Interrogating localism

What does 'Made in Portland' really mean?

Steve Marotta and Charles Heying

In April 2014, we were asked to observe a brainstorming session at ADX Portland, a makerspace based in Portland, Oregon. The setting was a funky, rehabbed industrial warehouse with concrete floors, retro lighting, an old beat-up piano and the lingering particulate haze of sawdust. A few six packs of locally brewed India Pale Ale sat in the middle of the table we all sat around. The meeting was populated by an angel investor,[1] representatives from a local entrepreneurial network and incubator experiment, ADX Portland's owner/director and marketing director of the ADX-affiliated Portland Made Collective. The meeting seemed very important, yet was nothing if not informal – beer took the place of water; capriciousness and profanity took the place of measured business-speak. Somehow, a conversation around seed funding for Portland Made Collective drifted seamlessly between formal, rational strategic planning and informal, ad-hoc expressions of Portland as an artisanal paradise. Throughout the meeting the emphasis was on all things local; it was this undercurrent of localism that really left a mark on us.

We had already begun to investigate the relationship between localism and the artisan/maker movement, but this meeting rewrote the questions that we wanted to ask. When the meeting was over, it was clear to us that this relationship must be based on a specific set of values that intertwine with the identity politics of Portland's maker community. As we have seen throughout our research, these values change rapidly and are constantly contested, and yet somehow seem to be shared among Portland's artisans, makers and social entrepreneurs (Heying 2010; Heying and Marotta 2016). It has become clear that *local* is an especially entangled concept; understanding what artisans and makers mean by local is at the core of our current inquiries.

Introducing localism

The political and spatial ambiguities embedded in the concept of *place* might be likened to a 'suitcase so overfilled one can never shut the lid' (Hayden 1995, p. 15). Like place, the concept of local is certainly overdetermined. At the outset of our research, we began hypothesizing on what local might mean to Portland's artisans. Perhaps it is place branding (e.g. 'Made in Portland'), a clustering of like-minded artisans that share resources and ideas; competitive advantage, boundary-related interpretations (e.g. 'local is my neighbourhood'), and sourcing and marketing interpretations (e.g. 'locally sourced' or 'buy local'). One constant, we guessed, would be a pushback against global forces, including mass production, off-shoring and race-to-the-bottom wages.

Many of our preconceived assumptions about local were theoretically informed. We first turned to the concept of authenticity (Relph 1976; Zukin 2010) to conceive of localism. Relph argues that authenticity arises as one 'dwells' (*Dasein*, following Heidegger) or invests time in a place and develops a sense of belonging; inauthenticity, on the other hand, is a sense of foreclosure on human possibility, reified for Relph in the form of total uniformity (a lack of particularity) or 'disneyfication' (c.f. Baudrillard 1994). Zukin (2010) largely adapts Walter Benjamin's notion of aura to describe authenticity, arguing that authenticity best comes into view as it is disappearing. Authenticity, for Zukin, is in crisis precisely because of the efforts to reproduce it. These efforts end up stripping away any sense of wholeness or connectedness from a place. A potent example is the attempted reproduction of bohemian artist districts all over the globe; most of these districts have rents too high to actually house artists. Space, in these cases, is produced in a way that bludgeons authenticity rather than locally re-contextualizing it.

There seems to be a split in terms of how local is perceived in the 'postmodern' or neo-liberal era. This split might be best envisioned in a debate about the nature of place. Cresswell (2004) frames this in terms of 'reactionary' versus 'progressive' senses of place. On the one hand, there is a variety of literature that sees place as a defensive position against globalization, occupied by neo-Marxian positions such as Harvey (1996) and Peck and Tickell (1994, 2002). These positions stress the downward pressure exerted on the local scale, in which the local acquires evermore responsibilities without the power necessary to execute them (Peck and Tickell 1994). In this literature, place and localism is always understood in the context of political economy, and it is normally the contradiction between mobile capital and fixed place that serves as a point of conflict. On the other hand, much of the recent literature on place attachment or sense of place moves away from the emphasis on political economy. Massey (1994) points out that colonized peoples have been experiencing 'the annihilation of space by time' for centuries – instead emphasizing localized multiplicities of identities and experiences (Gibson-Graham 2006; Hayden 1995; Massey 1994; Rose 1995). Place, locality and community are all concepts that are best thought of as fluid with negotiable borders. The local in this case can be thought of as a space where the ongoing performance of subjectivity constructs a negotiated foundation from which global processes can be engaged with (Gibson-Graham 2006).

Localism can also be thought of in terms of localization strategies that address certain imbalances. One example of localization is import substitution, whereby locally produced goods substitute for the importing of globally produced goods (Bellows and Hamm 2001); in many ways, the artisan-led 'maker movement' is performing import substitution on a variety of goods, from clothing to foods, by stressing the localization of production rather than the consumption of goods produced (under unknown conditions) elsewhere. Localization can embed place-specific knowledge in smaller, more manageable systems in ways in which state or global systems cannot (Helleiner 2000; Scott 1998). Embedding local knowledge, however, can actually problematize the purported relation between local and global (universal and particular). Geertz (1992) points out that there is no 'everything' to know (no universal); all knowledge must therefore be locally situated (particular). The benefit of dissolving the distinction between universal and particular is that it gives analysts a better vantage point to observe the flow of power regardless of its classification as global or local; locally situated knowledge, therefore, is still imbued with power relations (Diawara 2000).

A specific danger associated with localism is the 'local trap' (Purcell and Brown 2005; Purcell 2006; Sonnino 2010). At the core of the local trap argument is the fallacious assumption in social science literature that localization – 'scaling down' or relying on locals for knowledge or methods – will automatically lead to social justice, environmental remediation or a 'true' form of democracy (Purcell and Brown 2005). There is no necessary relation between scale (which the authors point out is socially produced) and equity, meaning the assumption of more just outcomes at smaller scales is not grounded in any evidence. In addition, Purcell is critical of the many literatures that empirically ignore cases in which 'going local' can be burdensome for communities rather than empowering. As Purcell (2006) points out, some groups feel as if they are suddenly 'being asked to do the work the state should be doing' (ibid., 1927).

Our findings have pointed to both confirmations and confrontations with the above theoretical notions. Local, as it turns out, is one of those complex concepts that encompass an array of nebulous, yet somehow shared, values. Rather than try to shoehorn our conclusions about localism into some previously existing theory or concept, we will present some of the common themes that we were able to distil through our yearlong empirical investigation. While this is not the forum for a detailed description of our research methods, over the past two years we have employed a community-embedded research strategy to engage Portland's artisan community. This has involved a variety of surveys, interviews, grounded theory and participant observation, as well as a general embeddedness in the community (see: Heying and Marotta 2016). What follows below is a variety of interpretations of 'local', as we could best reconstruct the notion through a series of interviews and interactions with Portland's artisan community.

Local and authenticity: tourism, space, place

One of the first things one notices on arrival in Portland is the amount of colourful storefronts that dot the trendiest part of downtown where the centre city meets the upscale Pearl District. Shops like Made Here PDX, Canoe, Boy's Fort, Tender Loving Empire and Crafty Wonderland are all located within five blocks of Powell's Books, the internationally known independent bookstore (and tourist favourite) that anchors this area. All of these shops feature local artisans, and many have identifiers of their 'localness' in their windows: stickers that advertise their membership in Supportland, a 'Portland is Happening Now' flyer, or 'Keep it Local' lettering across the threshold of the door. In these cases, the inclusion of the word "local" is often times a signifier of its authenticity to non-locals. These shops are the first exposure for tourists that have seen or heard about Portland's 'vibrant' and 'notorious hipster culture' ('Hip and Happening in Oregon' 2015) made famous in part by IFC's *Portlandia* and indie rock bands galore. These shops also serve as the contact point between Portland's artisans and tourists; many of the goods sold in these shops are marketed to the tourists looking for an *authentic* piece of Portland to bring back home with them.

According to many of our interviewees, Portland has a tourist economy that is unique when compared to other cities. The tourists that come to Portland are looking for a particularity that they cannot find elsewhere, a sense of urban openness that is simultaneously playful and unthreatening. To quote from one of our interviews: 'In a lot of the tourist areas in downtown New York and San Francisco and Seattle, they just sell crap junk from China, and people expect that'. But in Portland, the downtown boutiques largely eschew products like these in favour of quirky, local and handmade goods. The sentiment among artisans is that other urban tourist destinations have downtowns that resemble over-commercialized shopping malls, whereas Portland's downtown is not like this. Portland's boutique shops have caught the city's eccentricity in a bottle and sell it to tourists that seek authentic weirdness; this is an authenticity that apparently can't be found in the ho hum suburbs or other cities with fewer young and creative people.

Tourists looking for authentic pieces of Portland spend time reading labels in search of some sort of validation that a shop's products really are made locally by local people. Shop owners are aware of this and ask artisans to label their goods:

> When I was building out my retail line, I got the chance to talk to a couple buyers/retailers and I had not put 'Made in Portland' on my cards … a number of them highly recommended it because customers ask for and look for things that were made in Portland. … The focus and value of being made locally is really important.

Another artisan recalled the experience of selling his goods at a craft fair. Many of the consumers were not concerned with the price but instead were very concerned with whether *he* had made it and *where* he made it. The good would have not been authentic otherwise; it would not have the stories of Portland as a *place* locked within it.

Mixing business and pleasure: a local cultural economy

Many artisans see localism from a cultural vantage point, but to others the lack of economic context is bothersome. For instance, one artisan argued localism 'isn't necessarily about the farmer's market mentality', he argued, it 'is important because of the freshness, the factors of input, not because of the ethos'. This artisan was critical of the local 'maker' culture, arguing that it ignores many economic realities in favour of lifestyle choices and amenities. 'It has to be about economy. It has to be about making money and making it efficient'. His argument here is that localism is understood by many artisans as a way of *living* rather than a way of *making* (producing); he is interested in localism because he feels that Portland has some competitive advantages, a certain *terroir* that can bolster the city's economy. He was especially critical of the trend of barter and trade between artisans, because it cannot be measured: for him, this would confirm to investors that Portland is more about lifestyle than economic viability.

While many interviewees think of the financial aspect of their work as 'fully annoying', others do embrace the traditional business challenges of growing an enterprise in a new economic setting. One artisan envisions the local network of artisans and makers as a supply chain. Envisioning a local network as a supply chain is probably not new, but the way in which this particular supply chain functions might be. Rather than each enterprise providing an input to a finished good (this, of course, does happen in Portland's artisan economy), this perspective of supply chain is based on the potential for collaboration on 'one-off' projects and the cross-fertilization of ideas. From a business point of view, one of the objectives becomes deepening one's network of artisans in order to anticipate common economic interests. Since artisans are generally linked by culture more so than their industrial specializations, unique inter-sector collaborations are common. Furthermore, according to a few artisans, the diversity of specialties in the artisan network actually reduces competition between them, which allows them to work together without worrying about how much market share each might poach from the other. 'There's no reason to be cutthroat, that'll never happen around here', says one artisan of his relationships with others.

We can see from many of these examples that culture and economy intersect locally in some interesting ways. Are they new intersections or rearticulations of always-present (but often ignored) intersections? What seems more important than the possibility of newness are the ways in which these intersections seem to work for artisans. In posing the question of localism to artisans, we got a bounty of responses that blur the boundaries of culture and economy. It also seems that in many cases artisans are willing to sacrifice potential economic gain for cultural or value-based considerations. For example, two artisans went into detail about why they felt it necessary to locate their production house in the Central Eastside of Portland, an industrial neighbourhood that is under pressure from private-market gentrification and the looming possibility of a zoning change that could be disastrous for manufacturers. The artisans' decision to locate there, despite these pressures, had to do with the cultural space of the neighbourhood: their employees want to 'bike to work, they want to stop and have a beer on the way home', and these enterprise owners feel it important to provide these cultural amenities. And even though it would be far cheaper for them to locate in a suburban industrial park, they are 'uninterested in the lifestyle that accommodates being away from the inner core of the city'.

Localism as 'windows' into making processes

Most things are bought and consumed after they are produced. In this form of consumption, the production process is concealed; the conditions of a thing's production are obscured from the consumer. One of the values we have seen repeatedly in Portland's artisan economy is an effort to remedy this – the consumer is often invited by the producer (artisan/maker) to follow a product's journey into existence. Artisans have become hip to the possibilities here, often offering a 'window' into the various phases of the production process. Windows are 'opened' primarily through the internet and social media, over which the artisan provides progress reports to the consumer in the form of text, pictures and video. This was one of the most common responses we got to our questions about localism, although this clearly is not an analysis of localism based on strict geographical borders – *there is no need for the consumer to be local in order to feel local*.

Through the use of social media sites like Instagram, consumers actually become participants in the production process, and thus the windows are generative of new relationships between producer and consumer. It is important to recognize that the window into the production process (from the consumer's point of view) is also a window into the consumption process (from the artisan's point of view). This allows the artisan and the consumer to become familiar (local?) to each other in a way that strikes us as atypical of capitalist commodity production. For the consumer, the 'black box' of production gets opened; for the producer, the 'black box' of consumption (specific to their craft) gets opened. The window, then, serves as an 'other' space where the processes of making and consuming are in direct contact.

Practically speaking, what are these windows and how are they used? In a conversation with one artisan, we asked about this. Her response drifted towards a description of a shift in the way artisans go about handling the ordering process:

> This is where the independent, handmade thing comes in, and this is part of why I like it so much, connecting with your customers. They're not just buying off Amazon … it's usually much more personal, you know, back and forth depending on what type of order it is. And then they have that personal connection.

Her reply distinguished the exchange process of artisans from what we would consider a 'normal' purchase from a retailer like Amazon. She continued on to say that even if artisans are making items that are similar, this does not induce competition because the personal connection between consumer and artisan is what sets things apart. 'Some people end up having long relationships, they like this person's style … they've always bought from this person', she continued before we interrupted: 'Maybe [the consumer] know[s] something about the [the artisan]'s story?' To this she described how social media provides a unique (two-way) window:

> A lot of creative people really like Instagram, I love Instagram because I can have my business stuff with all these pictures … so when someone buys something from me I try to find them on Instagram and follow them so I can get their personal side … and they can see that this is me in my day-to-day … so that people feel connected to you.

The implications for interpretations of localism are substantial. On the one hand, we have the example of social media, which in terms of connectivity in the local artisan community is of significant value. But social media, especially when used on ubiquitous devices like iPhones, show how localness is stewarded in part by large multinational corporations such as Apple, Google and Instagram. On the other hand, if we see localism as a sense of familiarity or connectedness, then geographic location means little to how that connectedness is articulated. This is true, again, because of the functionality of social media and the internet.

Another artisan business owner made it explicit that successful artisan businesses are good at showing consumers the production process. She was talking about the difference between their production operation and a 'typical' factory operation, making the point that most other factories aren't going to 'feel local.' This feeling of localness, for this artisan, is a direct result of the closeness of the relationship between her and her clients. 'It's about giving them access to the making process' that makes their operation feel local. This is also despite the fact that many of their clients are not from Portland, but from around the United States and Canada. For many of their clients, especially considering the window this artisan provides into the production process, their enterprise is 'local enough.'

Localism(s): a synthesis

In our interviews, we were interested in exploring the meanings that emerge once we divorce the notion of 'local' from the map. Our strategy of asking questions that examine the intersection of *making* and *place* provided rich data about how localism is perceived by Portland's artisans. While this chapter has explored how some Portland artisans articulated their versions of localism, there were many more that we could not develop in this chapter. Table 13.1 summarizes the many ways in which our interviewees expressed their views on localism.

Many of the articulations of localism we experienced did indeed map back to theory: interpretations of localism as 'authenticity' (Relph 1976; Zukin 2010), 'situated knowledge' (Geertz 1992), and as 'fortress' (Harvey 1996; Tickell and Peck 2002) come directly from our literature review. Other interpretations had little to no relation to the literature. Design, for example, was often discussed in context of localism, especially in that Portland is thought to have a concentration of place-inspired designers ('couture'). Some artisans and makers see localism simply as a neighbourhood or a region ('strict geography'), but many others described localism in complex and unexpected ways. For example, many artisans and makers defined localism in terms of environmental awareness ('sustainability'), with many explicitly questioning how sourcing materials from distant lands can be ecologically sound. But the 'sustainability' interpretation often overlapped with the 'fortress' and 'windows' interpretations in the context of globalization: makers

Table 13.1 Localisms

Characterization of Localism	Occurrences in Interview Data	Our Interpretation
Localism as Strict Geography	3	As it sounds; interpretations of localism that don't leave the map
Localism as Fortress	3	Localism as a pushback against globalization, mass production and homogeneity
Localism as Authenticity	3	Localism as it relates to the insider/outsider relation (e.g. tourism)
Localism as Sustainability	2	A 'green' localism, with an emphasis on sourcing
Localism as a 'Window'	2	Localism that emphasizes familiarity and process across distances
Localism as Lifestyle	2	Localism as a richness of amenities
Localism as Couture	2	Localism as a place's aesthetic as captured in a product's design
Localism as 'Made in Portland'	2	Localism as 'zeitgeist'; the multiplicity of factors associated with making in a place; often used in a branding context
Localism as Localization	2	Localism that emphasizes the economic benefits of culture
Localism as Situated Knowledge	1	Localism as a particular knowledge unique to place and interest-based communities

are aware of the fact that their clients either are sensitive to factory conditions overseas (thus the importance of the 'window') or want their patronage to serve local ends (keeping the money local – creating a 'fortress' against the perceived ills of globalization).

Reflecting the title of this chapter, perhaps it is the 'Made in Portland' trope that best brings all of the disparate interpretations together. Portland has developed a reputation for harbouring most of the values listed on the table, and claiming something is made in a place with such values ostensibly locks a particular 'authenticity' into such products. Additionally, the term 'made' is often a proxy for 'handmade', which arguably is a proxy for 'authentic.' But then again, the 'Made in Portland' interpretation is often applied in the economic context of branding (often to people in places other than Portland). 'Made in Portland', then, attempts to convey 'local' meaning to people outside Portland that want to feel connected with such values.

Conclusion

Of course localism is overdetermined, but it is important to go through the deconstruction process in order to understand the specific entanglements that push the localism discourse forward. We have shown that localism is capable of incorporating everything from environmental and social justice to branding and tourism. As is the case in most investigations, looking at localism raises as many questions as it answers: How much of what we found is Portland-specific? What might we find if we did a similar investigation in Chicago or London? How does 'local' policy harness or even propagate the localism discourse, and to what ends? We may ask the same question of corporations – the aisles of Whole Foods, an upscale grocery chain in the United States, are blanketed with advertisements of 'locally made' goods. So who gets to tap into the local discourse? Who or what is made invisible by it? How does localism change as places change (e.g. through gentrification)?

Our goal for this chapter is to begin to tease apart the contradictory articulations of a particular value in a particular context. If there is a point to belabour, it is that we have seen the mobilization of a constellation of localisms function as one commonly understood value. These observations seem to give purchase to Massey's (1994) and Gibson-Graham's (2006) arguments for seeing places as fluid yet contested; the conflicting meanings of local we have seen are indeed constructive of a common ground for the artisan/maker community here in Portland. Localism is a diversity of articulations that has somehow ossified into one understanding and it seems to be enough to foster a sense of belonging among Portland's makers and artisans.

Note

1 An angel investor is a private investor that provides seed funding or other cash assistance to early-stage entrepreneurs, usually in exchange for some amount of equity stake in the business. Angel investors are typically individuals, whereas venture capital investments are made through investment firms.

References

Baudrillard, J. (1994), *Simulacra and Simulation*. Ann Arbor, MI: The University of Michigan Press.

Bellows, A. C. and Hamm, M. W. (2001), 'Local autonomy and sustainable development: Testing import substitution in more localized food systems', *Agriculture and Human Values*, 18 (3): 271–84. http://doi.org/10.1023/A:1011967021585

Cresswell, T. (2004), *Place: A Short Introduction*, Malden, MA: Blackwell Publishing.

Diawara, M. (2000), 'Globalization, development politics and local knowledge', *International Sociology*, 15 (2): 361–71. http://doi.org/10.1177/0268580900015002013

Geertz, C. (1992), '"Local knowledge" and its limits: some obiter dicta', *The Yale Journal of Criticism*, 5 (2): 129–35.

Gibson-Graham, J. K. (2006), *A Postcapitalist Politics*, Minneapolis, MN: University of Minnesota Press.

Harvey, D. (1996), *Justice, Nature, and the Geography of Difference*, Malden, MA: Blackwell Publishing.

Hayden, D. (1995), *The Power of Place*, Cambridge, MA: The MIT Press.

Helleiner, E. (2000), 'Think globally, transact locally: Green political economy and the local currency movement', *Global Society*, 14 (1): 35–51. http://doi.org/10.1080/13600820050001112

Heying, C. (2010), *Brew to Bikes: Portland's Artisan Economy*, Portland, OR: Ooligan Press.

Heying, C. and Marotta, S. (2016), 'Portland made: Building partnerships to support the local artisan/maker community', in *Sustainable Solutions: Let Knowledge Serve the City*, Sheffield, UK: Greenleaf Publishing.

Hip and Happening in Oregon. (2015), Retrieved 28 June 2015, from http://www.travelchannel.com/destinations/us/or/portland

Massey, D. (1994), 'A Global Sense of Place', in *Space, Place, and Gender*, Minneapolis, MN: University of Minnesota Press.

Peck, J. and Tickell, A. (1994), 'Jungle Law Breaks out: Neoliberalism and Global-Local Disorder', *Area*, 26 (4): 317–26. Retrieved from http://www.jstor.org/stable/20003479

Purcell, M. (2006), 'Urban democracy and the local trap', *Urban Studies*, 43: 1921–41. http://doi.org/10.1080/00420980600897826

Purcell, M. and Brown, J. C. (2005), 'Against the local trap: scale and the study of environment and development', *Progress in Development Studies*, 5: 279–97. http://doi.org/10.1191/1464993405ps122oa

Relph, E. (1976), 'A sense of place and authentic place making', in *Place and Placelessness*, 63–78, London: Pion.

Rose, G. (1995), 'Place and identity: A sense of place', in D. Massey and P. Jess (eds.), *A Place in the World?: Places, Cultures and Globalization*, 87–132, Oxford, UK: Oxford University Press.

Scott, J. (1998), *Seeing Like A State*, New Haven, CT: Yale University Press.

Sonnino, R. (2010), 'Escaping the Local Trap: Insights on Re-localization from School Food Reform', *Journal of Environment Policy & Planning*, 12 (1), 23–40. http://doi.org/10.1080/15239080903220120

Tickell, A. and Peck, J. (2002), 'Neoliberalizing Space', *Antipode*, 34 (3): 380–404. http://doi.org/DOI: 10.1111/1467-8330.00247

Zukin, S. (2010), *Naked City: The Death and Life of Authentic Urban Places*, Oxford, UK: Oxford University Press.

14

Policy, locality and networks in a cultural and creative countryside

The case of Jingdezhen, China

Zhen Troy Chen

Introduction

This chapter develops a qualitative study of a small creative cluster based in Sanbao International Ceramic Art Village, Jingdezhen, a city known as the capital of Chinese porcelain and ceramics for over 2,000 years (Dillon 1992). It will draw upon multiple sources including semi-structured interviews with artists, workers, managers and mentors in the craft, ceramics and painting sectors in Sanbao to analyse how locality, relationship and community networks work in maintaining and developing this rural cultural and creative cluster. In addition, the work of other researchers, policy documents and media releases will be used to contribute to the analyses. Fieldwork and participatory observation within the village will add some specificities and texture to the theoretical skeleton, revealing some details and complexity of the evolving discourse on cultural and creative industries (CCIs) in China. Further, the chapter hopes to enrich and contribute to existing research on creative industries, given the dominant urban bias towards creative clusters research in recent years.

Sanbao means 'three treasures' in Chinese, namely tea, bamboo and clay in Jingdezhen's case. Sanbao, a village regenerated from several derelict farmhouses sixteen years ago,[1] is now home to hundreds of artists and workers. It has been developed into a self-sustaining ceramic art village with an international reputation. It consists of multiple ceramic studios and kilns, a gallery and museum for artists to make and display ceramics. It also functions as an intermediary agency offering upstream and downstream services, such as raw material supply, training and consulting, organizing forum and exhibitions. Additionally, it hosts a UNESCO-recognized research institute offering cultural immersion programmes and ceramic workshops in and around Sanbao for artists and enthusiasts from around the world. There are also hostel, restaurant, café and tea house, accommodating artists-in-residence, students and tourists.

FIGURE 14.1 Sanbao Studio Area. Photo by Author 2014.

Given Sanbao's scale and organizational structure, it is quite different from the dominant narratives of urban, often purpose-built creative clusters in China. This chapter aims to extend the existing research on CCIs beyond metropolitan agglomeration and urban clustering. Among interdisciplinary literature, there is a lot dealing with the clustering of creative activities, including studies of creative cities, creative labour and creative class. However, recent years have seen emerging cultural geography research which challenges the urban bias towards creative industries. The 'other' geographies and stories from the margins shifted the attention towards the broader view of locality and networks within and across creative clusters (Coe 2000; Harvey, Hawkins and Thomas 2012; Luckman 2012; Waitt and Gibson 2009). Research into Chinese rural CCIs are even fewer as researchers tend to look at tier-one and tier-two cities, namely Beijing, Shanghai and Guangzhou; Suzhou, Hangzhou, Dalian and Ningbo (Keane 2011 and 2013; Montgomery 2010).

CCIs in China: The problematic and the pragmatic

Since the mainstream policy take-off of the term creative industry in 1998 (DCMS 1998), a plethora of policies and categorizations regarding CCIs have been raised, yet ambiguity and contests remain. The term is derived from the Frankfurt School's *culture industry*, which referred to the industrialization of culture, whereas *cultural industries* focus on the industry dynamics of cultural production in capitalist economies (Flew 2012). The term *creative industries* was initiated by the UK government as a response to the shift from a manufacturing economy to a knowledge-intensive, creative or experience economy (Keane 2013), and sought to embrace more than the *cultural industries* discourse, emergent digital content industries. Creative industry discourse thus grew out of cultural industry and transcended its original cultural aspect, emphasizing the importance of individual creativity and innovation. In China, the term has gone through a series of developments in the academic and policy circles. The concept also inspired policy within many developing 'Asian Tiger' economies. Singapore, Hong Kong and Taiwan all came up with their own long-term plans tailored for their local economy (Kong 2005).

Chinese policy normally starts from the top central government who develop overarching plans, followed by a series of regulations, which are often framed in broad terms that lack specification. This vagueness and ambiguity allows local governments to interpret and launch further reforms. Sometimes new ideas are fed in by relevant scholars and entrepreneurs through either formal consultation or other channels. Successful cases and entities will be used as models or demonstrations to showcase the policy in richer textures (Keane 2013). The post-1978 'Open-up' reforms initiated by Deng Xiaoping spread across various economic sectors. In Chinese cultural institutions and affairs, it first began with performing arts and then extended to other cultural and creative sectors. The ownership reform (privatization) of cultural industries was first conducted among state-owned cultural departments. From 2003, the focus for the cultural industries shifted from propaganda or reflections of socialist spiritual civilization to economic development with a rapid privatization of state-owned *cultural affairs* to privately owned *industry* or *enterprises*. The central government declared the official use of cultural industries as a key national task in their tenth Five-Year Plan. However, it was not until 2006 that China officially endorsed 'creative' in its policy documents (Hui 2006).

As creative industries discourse caught the attention of academics and policymakers in the West, technological innovations and cultural creativity were advocated for further policy development by 2011 in China. This has not meant China will break with its cultural past and embrace only individual creativity. Rather, this policy roll-out reflects the broader dynamics and tensions of cultural control or cultural nationalism and market liberalization currently under way in China. Thus, the reconciliation term 'cultural and creative industries' (CCIs) becomes a seemingly politically appropriate way to reflect the importance of both culture and creativity in a pragmatic way. Li Wuwei, an influential scholar and high-profile government official in China, has contended that creative industries and the creative economy are both driven by a dual engine of technological innovation and cultural creativity. CCIs follow a value logic which seeks value maximization; by exploiting human creativity, people can increase added value, both tangible and intangible (Keane 2013).

Xi Jinping's new government reaffirmed cultural creativity and technology innovation as two drivers for the whole nation; this state-level strategy will continue to support the cultural aspect as culture is deemed to offer an edge in China's competition in the global market. The encompassing list of CCIs China proposed consists of tourism, crafts, industrial design and R&D, among other sectors. Crafts and tourism are important components of the CCIs, which are often more evident in developing countries, as it is easier for start-ups to profit since these require less technological innovation and thus less financial capital. This also brings up the very question of the definition of 'creativity' at stake here. Even though defining creativity and CCIs is not my purpose and certainly beyond the scope of this short chapter, a quick summary of the literature will be helpful to make sense of these debates. The 'God-given individual genius' or elite-based notion of individual creativity has been criticized since the 1970s in Western cultural studies, cultural sociology and other disciplines. The emphasis on the social nature of creativity holds that creativity is not produced with some pure raw material by the selected few, but is a human capacity which can be trained and nurtured (O'Connor 2012). As Marx argued, raw materials are not natural givens but socially constructed and the democratized creativity is about 'social intercourse, mutual respect and the existence of other possibilities connecting creativity with social praxis' (Pang 2012, p. 44). This is very helpful in analysing Sanbao's case, as this empirical research looks particularly at the connections and networks within Sanbao and how these foster creativity.

Local policies

Sanbao is a representative case within China's CCIs as it is rural yet international. According to *Jingdezhen Daily*, the development of CCIs in Jingdezhen has reached an international and high-end stage. In 2010, the overall value of gross output of ceramic industry in Jingdezhen reached 16.02 billion RMB. In the first half of 2011 alone, ceramics exports totalled 89 million USD (JingdezhenDaily 2011). The local government has followed the evolving discourse about CCIs and made a list of policies aiming to develop its local economy mainly based on manufacturing, ceramics and the tourism industry. It believes the revitalization of the capital of Chinese porcelain and ceramics will bring competitive advantage and generate economic (and social) value. Sanbao has been mentioned repeatedly in local policies as well as in many national, provincial and local media releases as a municipal CCI demonstration base.

Prior to 2008, the local polices connected to Sanbao were mainly about ceramic industry, tourism and cultural industry in isolated terms. It was not until 2008, two years after the eleventh Five-Year Plan was announced, that Sanbao was connected with creative industries. The next year, Jiangxi Provincial government decided to list Sanbao as one of the five CCI Demonstration Bases and later granted official status of Sanbao Art Gallery.[2] In 2012, Sanbao finally got endorsed by the local government as both cultural and creative. In 2014, the municipal government issued an intellectual property right regulation to better support its ceramic industry. At the time of writing, the local government organized a high-profile forum named *Dialogue about Sanbao: Beautiful Nostalgia of the Millennium Porcelain Capital* to discuss the further development of Sanbao. The aim is to bring in investment and expertise to make Sanbao 'bigger and stronger'. It has created tension between the government and Sanbao due to the fear of turning Sanbao into one of those similar looking industrial creative zones based on a quintessentially urban playbook; similar cases can be found in other creative clusters in Chinese cities like Tianzi fang in Shanghai, 798 Art Zone in Beijing and Lijiang old town in Yunnan (Keane 2013; Pang 2012).

Crafts-making as cultural and economic pillars

Creative work in Sanbao reflects the convergent characteristics and functions of craft-making as a synergy of a cultural and natural endowment of uniquely place-specific raw materials, cultural heritage, traditions and skills. It involves learning and experience, display and exhibition, as well as sale of handcrafts and a supporting hospitality industry. The production and skills acquired are often not only based on imitating and replicating traditional forms or patterns, but also on innovation which differentiate itself from its competitors. The cultural and spatial proximity and agglomeration in Sanbao provides an excellent environment and networks for the uncodified and apprenticeship-based tacit knowledge to accumulate and stimulate creativity.

As discussed earlier, the definition of CCIs has a strong economic focus. Given its broadness, it is important that empirical research focus on detailed sub-sectors – crafts and ceramics in the case of this study – in order to examine the cultural and social aspect alongside the mere economic focus. This study covers all aspects of the ceramic production chain: it includes the design and manufacture of ceramic objects and paintings, table wares, ornamentation and decorations which are strongly linked to creativity, contributing to both their aesthetic and utility value. The popularity of crafts and tourism also coincides with the reconstruction of many rural economies in a post-productivist era with rising demand for consumption-based leisure and entertainment (Connell and Gibson 2004). In China today, more and more creative districts are being established, and people feel more comfortable staying and appreciating art works in diverse galleries as compared to a decade ago. Facilitated by government policies, creative tourism programmes in the countryside, such as ceramics classes in Jingdezhen and stitch-work seminars in Suzhou, are getting popular as part of the construction of new socialist countryside.

The Sanbao study

Pratt (2000) referred to networks as complicated interdependencies, which make a place convergent. Coe argues that 'networks of interpersonal relations' and 'the embeddedness and embodiment of economic processes' should be examined to study the agglomeration and regeneration of places (Coe 2000, p. 394). Current spatial theory has acknowledged that there is a relevance between place and both collective and individualized aesthetic creativity (Drake 2003; Harvey et al. 2012). The contention of this research is to further explore the role of locality and networks in prompting creativity in rural Sanbao. This study begins with the question of how the ceramic network was formed in Sanbao and to what extent the networked interactions and engagement foster creativity. It then examines the role of spatiality and to what extent locality creates and develops networks, relationships and community within and beyond this particular location. In seeking the answer to these questions, this empirical study conducted semi-structured interviews together with participatory observation from May 2014 to August 2015. A number of key people who setup, manage and maintain Sanbao were interviewed, including its founder, arts director and manager. Some artists-in-residence from China, Holland, South Korea and Italy were interviewed as well to investigate why Sanbao has an international reputation which differentiates itself from other creative clusters in Jingdezhen. Given the size of this art village, their significance is more evident than that of even key individuals in large metropolitan creative clusters. The qualitative data was then coded to create themes. I employ some key statements which best explain and illustrate the experience and thoughts of the respondents.

Brand and naming value: A millennium of ceramics history

In Jingdezhen, a series of polices initiated by the local government have sought to maximize the significance of the city's long history and traditions of porcelain and ceramics to maintain the position as one of the leading production centres and markets. Jingdezhen's myth is not only limited to China; the porcelain made there was called 'white gold' and became a luxury item in Europe dating back to Ming and Qing dynasties (Dillon 1992; Gerritsen 2011; Valenstein 1989). This 'china mania' was well documented in the historical fiction *The Arcanum* (Gleeson 1998). Therefore, it is not surprising for ceramic artists from around the world to exploit the reputational value of this long-established ceramic capital. In the ceramic community, Jingdezhen exemplifies quality in traditional fine Chinese porcelain and ceramics.

Most interviewees expressed the idea that Sanbao is a perfect place to do porcelain and ceramics, not only because it sits within Jingdezhen, but also because of the way it is built and managed by the founder Jianshen Li.[3] The atmosphere and environment, they all agree, provides a good reason for ceramicists from around the globe to come, exchange ideas and make ceramics. The living and working experience certainly is a crucial emotional and creative wellspring for them as both artists and human beings. For example, Lee YoungMi came to Sanbao for the first time when she was a PhD student at the China Central Academy of Fine Arts. She studied ceramic sculpture in South Korea, but chose to settle down in Sanbao because of its porcelain history and culture. She has lived in Sanbao for eight years while teaching at the Jingdezhen Ceramics Institute. She likes Sanbao because of its complete and well-developed ceramic industry supply chain, starting from raw materials and moving through to firing and transportation, as well as training and education. Sanbao is perfect to do 'real creative work', she feels, as it is so dynamic yet quiet enough to focus on crafts. Enzo D'Agostino, an Italian artist, talks about his own experience with Sanbao as one which enables him to do creative work from a fresh perspective. He came to Jingdezhen because of its porcelain history and tradition. He spoke about how a sense of history has merged with a sense of raw materiality here, giving him a feeling of authenticity. He treats the clay as a surface, a carrier and a medium for his conceptual art.

The interviews show evidence that some respondents find Sanbao's creative atmosphere stimulates their creativity. But it appears for others that locality is conceived of as not as important in terms of prompting creativity. In these cases, Sanbao is attractive because of its cheap and comfortable idyllic environment where their family and friends stay as revealed by Director of Sanbao Art Gallery, oil painter, Xileng Cao. However Wenying Li, Manager of Sanbao, even fears that this success might not be a good thing in the long run for Sanbao, as some so-called production-oriented artists will take advantage of the name of Jingdezhen without

FIGURE 14.2 Lee YoungMi's unfinished ceramic sculptures in her Studio at Sanbao. Photo by Author 2014.

contributing anything valuable to it. But it is important to note that, as Xileng Cao commented, the locality-based reputation and the tradition of ceramic making is not so significant for him in terms of enabling him to be more creative. The reason might be that he is not a ceramic artist, rather he did find creative stimulus in Sanbao's visual environment and nature as revealed below.

Spatiality as visual raw ingredients

Reference has been made in the literature review to the place of landscape as a visual influence potentially enabling creativity. In the context of this study, a number of respondents made clear that the local visual environment has functioned as the wellspring of their creative crafts-making. Xileng Cao explained he realizes Dao (truth or order) while living and working in Sanbao. His art project, Wander and Image, reflects the natural order of the endless four seasons in Sanbao. Tea, mountains and trees were featured in the series. Obviously, very specific visual symbols and signs are used by Xileng Cao, but Jianshen Li talks more about his excitement at being immersed in the rural surroundings in Sanbao. For him it is not the specific seasons or mountains which inspire; rather it is the architecture and rural lifestyle that stimulates and shapes his crafts-making. Overall, the interview data reveals that locality and spatiality can actually work as raw materials to prompt creativity. However, Xileng Cao

FIGURE 14.3 Sanbao Raku-firing Workshop. Photo by Author 2015.

suggested that any locality would do a similar thing. He pointed out that the inspiration of the natural order could have occurred anywhere, it just happened to be Sanbao in his case.

Intensive social and cultural networks

Respondents also gave credit to the intensive social and cultural activities in Sanbao which provoke creativity. Jianshen Li emphasized the role of various forums, seminars and exhibitions which foster a mutual learning and sharing community. As a world famous porcelain and ceramic city, Jingdezhen has become a meeting point where dynamic cultures and novel ideas converge, and where locality serves as the venue for this to happen among which Sanbao is one of the most striking cases. However, this does not mean that co-present locality is the only source for inspirational stimuli. What the respondents mean is not simply that it provides a collection of creative people; rather it is the engagement and meaning created between them that matters. This echoes the conceptualization of Scott (2001, p. 12) regarding 'the tendency of cities to engender multiplicity, flux, and unexpected event or experiences'. Sanbao proves that such synergies can also happen in a rural, internationally networked creative cluster. This evidently links back to the social and cultural networks and connections that have been built around Sanbao, sometimes in a very random and temporal fashion, such as during a visit, a seminar or an exhibition, which nonetheless can be of considerable value to the creative process.

Locality-specific creative community

Among interdisciplinary literature, there are a body of works theorizing the relationship between locality and creativity. One interesting direction to emerge from this is the collective creativity contributed by the local community of creative workers (Coe 2000; Drake 2003; Harvey, Hawkins and Thomas 2012; Pratt 2000), as creativity is also, as previous reinforced, a socially constructed process. The research respondents acknowledged the influence of networks and the community of creative craftspeople in Sanbao on their creativity, some of which has been reflected through their works. In some cases, this was channelled through a mutual learning community which fosters and promotes new ideas and novel perspectives. Enzo, for example, talks about how he got inspired by Chinese painting and calligraphy when learning and practicing it with local artists in his studio. His current ceramic art project is based on Chinese philosopher Mencius whom he draws a comparison with Socrates.

Wenying Li looked back at what they did over the years to help create a culturally rich community which fosters mutual leaning and stimulates artists from around the world create ceramics in new ways. She mentioned that in Sanbao a lot of traditions and cultures are preserved, including some ceramics making techniques and tools. They frequently invite senior ceramic masters (*shifu*) to come to Sanbao and showcase their works and techniques. The museum and gallery offers a marketing and display platform. It also functions as an educational place, facilitating both temporary and long-term networks within the community. Lectures and seminars take place on a regular basis and are a haven for the exchange of ideas and knowledge. As Wenying Li mentioned, there are no restrictions or particular obstacles for people from different backgrounds to form a new community or become part of the current community. But it is interesting to note that she also talked about some disconnections within this dynamic community, where some senior engraving artists were not willing to cooperate with ceramists and painters. While most of the participants advocate and agree that locality-based creative community prompts creativity, some artists hold slightly different ideas towards it. They prefer to stay and work in more isolated places where they can focus on their work. Even though most participants acknowledged the cooperation within the community, some also mentioned the competition and tensions within it. But overall they believe competition actually facilitates creativity.

Concluding remarks

This study employs semi-structured interviews followed by fieldwork to develop a qualitative case study of a small-scale, rural-based creative cluster, Sanbao. It illustrates Sanbao's complicated interdependencies and points out how networks, both connections and disconnections, power up this place. This empirical research complements the existing creative place literature's urban-based creative clusters and agglomerations by providing empirical nuance from beyond cities and the metropolis. Although Sanbao may be a small and individual case, especially when compared to international cities like London and New York, it is important in that it contributes to the diversity of the research on CCIs. Furthermore, in ceramics circles, Sanbao is now a globally significant player. While Sanbao is located in the hidden hills of Jingdezhen, the engagement and interactions with the outside world extend far beyond its studios and museums, influencing artists, creative workers, students and educators at home and abroad. One implication this chapter might contribute is that it illustrates the ambiguity and 'structured uncertainty' of policy in CCIs in China (Keane 2013, p. 22), which both helps and hinders the development of the creative industries. This comes from the fact that the ambiguity from the top actually leaves room for local governments to make policies that adapt to their own situations, while the unified and oversimplified policy lacks sufficient understanding of the politics embedded in disparate clusters and geographies.

The empirical data generated by this study extend our understanding of the way in which creative people respond to locality and spatiality. Using crafts as a sub-sector of CCIs in rural China, the themes provide evidence of how different places may offer different types of creativity stimuli, namely history and tradition, visual raw materials, social and cultural networks, brand and naming value, as well as place-based creative community. These all complement the lack of research into discovering and mapping the relationship between locality and creativity in rural clusters which challenges the traditional narrative of creative clusters, in terms of the forms, patterns and politics and thus possibilities (Harvey, Hawkins and Thomas 2012). Furthermore, the texture of creative work and life in Sanbao depicted a more recent and fresh picture of networks and community in a rural creative cluster, with both connections and disconnections. It allows researchers and policymakers to reflect on the oversimplified understanding of CCIs. This echoes the critique on neglecting the contradictions, problems and limitations different CCIs may have in their specific scenarios, which is more evident and severe in rural areas (Bell and Jayne 2010). Finally, it points to the danger of the unsophisticated development of CCIs which leads to the unquestioning transplantation of formulaic policy to disparate places and regions (Harvey, Hawkins and Thomas 2012). In order to notice and value the nuances of a particular cluster, further research is needed to explore the life and texture of creative clusters such as Sanbao. Before we go into detail mapping the cluster and policy initiatives, we need to abandon the presumption that certain policy blueprints will fit all places and clusters. It has been sixteen years since the inception of Sanbao village, but the insights here are drawn from legacies that date back thousands of years in terms of its culture, history and creativity.

Notes

1 The village used to have kilns and kaolin clay-making workshops. It is close to the mountain which provides both clay and wood for ceramics-making and firing. However, with the advancement of technology and industrialization in Jingdezhen city, craftspeople gradually moved out of the village to work for bigger companies and workshops, which left their houses into ruin. This is not uncommon for the other villages around Jingdezhen.

2 Sanbao Art Gallery together with other four private-owned museums was officially approved in 2012. Sanbao was first built in 1995, which focuses on ceramic art making and research, cultural exchange and tourism. It also serves as one of the most important exchange hubs in Jingdezhen with a global focus. It became a member of IAC (UNESCO International Academy of Ceramics) in 2002.

3 Jianshen Li bought several rundown farmer houses in Sanbao in 1998 which have been developed into a small cultural and creative village in Jingdezhen. He had this idea when he was

doing his Master of Fine Arts (MFA) degree at Jingdezhen Ceramic Institute, the only university specifically focusing on ceramics and porcelain design and production in China. He later obtained another MFA degree from Alfred University, New York. He was enlightened by the concept of modernity and postmodernism, which influenced his works from then on. Upon his graduation, he worked for Jingdezhen Ceramic Institute and founded Jingdezhen Sanbao Ceramic Institute. He made an award-winning documentary film named *Tao Yao* (Tao kiln or ceramic kiln, awarded by Heritage Foundation and UNESCO, France) telling stories about the handmade techniques and traditions of ceramic ware in the traditional dragon wood-firing kiln. The houses in Sanbao were rebuilt in a traditional way, which used only mud and wood. He started this art village with a 'utopia dream' to attract ceramic artists around the world to live and get inspired in this traditional and eco-friendly ceramic holy land. As an established ceramic artist, he started the neo-royal china ware (*xin guanyao*) and neo-pop (*xin minyao*) china ware movement. The works attracted the attention of the Forbidden City Palace in Beijing and went on exhibition there. From 2000 onwards, he combined both Eastern and Western cultures and aesthetic taste, stimulating audience to contemplate and re-evaluate the meaning of both classic and contemporary art. Instead of merely focusing on the perfection and refining of the shape and details, he featured a small portion of traditional china ware's characteristics and highlights the beauty of the ware itself through deconstructing and reconstructing strategies.

References

Bell, D. and Jayne, M. (2010), 'The creative countryside: policy and practice in the UK rural cultural economy', *Journal of Rural Studies*, 3: 209–18.

Coe, N. (2000), 'The view from out West: embeddedness, inter-personal relations and the development of an indigenous film industry in Vancouver', *Geoforum*, 31 (4): 391–407.

Connell, J. and Gibson, C. (2004), 'World music: Deterritorialising place and identity', *Progress in Human Geography*, 28 (3): 342–61.

DCMS. (1998), *Creative Industries Mapping Document*, London, London: DCMS.

Dillon, M. (1992), 'Transport and Marketing in the Development of the Jingdezhen Porcelain Industry during the Ming and Qing Dynasties', *Journal of the Economic and Social history of the Orient*, 35 (3): 278–90.

Drake, G. (2003), 'This place gives me space: place and creativity in the creative industries', *Geoforum*, 34 (4): 511–24.

Flew, T. (2012), *The Creative Industries: Culture and Policy*, London: Sage.

Gerritsen, A. (2011), 'Global Design in Jingdezhen: Local production and global connections', in G. R. Glenn Adamson, Sarah Teasley (ed.), *Global Design History* (1st ed.), 25–36, New York: Routledge.

Gleeson, J. (1998), '*The Arcanum: Extraordinary True Story of the Invention of European Porcelain*', New York: Warner Books, Inc.

Harvey, D., Hawkins, H. and Thomas, N. (2012), 'Thinking creative clusters beyond the city: People, places and networks', *Geoforum*, 43 (3): 529–39.

Hui, D. (2006), 'From cultural to creative industries: Strategies for Chaoyang District, Beijing', *International Journal of Cultural Policy*, 9 (3): 317–31.

JingdezhenDaily. (2011), 'An impact wave of culture and creativity – Jingdezhen vigorously develops its ceramic cultural and creative industry (wenhua dachao chuangyi yongdong – Jingdezhen dali tuijin taoci wenhua chuangyi chanye fazhan dianji)', *Jingdezhen Daily*. Retrieved from http://www.jdzol.com/2011/0726/17599.html

Keane, M. (2011), *China's New Creative Clusters: Governance, Human Capital and Investment*, London: Routledge.

Keane, M. (2013), *Creative Industries in China: Art, Design and Media*, Cambridge: Polity Press.

Kong, L. (2005), 'The sociality of cultural industries: Hong Kong's cultural policy and film industry', *International Journal of Cultural Policy*, 11 (10): 63-75.

Luckman, S. (2012), *Locating Cultural Work: The Politics and Poetics of Rural, Regional and Remote Creativity*, London: Palgrave Macmillan.

Montgomery, L. (2010), *China's Creative Industries: Copyright, Social Network markets and The Business of Culture in a Digital Age*, Northampton: Edward Elgar.

O'Connor, J. (2012), 'Creativity and Its Discontents: China's Creative Industries and Intellectual Property Rights Offences by Laikwan Pang (review)', *China Review International*, 19 (2): 319–28.

Pang, L. K. (2012), *Creativity and Its Discontents: China's Creative Industries and Intellectual Property Rights Offences*, Durham, NC: Duke University Press.

Pratt, A. (2000), 'New media, the new economy and new spaces', *Geoforum*, 31 (4): 425–36.

Scott, A. (2001), 'Capitalism, cities and the production of symbolic forms', *Transactions of the Institute of British Geographers*, 26 (1): 11–23.

Valenstein, S. G. (1989), *A Handbook of Chinese Ceramics*, New York: The Metropolitan Museum of Art, New York.

Waitt, G. and Gibson, C. (2009), 'Creative small cities: Rethinking the creative economy in place', *Urban Studies*, 46 (5–6): 1223–46.

15

Design Recycle meets the product introduction hall

Craft, locality and agency in northern Japan

Sarah Teasley

Introduction

In December 2012, a second-hand housewares shop appeared in Yamagata, a city in northern Japan. Items for sale included brightly coloured dishes, glasses and cookware from the 1960s and 1970s. Pots, pans and plates from Japanese, European and American manufacturers were displayed on sculptural wood furniture, itself also for sale. A sign explained the shop's concept:

> Amongst already created products are long-life products that possess a universally-recognisable design sense, and can continue to enjoy steady sales and use. [We have] gathered products like this from each area of Yamagata. There may be things here just like those you use in your own home. A perspective unfettered by the distinction between 'old' and 'new' brings new discoveries. (Design Recycle 2012)

Second-hand housewares shops are common in Japanese cities, and the shop's focus on postwar housewares and furnishings with a distinctively modernist aesthetic – clean lines, bright colours, abstract patterns and sculptural forms – corresponds to the revival and popularity of 'mid-century modern' style since 2000. Indeed, the second-hand furniture was entirely comprised of pieces by Tendo Mokko, a furniture manufacturer located in the same prefecture whose modernist pieces are prized by collectors and found in museum collections worldwide.

Unusually for a design shop, Design Recycle was located within a 'product introduction hall' (bussan shokai shitsu) for traditional local craft and food products (see Figure 15.1). Scandinavian-style juice glasses intermingled with iconic Yamagata crafts such as carved wooden roosters, papier mâché dolls and patterned towels, alongside tins of apple juice and other agricultural products, presented in cheerily bright packaging. This unusual combination formed part of the

FIGURE 15.1 The product introduction hall at the Manabikan Mono School, Yamagata Japan, December 2012. Local crafts and foodstuffs were displayed alongside postwar housewares on used tables and stools from legendary modernist furniture manufacturer and local firm Tendo Mokko, also for sale. Photograph: Sarah Teasley.

Manabikan Mono School, a public facility in central Yamagata. As operated by Colon Design, a local design agency under contract from the Yamagata city government, the Manabikan Mono School aimed to connect Yamagata's existing crafts industries with the city's new creative communities and with new markets, and to promote 'making' to local residents generally. Like the Design Recycle pop-up, which reframed ordinary household objects as valuable items of modernist heritage for casual visitors, the product introduction hall reframed traditional crafts and foodstuffs as contemporary craft for a new, younger audience of residents and tourists alike.

Yamagata city is a regional centre for craft production, known particularly for iron casting and lacquered wooden Buddhist altars. Since the 1990s, craft industries in the city and surrounding Yamagata Prefecture have weathered economic and demographic challenges. In response, industry organizations, local and national government and design activists have experimented with new support mechanisms. In some cases, as with the Manabikan Mono School, these actions have brought members of craft communities into collaboration with new industries, technologies and markets – both within Yamagata and further afield.

This chapter articulates how Colon Design and Chobundo, a Yamagata iron-casting firm, have engaged with new actors and technologies to reframe local crafts products as lifestyle goods for new markets, as a way to secure a future for Yamagata crafts. A key theme is 'the local' and how the various actors – at the national as well as local level – understand and employ the concept within crafts promotion activities in Yamagata. I suggest that 'the local' is subject to interpretive flexibility (Kline and Pinch 1996) and that actors have varying investments in Yamagata as a locale, but that these differing understandings and investments do not impede collaboration. Rather, the interactions discussed here are pragmatic collaborations to achieve differing aims through shared results. In a short chapter it is impossible to name all actors and interactions, let alone to assess their impact. However, a further hope is that presenting some actors and interactions might offer a model for carrying out similar initiatives elsewhere.

Anthropologists, geographers and historians have articulated how crafts industries and external actors adapt to changing conditions within globalizing economies, in Japan as elsewhere. A key strategy identified has been an emphasis on the local nature of craft production as a way to signify authenticity and value, particularly for consumers operating within globalized economies (Kirshenblatt-Gimblett 1998; Comaroff and Comaroff 2009; Cavanaugh and Shankar 2014; Boyd Gillette 2016; Wilkinson-Weber and DeNicola 2016). As Susan J. Terrio writes:

> Indeed it is the politics of cultural authenticity in global markets that enables genuine craft businesses and commodities produced over time in a specific place to be maintained, revived and/ or reinvented precisely because they can be commoditized and sold as such. Within the framework of international capitalism, a regional identity tied closely to a specific production mode, labor practices, associational forms, or indigenous goods becomes a valuable commodity which can be readily marketed to and purchased by tourists eager to consume tradition. (Terrio 1999, p. 129)

Since the early twentieth century, intellectuals, civil servants and entrepreneurs have regularly publicized 'the regions' (chiiki) as a more 'authentic' Japan, in hopes that doing so might support regional economies through tourism and the consumption of regional products (Moeran 1990; Ikuta, Yukawa and Hamasaki 2007; Ivy 1995; Creighton 1997; Wigen 1996; Kikuchi 2004; Brandt 2007; Love 2010). Most recently, in the late 2000s, influential Tokyo-based designers and curators previously associated with product design, graphic design and branding began to promote the consumption of regional tourist experiences and products – light industry and foodstuffs as well as craft – as a vehicle for accessing Japanese cultural heritage (Nagaoka 2015). At the same time, other design activists began promoting 'endogenous' (naihatsu-teki) development on a national scale (Dimmer 2017). This chapter contextualizes these actions within the longer history of centralized promotion of local culture and industry, but the main focus is to articulate how industry actors in Yamagata have interacted with these external actors and their concept of 'local craft' (Klien 2010). In doing so the object is also to displace the view to 'the regions' and to argue for an expanded understanding of new craft economies as formed of old and new actors alike (Edgerton 2006; Mohlman 1999; Pollard 2002; Matanle 2006; Teasley 2013).

Chobundo: A 'traditional crafts producer'

Iron casting is one of two Yamagata city products officially designated as a traditional craft product under the 1974 Law for the Protection of Traditional Craft Industries, but this designation belies iron casting's history as industrial production. Yamagata iron casting dates to the sixteenth century, when material availability, urbanization and population growth drew both iron and bronze casters to the area. Principal products included kettles, stoves and religious artefacts. Thanks partly to their popularity with pilgrims to a nearby shrine as souvenirs, Yamagata iron casting gained a national reputation in the eighteenth century.

Yamagata iron casting became 'craft' in the mid-twentieth century as a self-conscious, urgent response to a changing product landscape and daily life habits. The 1937 Yamagata City Commercial and Industrial Directory described iron casting as 'an important industry for this city' and listed 118 ironware firms located within city boundaries (Yamagata Shoko Kaigijo 1937: 20). After the Second World War, some firms diversified to agricultural, weaving and mining machinery and to car parts, becoming suppliers to larger local and regional industries (Yamagata Imono Kogyo Danchi Kyodo Kumiai n.d. a). Others began producing sewing machines, a popular product on domestic and export markets (Yamagata-ken Kikaku-bu Kikaku Kaihatsu-ka 1963). For the remaining iron-casting firms, domestic electrification and the arrival of affordable, mass-produced tin and aluminium kettles in the mid-1960s rendered cast iron kettles superfluous 'craft' items. Some producers rebranded their products for use in the tea ceremony, and others joined the world of 'artistic crafts' (bijutsu kogei), singular pieces sought after by collectors (Figure 15.2).

Support mechanisms played a role in making iron-casting craft. From the 1900s to the 1960s, prefectural and national industrial research institutes helped local industries adapt to change through design, technical and marketing support and training (Hayasaka and Atsumi 2013; Kogyo Gijutsuin Sangyo Kogei Shikenjo 1960). In the late 1960s, many institutes' focus shifted towards high-value technology and human factors, as mass-produced products replaced handmade light industries' products as everyday housewares (Kogyo Gijutsuin Seihin Kagaku Kenkyujo 1976). The 1974 Law for the Promotion of Traditional Craft Industries, backed by the Ministry of International Trade and Industry (MITI) and sponsored by the newly created Association for the Promotion of Traditional Crafts Industries, rebranded traditional industry as 'craft'. Promulgation allowed industries like Yamagata

FIGURE 15.2 'Yamagata ironwork': teapots for sale at Chobundo in Yamagata, Japan, December 2012. The ironwork kettles, teapots and vases for which Yamagata metalwork is best known are characterized by thin, lacquered skin, low-relief decoration and a tactile quality to the surface. Photograph: Sarah Teasley.

iron casting to apply for official designation (1975) as a recognized traditional craft, thus transitioning to luxury or lifestyle goods outside competition with novel, cheaper mass-produced goods (Tohoku Keizai Sangyo Kyoku n.d. a). Designation provides access to promotion mechanisms such as national and overseas exhibitions and branding, funding for new product and market development, the recording and preservation of skills and techniques, and materials and training schemes to secure successors and for new marketing (Hayasaka and Atsumi 2013; Japan Brand Ikusei shien jigyo' (n.d.), Keizai Sangyo Sho Daijin Kanbo Chosa Tokyo Guruppu (2014); Keizai Sangyo Sho 2015). In effect, the law offers similar support to that provided by the industrial research institutes, but differentiates products as craft – with the added urgency to retain technical knowledge and skills as makers die without successors (Tohoku Keizai Sangyo Kyoku n.d. c). Furthermore, marketing rhetoric and the well-publicized criteria for designation – local materials, techniques and tools, a minimum of 100 years' history, 'handcraft-ish' (shukyogyo-teki) processes and products predominantly used in everyday life use products – emphasize products' local and handmade identity, creating an aura of authenticity directed to market appeal (Sangyo Keizai Sho n.d.; Tohoku Keizai Sangyokyoku n.d.).

In the mid-2010s, the city of Yamagata was home to twenty-four traditional iron-casting firms (Tohoku Keizai Sangyo Kyoku n.d.). Small and micro-businesses predominate, and include workshops going back several generations as well as relocated designer-artisans. Firms operate a cooperative association to liaise with state support mechanisms and organize promotional activities; a small museum is currently closed for lack of funding. External economic challenges include two decades of recession and the loss of central government subsidies to regions (Keizai Sangyo Sho Daijin Kanbo Chosa Tokyo Guruppu (2014); Rausch 2010; 2014), as well as import competition from China and the 3.11 earthquake and tsunami disaster, which had little physical impact on Yamagata but disrupted infrastructure and caused emotional distress. Japan's ageing population and low birth rate have resulted in regional depopulation, including in Yamagata Prefecture (Yamagata-ken Kikaku Fukko-bu Tokei Kikaku-ka 2016), further destabilizing northeastern Japan's economic base and social fabric (Assmann 2016; Brown 2006; Matanle and Rausch 2011); demographic change presents crafts industries like iron casting with a dwindling market and challenges finding successors (Yubido n.d.).

The iron-casting industry demonstrates the clear impact of these changes. Chobundo is a family micro-business founded in 1952, currently run by father and son Hasegawa Fumio and Hasegawa Mitsuaki (Hasegawa 2012). Shrinking demand and production volumes have changed labour structure and skills: in the 1950s and 1960s, the firm employed specialists for specific processes such as lacquering the exterior. In 2012, the Hasegawas performed all processes themselves. They retain batch production and hand tools, but employ a new workflow allowing more efficient throughput. They have retained the founder's materials and aesthetic but innovate within them to create new products and designs (Hasegawa 2012). Product design combines components of the founder's designs in novel ways rather than to create new objects, for example, transforming the pattern from the wall of a pot into a handle on the lid. The Hasegawas also, however, develop new product types for changing uses and markets. A rare decision to modify the form of Chobundo kettles resulted from the decision to create a kettle for induction hobs – in this case, to broaden the base, to fit the diameter of induction hobs. And while Chobundo is known for formal kettles and teapots for use in tea ceremony, less-expensive teapots for everyday use invite more casual purchases. Products in the Mono School product introduction hall included whale-shaped chopstick rests, designed and priced to appeal to the Mono School's younger, design-savvy visitors, not conventionally a market for local products or traditional crafts (Hasegawa 2012).

As participation in the Mono School suggests, Chobundo have accessed new technologies and aesthetics for marketing their products to new audiences, including a Facebook page launched in 2013 (Chobundo 2016b). Chobundo has also tapped into d design travel (2009), a privately run mechanism for promoting Japanese regional products and tourism to new domestic markets. As created by designer Nagaoka Kenmei within the multidisciplinary practice D&DEPARTMENT, d design travel publicizes regional businesses, categorized by prefecture, through print, online and social media; physical and online shops; exhibitions and promotional events (D&DEPARTMENT n.d. a). Since 2014, Chobundo has sold products through d design travel shops and appeared in events and blog posts. The firm's image – on its own media as well as in D&DEPARTMENT's – emphasizes skill, the handmade and materiality (Kendall 2014), combining fashionable rhetoric around the authenticity of craft making with D&DEPARTMENT's contemporary visual aesthetic to promote Chobundo products to new markets while retaining its existing market of tea ceremony practitioners and traditional crafts aficionados (Shibuya Hikarie 8 2014, d47 design travel store Shindo 2015). In this framing, Chobundo's craft qualities are highlighted more prominently than its localness, indicating the shared presence of two rhetorics of authenticity – within d design travel as well.

Chobundo is also adept at framing its products through locale. By late 2012, Chobundo had refused several invitations to create a factory and showroom in China, Chinese market-specific designs and a diffusion line, after Chinese entrepreneurs recognized the appeal of Chobundo's products to a growing market of wealthy, aesthetics-conscious Chinese consumers interested in luxury tea wares. According to Hasegawa Mitsuaki, the firm preferred to retain a waiting list and current production volumes, to keep full control of the brand and quality and to not dilute their brand image and attention to managing existing production and sales (Hasegawa 2012). And yet the firm had also recombined classic design elements to create new products with the larger, more elaborate designs popular with its Chinese consumers and was clearly actively engaging with this new, unexpected market. In sum, affiliation with external actors and conditions and the ability to maintain multiple framing devices for a largely standard set of products, in part by setting clear parameters for adaptations, has allowed Chobundo to further its aims.

Design, making and activism at the Manabikan Mono School

Unlike Chobundo, Colon Design is a newcomer to Yamagata: a design firm launched in 2001 whose founder and chief designer, graduates of Yamagata's art and design university, remained after graduation to promote Yamagata's sense of local pride and community and visibility as a tourist destination through design (Takahashi 2013b). The motivation was not new. Since the 1990s, mass manufacturing itself encountered difficulties due to economic recession and rising competition from Chinese and South-East Asian imports. Municipal and prefectural branding, place-making (machizukuri) and regional vitalization (chiiki kasseika) initiatives followed, in Yamagata (Yamagata-ken 2010, Yamagata-shi Machizukuri Suishin-bu Toshi Seisaku-ka 2011) and across Japan (Yoshida 2007, Rausch 2008, Love 2010, Love 2013, Favell 2016; Okamoto 2013; Sorensen and Funck

2007). Design-specific responses aimed at manufacturing communities included the NPO Yamagata Design Network (1990), which provided promotional activities and design consulting, and Colon Design's alma mater, the Tohoku University of Art and Design (1992).

The Manabikan is located in a former elementary school in Yamagata's centre. From 2010 to 2013, Colon Design operated the facility as the 'Manabikan Mono School'. In its bid, the firm proposed that the facility serve three functions: town centre vitalization through attracting tourism, support for making and a place for learning (Takahashi 2013b). A product introduction hall, café, reading room, wood and metal workshops and events programming supported all three functions. In addition, Hagiwara desired to use the Mono School to connect Yamagata's crafts industries with members of the new artistic and craft community – for industrial revitalization and to help new arrivals ground themselves in the city. The two remits could be seen to sit uneasily alongside each other – the reading room offered tourist material alongside design periodicals – but aimed to support Yamagata's economic base and social cohesion by convening previously divergent communities through a shared investment in making and its products.

Here we should consider Colon Design's use of 'the local' in this schema. Hagiwara has ascribed his motivation for undertaking public facility management as derived from meeting D&DEPARTMENT's Nagaoka (Takahashi 2013a). Indeed, the desire to contribute to community and industrial revitalization mirrored Nagaoka directly, as did the combination of product information hall and Design Recycle: d design travel developed from Nagaoka's broader interest in 'long-life' design, which in the early 2000s consisted of reframing post war Japanese housewares and furnishings in a display environment to render them internationally legible modernist design (d design travel' n.d.; Ki ni naru kaisha intabyu 60 Bijon no mezasu mono' 2008; Nippon Vision Exhibition Tokyo' 2008; Rokumaru 60 Vision: Concept n.d.). Within this framing, the valuing of local well-being merged with a broader desire for authenticity. d design travel promotes regional tourism and 'good design' consumption as a socially responsible, aesthetically satisfying choice but offers authenticity as proof of value, with product selection criteria that include 'communicating that place's important message' and editorial guidelines that include 'not hiding behind special lenses in the photography. Photographing things as they are'. (D&DEPARTMENT n.d. a) In other words, D&DEPARTMENT projects locate the draw of local products and experiences in their ability to offer authenticity, and local origin – like heritage – is a mode for delivering it.

Like twentieth-century schemes to brand Japanese towns and regions through an appeal to nostalgia (Ivy 1995; Creighton 1997), D&Department positions both itself and its consumers outside (Tokyo shiten to chiiki no miryoku o kosa sasete iku: Nagaoka Kenmei D&DEPARTMENT (2012)). Hagiwara, by contrast, situates Colon Design's practice as a go-between:

> People like Yamazaki-san and Nagaoka Kenmei-san bring delicious seeds from the outside like birds or the wind. I'd like to take them, germinate them and plant them in this place called Yamagata. Vitalising the city's human potential is important, but stimulus from the outside and places for people from inside and outside the city – from inside and outside the prefecture – are also necessary. Now, I can't help but think that's our role.

We might see Colon Design, then, as an actor positioned at the interstices between inside and outside, mediating information – and capital – between the two through the act of reframing.

Conclusion

Chobundo, Colon Design and D&Department's actions and interactions indicate how one's situation in relation to 'the local' might shade the meanings one assigns it. Designers with a sense of social obligation transform everyday artefacts into fashionable commodities through the aesthetics and rhetoric of 'design'. They collaborate with city officials to create framing devices for local products, tapping into the now-historical rhetoric of 'the local' and of crafts products as an authentic, real alternative and pragmatic craftspeople join these frameworks for their own livelihood, in addition to a similar spirit of social contribution, but frame their products within the rhetoric of making, not locality. More poignantly given the predilection both within and outside Japan to speak of 'Japanese craft', the only actor of the three to refer regularly to Japaneseness is D&Department, the actor situated furthest from the local products categorized as such. Calls for consumers to take pride in their country – through its modernist design as much as its authentic local crafts – sit alongside products' promotion through appeals to the local and the handmade. For the actors, however, the rhetoric may not matter as long as the objectives are accomplished.

Acknowledgements

I would like to express my profound thanks to Sugasawa Mitsuhiro, Hasegawa Mitsuaki and Sekine Yasumasa for their generosity in introducing me to Chobundo and the Manabikan Mono School and encouraging this research, and to Susan Luckman and Nicola Thomas for their patience. This research was supported by funding from the Arts and Humanities Research Council (AHRC) and the Japan Society for the Promotion of Science (JSPS).

References

Assmann, S., ed. (2016), *Sustainability in Contemporary Rural Japan: Challenges and Opportunities*, London: Routledge.

Boyd Gillette, M. (2016), *China's Porcelain Capital: The Rise, Fall and Reinvention of Ceramics in Jingdezhen* London: Bloomsbury Academic.

Brandt, K. (2007), *Kingdom of Beauty: Mingei and the Politics of Folk Art in Imperial Japan*, Durham, NC: Duke University Press.

Brown, L. K. (2006), 'Epilogue: Tohoku: A Place', in C. Thompson and J. Traphagan (eds.), *Wearing Cultural Styles in Japan: Concepts of Tradition and Modernity in Practice*, 196–206, Albany NY: SUNY Press.

Cavanaugh, J. R., and S. Shankar (2014), 'Producing authenticity in global capitalism: Language, materiality, and value', *American Anthropologist*, 116: 51–64.

Chobundo (2016), 'Chobundo', Facebook. Available online: https://www.facebook.com/chobundo (accessed 18 August 2016).

Colon Design (2012), Introductory caption for the Manabikan Mono School 'Design Recycle' pop-up shop, Yamagata Manabikan Mono School.

Comaroff, J. L., and J. Comaroff (2009), *Ethnicity, Inc.*, Chicago: University of Chicago Press.

Creighton, M. (1997), 'Consuming rural Japan: The marketing of tradition and Nostalgia in the Japanese travel industry', *Ethnology*, 36 (3): 239–54.

d design travel' (n.d.), D&Department. Available online: http://www.d-department.com/jp/d-design-travel (accessed 27 September 2016).

d47 design travel store Shindo (2015), 'Chobundo no dezain' (The design of Chobundo), D&Department. Available online: http://www.d-department.com/jp/archives/shops/25755 (accessed 18 August 2016).

d school Wakariyasui sanchi: Yamagata mono Chobundo no tetsubin' (2014), (d school easily understandable production region: products from Yamagata, Chobundo's iron kettles), Shibuya Hikarie 8. Available online: http://www.hikarie8.com/d47designtravelstore/event/2014/11/d-school—. shtml (accessed 18 August 2016).

Dimmer, C. (2017), 'Place-making before and after 3.11: The emergence of social design in Post-Disaster, Post-Growth Japan', *Josai Review of Japanese Culture and Society*, XXVIII.

Edgerton, D. (2006), *The Shock of the Old: Technology and Global History since 1900*, London: Profile Books.

Favell, A. (2016), 'Islands for life: artistic responses to remote social polarisation and population decline in Japan', in S. Assmann (ed.), *Sustainability in Contemporary Rural Japan: Challenges and Opportunities*, 109–24, London: Routledge.

Hasegawa, M. (2012), Interviewed by Sarah Teasley, Yamagata, Japan, 18 December.

Hayasaka, T., and H. Atsumi (2013), 'Yamagata', in Geijutsu Kogakukai Chiiki Dezain-shi Tokusetsu Iinkai. (ed.), *Nihon Chiiki Dezain-shi I* (The Design History of Japan's Regions I), 57–82, Tokyo: Bigaku Shuppan.

Ikuta, T., K. Yukawa, and H. Hamasaki (2007), 'Regional branding measures in Japan: Efforts in 12 major prefectural and city governments', *Place Branding and Public Diplomacy*, 3 (2): 131–43.

Ivy, M. (1995), *Discourses of the Vanishing: Modernity, Phantasm, Japan*, Chicago: University of Chicago Press.

Keizai Sangyo Sho (2015), 'Dento kogei-hin sangyo shien hojokin kofu yoko (Guidance for the delivery of support funding schemes for traditional craft product industries), Keizai Sangyo Sho. Available online: http://www.meti.go.jp/policy/mono_info_service/mono/nichiyo-densan/koufuyoukou/H27FYshien_koufuyoukou.pdf (accessed 29 September 2016).

Keizai Sangyo Sho Daijin Kanbo Chosa Tokyo Guruppu (2014), 'Kogyo tokei chosa Heisei 24-nen kakuho shikuchoson-hen' (Heisei 24 Industrial Statistics Survey: City, Town and Village Edition), Keizai Sangyo Sho. Available online: http://www.meti.go.jp/statistics/tyo/kougyo/result-2/h24/kakuho/sichoson/index.html (accessed 29 September 2016).

Kendall, L. (2014), 'Intangible traces and material things: The performance of heritage handicraft', *Acta Koreana*, 17 (2): 537–55.

Ki ni naru kaisha intabyu 60 Bijon no mezasu mono' (Interviews with Companies That Catch Our Attention: What 60 Vision Is Aiming At) (2008), *Pakkeiji Dezain* (Package design), 8: 10–16.

Kikuchi, Y. (2004), *Japanese Modernisation and Mingei Theory: Cultural Nationalism and Oriental Orientalism*, London: RoutledgeCurzon.

Kirshenblatt-Gimblett, B. (1998), *Destination Culture*, Berkeley and London: University of California Press.

Klien S. (2010), 'Collaboration or confrontation? Local and non-local actors in the Echigo-Tsumari Art Triennial 2000-6', *Contemporary Japan*, 22 (1–2): 1–25.

Kline, R., and T. Pinch (1996), 'Users as agents of technological change: The social construction of the automobile in the Rural United States', *Technology and* Culture, 37: 763–95.

Kogyo Gijutsuin Kogei Sangyo Shikenjo (1960), *Kogei Shikenjo 30-nen shi* (The 30-year history of the Industrial Art Research Institute), Tokyo: Kogyo Gijutsuin Sangyo Kogei Shikenjo.

Kogyo Gijutsuin Seihin Kagaku Kenkyujo (1976), *Sangyo Kogei Shikenjo 40-nen shi* (The 40-year history of the Industrial Art Research Institute), Tokyo: Kogyo Gijutsuin Seihin Kagaku Kenkyujo.

Love, B. (2010), 'Mountain vegetables and the politics of local flavor' in Assmann., ed. *Japanese Foodways, Past and Present*, 221–38. Urbana, University of Illinois Press.

Love, B. (2013), 'Treasure hunts in Rural Japan: Place making at the limits of sustainability'. *American Anthropologist* 115:1, 112–24.

Matanle, P. (2006), 'Organic sources for the revitalisation of Rural Japan: The craft potters of Sado', *Japanstudien*, 18: 149–80.

Matanle, P., and A. Rausch with the Shrinking Regions Research Group (2011), *Japan's Shrinking Regions in the 21st Century*, Amherst, NY: Cambria Press.

Moeran, B. (1990), 'Japanese Ceramics and the Discourse of 'Tradition'', *Journal of Design History*, 3 (4): 213–25.

Mohlman, K. (1999), 'Craft-as-industry and craft-as-culture: Analysing handicraft production in commercialized Asia and beyond', *Southeast Asian Journal Of Social Science*, 27 (1): 113.

'Nagaoka Kenmei-shi koenkai: Rongu raifu dezain ga umareru riyu: 'rashisa' ni tsuite' (A lecture by Mr. Nagaoke Kenmei: The reasons why long-life design is born) (2016), Yamagata Manabikan Mono School. Available online: http://www.y-manabikan.com/archive/nagaoka.html (accessed 11 August 2016).

Nippon Vision Exhibition Tokyo' (2008), D&Department. Available online: http://www.d-department.com/event/event.shtml?id=6492574060335756 (accessed 5 May 2014).

Okamoto S. (2013), 'Dento kogei sangyo kara no sangaku renkei ni yoru chiiki inobeshon soshutsu ni kansuru kadai to teigen: Kyoto chiiki oyobi Ishikawa chiiki ni okeru jirei kenkyu' (Issues and Proposals for Generating Regional Innovation through Industry-Academic Collaborations Deriving from Traditional Crafts Industries), *Kenkyu Gijutsu Keikaku* (The Journal of Science Policy and Research Management) 23 (4), 367–82.

Pollard, C. (2002), *Master potter of Meiji Japan: Makuzu K zan (1842-1916) and his workshop*, Oxford: Oxford University Press.

Rausch, A. (2010), *Cultural commodities in Japanese rural revitalization: Tsugaru Nuri Lacquerware and Tsugaru Shamisen*, Leiden: Brill.

Rausch, A. S. (2008), 'Place branding in rural Japan: Cultural commodities as local brands', *Place Branding and Public Diplomacy*, 4: 136–46.

Rausch, A. S. (2014), 'Japan's Heisei municipal mergers and the contradictions of neo-liberal administrative planning' *Asia Pacific Journal of Public Administration*, 36: 135–49.

Rokumaru (60) Vision: Concept (n.d.), 60Vision. Available online: http://www.60vision.com/concept/index.html (accessed 27 September 2016).

Sangyo Keizai Sho (n.d.) 'Dentoteki Kogeihin no Shitei no Yoken' (Requirements for Designation as a Traditional Craft Product), Tohoku Keizai Sangyo Kyoku. Available online: http://www.tohoku.meti.go.jp/s_cyusyo/densan-ver3/html/pdf/1_1.pdf (accessed 6 January 2015).

Sorensen, A., and C. Funck, eds. (2007), *Living Cities in Japan: Citizens' Movements, Machizukuri and Local Environments*, London: Nissan Institute/Routledge.

Takahashi M. (2013a), 'Yamagata Part 1: Dakara koso 'atsui hito' ga hitsuyo nan da' (Yamagata Part I: That's Why 'Heated-Up People' Are So Important), Colocal. Available online: http://colocal.jp/topics/think-japan/local-design/20130311_16211.html (accessed 11 August 2016).

Takahashi M. (2013b), 'Yamagata Part 2: Yamagata Manabikan no naritachi ni tsuite' (Yamagata Part 2: On the Origins of the Yamagata Manabikan), Colocal. Available online: http://colocal.jp/topics/think-japan/local-design/20130315_16309.html (accessed 9 August 2016).

Teasley, S. (2013), 'Why furniture is a global concern: Local industry and global networks, through the lens of Shizuoka furniture-making', in J. Kaner and F. Ionas (eds.), *Current Issues in Global Furniture: Proceedings of the 8th Biennial Furniture Research Group Conference*, Bucks New University, 41–64.

Terrio, S. J. (1999), 'Performing craft for heritage tourists in Southwest France', *City & Society*, 11 (1/2): 124–44.

Tickell, A. and Peck, J. (2002), 'Neoliberalizing Space', *Antipode*, 34 (3): 380–404. http://doi.org/DOI: 10.1111/1467-8330.00247

Tohoku Keizai Sangyo Kyoku (n.d. a), 'Yamagata-ken: Yamagata imono' (Yamagata Prefecture: Yamagata Cast Iron), Tohoku Keizai Sangyo Kyoku. Available online: http://www.tohoku.meti.go.jp/s_cyusyo/densan-ver3/html/item/yamagata_01.htm (accessed 18 August 2016).

Tohoku Keizai Sangyo Kyoku (n.d. b), 'Yamagata-ken: Yamagata imono no seiho ya kotei ni tsuite' (Yamagata Prefecture: On the production techniques and process of Yamagata cast iron), Tohoku

Keizai Sangyo Kyoku. Available online: http://www.tohoku.meti.go.jp/s_cyusyo/densan-ver3/html/item/yamagata_01b.htm (accessed18 August 2016).

Tohoku Keizai Sangyo-kyoku (n.d. c) 'Dento Kogei Shi ni tsuite' (Regarding the Traditional Crafts Master [designation]), Tohoku Keizai Sangyo Kyoku. Available online: http://www.tohoku.meti.go.jp/s_cyusyo/densan-ver3/html/top_2.html (accessed 29 September 2016).

Tohoku Keizai Sangyo Kyoku (n.d. d), 'Dentoteki kogeihin no shitei no yoken' (Requirements for designation as a traditional craft product), Tohoku Keizai Sangyo Kyoku. Available online: http://www.tohoku.meti.go.jp/s_cyusyo/densan-ver3/html/pdf/1_1.pdf (accessed 6 January 2015).

Tokubetsu intabyu: Ima, wakamono ga tabi ni motomeru no ha sono tochi 'rashisa' yonda hitotachi ga tabi ni detakunaru 'kikkake' wo teian shite iku' (Special Interview: Now, What Young People Seek from Travel Is the 'Likeness' of That Place: Proposing 'Reasons' Why People Who Have Read This Article Will Want to Go Traveling) (2012), *Reja sangyo shiryo* (Resources for Leisure Industries), 45 (11): 22–5.

'Tokyo shiten to chiiki no miryoku o kosa sasete iku: Nagaoka Kenmei D&DEPARTMENT' (Crossing a Tokyo Perspective with the Appeal of the Regions: Nagaoka Kenmei D&DEPARTMENT) (2012), *Burein* (Brain), 55(11): 55–7.

Wigen, K. (1996), 'Politics and Piety in Japanese Native-Place Studies: The Rhetoric of Solidarity in Shinano', *Positions*, 4 (3): 491–517.

Wilkinson-Weber, C. M., and A. O. DeNicola, eds. (2016), *Critical Craft: Technology, Globalization, and Capitalism*, London: Bloomsbury Academic.

Yamagata Imono Kogyo Danchi Kyodo Kumiai (n.d. a), 'Yamagata imono to ha' (What is Yamagata cast iron?), Yamagata Imono Kogyo Danchi Kyodo Kumiai. Available online: http://www.chuokai-yamagata.or.jp/imono/ (accessed 10 January 2016).

Yamagata Imono Kogyo Danchi Kyodo Kumiai (n.d. b), 'Yamagata Imono Kogyo Danchi Kyodo Kumiai' (The Yamagata Cast Iron Industrial District Cooperative Association), Yamagata Imono Kogyo Danchi Kyodo Kumiai. Available online: http://www.chuokai-yamagata.or.jp/imono/kumiai.html (accessed 10 January 2016).

Yamagata Shoko Kaigijo., ed. (1937), *Showa juni-nen hen Yamagata-shi shokojin kakuroku* (Directory of Commercial and Industrial Workers in Yamagata City, Showa 12 Edition), Yamagata: Yamagata Shoko Kaigijo.

Yamagata-ken Kikaku Fukko-bu Tokei Kikaku-ka (2016), 'Yamagata-ken no jinko to setai-su (suikei)' (Population and household figures for Yamagata Prefecture (Estimated), Yamagata-ken. Available online: http://www.pref.yamagata.jp/ou/kikakushinko/020052/tokei/copy_of_jinkm.html

Yamagata-ken Kikaku-bu Kikaku Kaihatsu-ka (1963), *Susunda fudo no kaihatsu: Sengo no sogo kaihatsu hakusho* (The Development of a Culture and Climate That Has Progressed: White Paper on Postwar Comprehensive Development), Yamagata: Yamagata-ken.

Yamagata-ken (2010), 'Yamagata-ken Sogo Burando Senryaku' (The strategy for a comprehensive brand for Yamagata Prefecture), Yamagata-ken. Available online: http://www.pref.yamagata.jp/ou/shokokanko/110010/brandsenryakufolder/burandosenryaku-zenbunn.pdf (accessed 29 September 2016).

Yamagata-shi Machizukuri Suishin-bu Toshi Seisaku-ka (2011), (2011)-ka chushin shigaichi runesansu koso (Gaiyohan)a (Plan for the renaissance of central Yamagata's urban fabric (Summary)), Yamagata-shi. Available online: http://www.city.yamagata-yamagata.lg.jp/kakuka/machizukuri/toshiseisaku/sogo/gazoufile/shigaichi/renaissance.pdf (accessed 29 September 2016).

Yoshida H. (2007), 'Chiiki burando to chiiki kasseika: Morioka Burando no tenkai' (Revitalisation of local economy building in Local Brand), *Niigata Hokusai Joho Daigaku Joho Bunka Gakubu Kiyo* (Bulletin of Niigata University of International and Information Studies Department of Information Culture), 10: 135–42.

Yubido. (2016), 'Yamagata mirai no shokai: Dento no gi, hokori to shinka' (Introduction to the future of Yamagata: The pride and progression of traditional skills), Yubido. Available online: http://h-yubido.com/index.php?山形みらいの匠会, (accessed 29 September 2016).

16

Crafted places/places for craft

Pop-up and the politics of the 'crafted' city

Ella Harris

In recent years cities across the Global North have experienced the rapid rise of 'pop-up' culture, a trend for creating temporary places in disused sites and buildings. Pop-up has been widely promoted within the creative industries as providing cheap and flexible access to space and is now a popular format for craft makers and sellers. In this chapter I propose that examining pop-up's intersections with the craft economy offers important insights into craft's impact in contemporary cities. I explore pop-up as a geography through which craft's logics of one-off, handmade production and flexible labour are transforming the urban fabric. I consider how craft's emphasis on the unique and the handmade is, through pop-up, infused into the materiality of the city and how its labour logics of flexibility also find spatiotemporal form in pop-up's own versatile urban landscape. The growing intersection of craft and pop-up cultures begs a pertinent question: if craft's sensibilities are being advanced and extended in the city through pop-up, then what does the politics of this 'crafted' city look like? More specifically, in a contemporary condition characterized by widespread precarity (Gill and Pratt 2008), how does this extension of craft's logics reflect and shape assumptions about how cities should be lived, governed and reproduced?

Pop-up culture's shared sensibility with craft is clearly discernible. Pop-up sites are customarily handmade by their organizers; reused materials are employed to craft personalized temporary spaces that, like craft products, are celebrated as one-off, DIY creations. Pop-up is also tied up with the same economic shifts towards post-Fordist economies within which craft is implicated. It is, like craft, an arena where 'flexible' work patterns are normalized and glamorized (Deslandes 2013; Ferreri 2015; Graziano and Ferreri 2014). It is also rooted in the 'hipster' economy within which craft has been situated, a scene whose sensibilities include a return to domestic practices of 'making, cooking and growing' (Luckman 2015, p. 44) which can be partially understood in relation to the austerity aesthetics ensuing from the global financial crash (Jakob 2013; Luckman 2015; McRobbie 2013; Luckman 2013).

Pop-up has, so far, been mainly considered in relation to creative cities (Mould 2014), artistic and cultural practice (Graziano and Ferreri 2014; Harvie 2013), gentrification, (Harvie 2013;

Mould 2014; Colomb 2012) and austerity urbanisms (Tonkiss 2013; Ferreri 2015). There has been little discussion of pop-up in relation to the craft economy, although the connections between the two are evidents. In this chapter I approach pop-up and craft together through an empirical focus on Netil Market, a temporary place for craft production and consumption in Hackney, East London. In doing so, I consider craft as an urban imaginary and pop-up as a geography in which that imaginary is being embedded and reproduced. I argue that tracing the ways that craft's logics of production and consumption are engaged in pop-up culture will illuminate how those logics are shaping contemporary cities. Analysts of the craft economy have considered craft's role in creating communities (Gauntlett 2011) and shaping the identity of local areas and regions (Schenll and Reese 2009; Thomas, Harvey and Hawkins 2012). Within this, craft's capacity to aestheticize postindustrial landscapes and intensify gentrification has been noted (Mathews and Picton 2014; Dawkins 2011). This approach implicitly considers craft as an urban imaginary, in that its sensibilities are understood to transform how cities are imagined and produced. I bring this to the foreground, drawing pop-up culture into conversation with craft to consider how contemporary cities are themselves 'crafted' through the logics of the craft economy.

Building on discussion of Netil Market, I make two arguments about how craft and pop-up can be considered together to illuminate craft's urban imaginary and its politics. First, I address pop-ups as *crafted places*, exploring them as handmade, customized sites and examining how they craft a particular kind of community. The aim of this section is to explore how craft's logics are mobilized by pop-up to 'craft' the urban environment in particular ways. Secondly, I explore pop-ups as *places for craft*. Having identified pop-up as a geography within which craft takes place, I argue that pop-up is an infrastructure for craft production which intensifies certain elements of craft's imaginary, in particular reinforcing the precarity of the craft economy.

Crafted places

Netil Market is located in Hackney, East London. Hackney is the epicentre of London's 'hipster' scene and, increasingly, a renowned area for craft production and retail (Schreiber and Treggiden 2015). However, as rental prices in the area continue to rise, there is growing financial pressure on Hackney's creative community, and Netil Market is one of several sites that has sprung up to provide affordable, albeit temporary and makeshift, space for craft makers and sellers. As Sarah, the market manager, describes it, Netil Market is 'a space for creative professionals to conduct their work in a flexible environment'[1]. Occupying what was once a derelict carpark, the market now contains several temporary units, mostly made from shipping containers, within which these professionals work and trade throughout the week. The container units line the perimeter of the market, leaving space in the middle for other traders to join the market at the weekends, setting up on traditional counter market stalls. The market is affiliated with Netil House, one of three indoor spaces run by the company 'Eat Work Art' who 'transform empty buildings into studio spaces that become home to exceptional communities' (Eatworkart 2015). The traders in Netil Market explicitly position themselves as craft makers and sellers. Their websites promote their products as unique, emphasize the careful attention to their crafting and celebrate craft's shift away from globalized production and retail towards the handmade (Luckman 2015; Sennett 2008;

Dawkins 2011). Natalie from 'The Worshipful Little Shop of Spectacles' describes how she designs and crafts 'one off handmade spectacle frames … a rare art in a world of mass, factory-line production' (Theworshipfullittleshopofspectacles 2015), while Tatiana from the jewellery shop 'WeAreArrow' stresses that her jewellery is all handmade 'in her small workshop she and her husband built inside a shipping container' (WeAreArrow 2015).

Indeed, the use of customized shipping containers is crucial to the craft sensibilities of Netil Market. In this section I make two arguments about what it means to understand these pop-up sites as 'crafted', paying particular attention to the importance of shipping containers (a popular building material within pop-up culture) for the 'crafting' of place. First, I argue that the use of container architectures extends the characteristics of craft products to the crafting of place, creating unique and personal units, which reinforce the creative identities of the traders. It is increasingly commonplace to characterize temporary and mobile architectures as 'crafted' (the 'office for crafted architecture' in Southwark, South London, is an interesting example of this[2]), and I consider how the units in Netil Market could be considered as crafted places. Secondly, I argue that the symbolic value of containers is also crucial to the 'crafting' of place, which takes place in Netil Market and specifically relates to the crafting of community.

To address my first point, that container architectures extend the logics of craft into the production of place, it is easy to see how the container units in Netil Market embody craft's sense of the unique and the personal. Most of the containers were bought from the company 'Bell',[3] who specialize in container conversions, and each trader has customized their container to express the style and ethos of their business, making architectural as well as decorative adjustments. For instance, Tatiana's container is fitted with an internal wall of white-painted wooden boards and shelves made of reclaimed wood. She uses a log for a stool. Bare light bulbs hang on exposed wires, and the inside is decorated with leaves, reiterating the aesthetics of her jewellery which, at the moment, is inspired by 'found plant parts' including 'seeds, pods and petals' (WeAreArrow 2015).

FIGURE 16.1 Tatiana in her studio. Photograph by Jan Vrhovnik, 2015.

In contrast, another container used by The General's Barber Shop's, a hairdresser, is decorated to feel more like an old-fashioned North American ranch workshop. Brooms, metal dust pans and hair brushes hang from chains, and products are stored in chests. The barber chairs and bottles for shampoo and lotion are all vintage or, at least, made to look old fashioned. On top of the container a typical red, blue and white stripy barber shop pole has been fitted. Customers can also buy beers, which the barbers brew themselves. The pseudo-workshop environment that 'The General's Barber Shop' has created affiliates their hairdressing practice with craft production. The effort put into the unit's design, as well as the brewing of their own (craft) beer, is aesthetic labour (Hracs and Leslie 2014; Warhurst and Dennis 2009), which assists in the crafting of identity for the barber shop.

The upkeep of a particular 'look' is crucial within the creative industries, where crafting an identity is equally as important as creating a product or service (Hracs and Leslie 2014; Luckman 2013). In Netil Market this is clearly achieved through the customization of containers. The personalized design and decoration of the units extends the sense of intimacy with the makers that customers find in their handmade products, creating places that are also 'imbued with touch' (Luckman 2015, p. 2). The units perform a version of what Thrift has described as 'worlding', the construction of a '*digestible* environment' (Thrift 2008, p. 13) that captures the imagination of the consumer. Inside each container a stylized world is created of which the traders are the epicentre. Going to 'The General's Barber Shop' or browsing Tatiana's products is to enter into a world infused with their creative identities, and the allure of the products and services stems from the potential to consume a small part of this world.

FIGURE 16.2 The General's Barber Shop. Photograph by Lee Wells.

As well as decorative adjustments to the containers, the symbolic value of their transformation from industrial, mass-produced objects to handmade, personalized units is also important to the crafting of place and 'worlding' of the products. Shipping containers are routinely positioned as emblematic of commercial standardization and related imaginaries of 'smooth space' (Martin 2013). It is argued that the intermodality of containers enables goods to travel seamlessly across space-time and thereby smooths over the heterogeneous characteristics of the environments they traverse (Martin 2013). Moreover, the standardized design of the boxes means that 'one is never privy to the contents. ... Everything is hidden from view to the extent that all that is given to the eye is the spectacle of efficiency' (Martin 2012, p. 154). In stark contrast, the containers in Netil Market aim to evoke individuality (although there is an irony to this given the increasing ubiquity of container spaces in London). Where the exteriors of industrial containers hide the contents of the box, those in Netil Market signpost their contents even when locked up as, for example, achieved by the barber sign on top of 'The General's Barber Shop . The customizing of the containers thereby creates 'crafted places' which mirror the movement of craft products away from the logics of mass production towards the unique and reinforce the uniqueness of those products by creating a distinctive world around them. Similarly, while cargo containers in global circulation smooth over the heterogeneous characteristics of environments in Netil Market, the containers are used to craft an environment that stands out from routine city spaces.

The reason that containers are so widely available for repurposing as architectures is that 'it is often cheaper for exporting countries to make new containers than it is to ship the empty ones back again' (Parker 2012, p. 9). Overproduction is *required* for economic efficiency, so surplus containers pile up and are repurposed for 'housing, office space, pop-up events and so on' (Parker 2012, p. 9). During recession in particular 'there is an oversupply of containers' (Parker 2012, p. 13), which explains why temporary container architectures have become so popular since 2008. That the containers are a waste product of globalized commercial production is important to the second kind of crafting of place which Netil Market is implicated in: the crafting of community.

It has been argued that the ruins of capitalist infrastructures provide fissures within which craft has the power to experiment with alternative forms of community and economy (Bratich and Brush 2011), and this is certainly the imaginary engaged by the repurposing of containers in Netil Market. Gregson and Crewe have suggested that the former meanings of a second-hand object can be reimagined, taking on new significance in the reused or repurposed product (Gregson and Crewe 2003). Here, the meanings of containers are reimagined through their customization. Once emblematic of wasteful hyperproduction, in pop-up spaces the containers can come to connote practices of mindful reuse and slow, small-scale production. As has been argued, craft production reacts to anxieties around waste with a focus on recycling (Harrod 2013). This has particular purchase at a time of recession and austerity during which a 'culture of thrift' has emerged (Potter and Claire 2013, p. 155) and been taken up, in particular within the hipster scene. Despite the way that trends for waste reduction and DIY have been highly commercialized, not just within the urban hipster scene but also in popular culture and television (Luckman 2015; Potter and Claire 2013), they evoke a 'vague anti-capitalist positioning' (Potter and Claire 2013, p. 162). This is attractive to the many young creative people disenfranchised and disillusioned by recession. The repurposed containers, in evoking this imaginary of reuse, thereby draw together a community of craft traders seeking to share in that ethos. Indeed, there is a pervasive emphasis on environmental sustainability in the food and drink produced and sold in Netil Market, as well as from the cycle shack who promote biking as an alternative form of transport in the city. Suwun, who also operate out of a container, run a 'Gender-neutral ethical lifestyle shop' which mainly sells clothing, extending the 'utopian' promises of craft (Banks 2010, p. 311) to tackle contemporary gender norms embedded in consumption.

Of course, while Netil Market crafts a community which, typical of hipster economies, has 'an aesthetics informed by environmental and labour concerns' (Luckman 2015, p. 41), the same aesthetics are implicated in the crafting of geographies of exclusion. These days Hackney is almost synonymous with gentrification. As the epicentre of London's hipster economy, and an increasingly popular residential location for upper-middle-class professionals and families, it has undergone significant changes over recent decades (Butler, Hamnett and Ramsden 2013; Duman 2012). Sarah explains how Netil House occupies what was a community college before it became derelict and was squatted. She says that in the early days after Eat Work Art took the property over, her boss would show people around 'with the light from his Nokia phone, promising they'd be a studio there if they put a deposit down'. The carpark that is now the market was also 'awful, completely overgrown', strewn with 'mattresses, syringes, the kind of things you'd expect in East London', but Sarah's predecessor cleaned it up and started to find traders to fill it.

This description of Netil House's takeover of a dilapidated site resonates with arguments that temporary, creative businesses act as urban pioneers which colonize formerly working-class areas of the city (Colomb 2012; Harris 2015; Harvie 2013; Mould 2014). In London, pop-up culture, and the 'meanwhile use lease' template (Gov.uk 2013) developed to facilitate it, has codified in policy and redevelopment discourse the repurposing of derelict spaces that has long taken place in the city. Temporary creative spaces like Netil Market now abound in East London and, while many are organized by small creative businesses, social enterprises or community groups, the format 'now come[s] as readily to property developers, alert to the speculative possibilities' (Tonkiss 2013, p. 318) of temporary creative places. As such, pop-up has exacerbated the trajectories of gentrification which craft has long been implicated in (Mathews and Picton 2014; Smith 1996) by helping to popularize the repurposing of derelict spaces for creative use. Indeed, Sarah recognizes that the success of the market has contributed to rapidly rising house prices in the immediate area. Approaching Netil Market as a crafted place therefore reveals the political contradictions embedded in craft's urban imaginary. The 'crafted' units in Netil Market are implicated in two conflicted forms of urban 'crafting': first, the crafting of creative communities organized around craft's ethos of production and, secondly, the crafting of the exclusionary geographies of gentrification.

Places for craft

Having considered the pop-ups in Netil Market as 'crafted places', this section explores pop-up as a geography *for* craft. I address how pop-up, as a temporary and mobile infrastructure for craft production and consumption, helps craft businesses to mitigate some of the impacts of precarity while also cementing that precarity. It has been argued that craft 'creates slow space ... at odds with the imperative towards hyperproduction' (Bratich and Brush 2011, p. 236). At first glance this would seem to be confirmed by Netil Market, where decommissioned containers, a direct result of that hyperproduction, are repurposed as units for the slow and careful making of craft goods and services. Yet, as Sharma has argued, imaginaries of 'slow' production and consumption are often based on unfounded and idealized assumptions and mask what are in reality precarious and demanding temporalities of labour (Sharma 2014). Indeed, a closer look at the spatiotemporal logics of crafted pop-up places troubles the notion that they offer an antidote to the temporalities of capitalist hyperproduction.

As is widely recognized, the craft economy is at the forefront of shifts towards 'flexible' labour and experiences of precarity are widespread (Banks, Gill and Taylor 2013; Gill and Pratt 2008). Binge work patterns are usual, with dry spells punctuating intense periods of labour, and securities such as sick pay and holiday pay are lacking. Yet regardless of oscillations in work, and importantly income, workers must be 'always on', constantly putting energy into the maintenance of a business identity that 'becomes increasingly difficult' to separate from their personal lives and leisure time (Hracs and Leslie 2014, p. 67). Pop-up culture provides an infrastructure which exacerbates these conditions of precarity. It is normal for pop-ups to occupy a space for only a few months, weeks, days or even hours, responding to availability. Furthermore, under the terms of meanwhile lease contracts, pop-ups usually have short notice periods so can be easily evicted at any point. As a place for craft, pop-up therefore normalizes and intensifies craft's unstable temporalities and matches them with an unpredictable, 'flexible' geography (Harris 2015). Businesses get used to moving nomadically from site to site as and when cheap space is available.

Sjöholm has questioned the nature of the modern studio at a time when 'artistic practices' are increasingly 'nomadic', 'fragmented' and 'precarious' (Sjöholm 2013, p. 506), and in Netil Market, the craft makers mobilize the pop-up format to respond to this precarity with studios that are themselves nomadic, built from containers specifically designed to be moved and transported. Sarah was initially hesitant to allow too many containers in the market because of the growing ubiquity of container spaces (East London alone is also home to several including Boxpark, Containerville, Bootyard and Container City). But as she says, 'The market is a transient thing, daily it changes [and] monthly we have new people coming in' and in these instances it is 'much easier to have a container'.

Designed to withstand transoceanic travel, containers are strong and secure. Although moving them does require forklifts, containers do not need to be dismantled so can be relocated without risking damage. They can also be locked up anywhere they need to be left, keeping their contents safe from theft. As Egle, one of the owners of Suwun, explained to me in an interview, 'You just lock the container door at night and that's it; nobody can get in.' In this way, containers provide an architecture for craft production and consumption which enables the traders to both withstand and succumb to the flux they face.

The nomadism that the pop-up format enables for craft practitioners also relates to an expectation that craft makers and traders should be instrumental in making the city more efficient and resourceful. Containers, as used in pop-up, ironically create a revised version of the 'spectacle of efficiency' they evoke in geographies of mass production (Martin 2012). As Ferreri has argued, in post-austerity London, pop-up carries a 'moral imperative' to make use of 'waste spaces' at a time of '(alleged) social and economic scarcity' (Ferreri 2015). In a city where space is expensive and in high demand, and at a time when funding for creative projects is scarce, disused sites are framed as opportunities for temporary creative use which it would be wasteful not to take up. This emphasis on thrift and resourcefulness within pop-up culture resonates with craft's own imperatives to reuse and re/upcycle as well as to reduce the production of waste. As a place for craft, pop-up extends craft's imaginary of waste and reuse to include a prerogative to reuse 'wasted' urban space-time. In doing so, I would argue, it also further precaritizes craft production in two mains ways.

First, the way that pop-ups occupy 'wasted', interim space-times between more routine uses of sites can make them subservient to other investment cycles. One of the reasons that pop-ups are valued by stakeholders, such as private landlords and local governments, is that they are thought to attract investment to disused sites (Ferreri 2015). Indeed, this is why they are given short notice periods, so that they can be easily moved on when that investment is found. As such, pop-up is a precarious urban form, easily mobilized to rejuvenate a 'wasted' space-time but just as easily displaced when a more profitable use is identified. Sarah's comments on Netil Market confirm this sense of precarity. Asked about the future of Netil Market, Sarah points to the many new housing developments which surround it and suggests that the future of the market is uncertain as the space becomes increasingly desirable for investment. 'We only get brief opportunities to use these spaces', she comments 'before they're developed … And the way things are going around here, if there's any chance of developing it, it will be'. So, if pop-ups are increasingly providing spaces for craft to take place, then in doing so they are extending the precarity embedded in craft imaginaries by providing an infrastructure within which it is normal for craft businesses to be nomadic, temporary and, crucially, subservient to the prerogatives and time scales of investment.

Secondly, the use of pop-up as an infrastructure for craft also extends the way that labour is 'deterritorialized, dispersed and decentralised' (Gill and Pratt 2008, p. 7) within the craft economy. The imperative within pop-up to seize 'wasted' space-times positions the whole city as a prospective site of work. In pop-up culture empty car parks, roof tops, shops after hours, gardens, parks, yards, derelict buildings and much more all become potential sites of labour. Within this imaginary it is the creative classes, including craft workers, who are expected to activate the latent work spaces of the city (Ferreri 2015). Pop-up's impetus for creative people to find and utilize such 'wasted' urban spaces makes the whole city a 'factory without walls' (Negri 1989, p. 79 in Gill and Pratt 2008, p. 7). Furthermore, the discourse of 'waste' gives this expectation more weight, positioning it as an ethical prerogative (Ferreri 2015). The precarity of the craft economy is thus further intensified through pop-up. If leisure time and domestic space have already been colonized through its logics, then the way that craft is engaged by pop-up culture subsumes new urban geographies into the 'social factory' (Gill and Pratt 2008).

Conclusion

In this chapter I have approached craft and pop-up culture together through a focus on Netil Market as a crafted place and a place for craft. In doing so, I have illuminated ways that craft's urban imaginary is playing out in contemporary London. As we have seen, pop-ups are crafted places that carry craft's emphasis on the handmade and the one-off into the production of temporary urban sites. These crafted sites then have an important role in 'crafting communities' where this entails both the production of creative communities positioned against mass production and the crafting of geographies of exclusion. As places for craft, I have argued that container units give craft traders resilience in a city where craft work is increasingly nomadic and unstable. I have also suggested that, as an infrastructure for craft production and consumption, pop-up is extending the precarity of the craft economy. In particular, I have explored how pop-up is mobilized to produce a city in which spatiotemporal precarity for craft workers is normalized in order to favour the interests of larger scale investment, and in which any space-time is positioned as a potential site of labour.

Thinking about the common sensibilities of craft and pop-up can also shed light on the purchase of both phenomena in the contemporary moment. Craft has become so popular in recent years, both as a term and as an aesthetic, that many argue it is now almost meaningless (Walker 2015), applied to practices that have little to do with craft in the traditional sense. The term 'pop-up' too seems to have lost in precision what it has rapidly gained in currency, often now used to refer to fairly long-term developments or, conversely, to things that are inherently temporary or mobile. This accusation that craft has become meaningless could certainly be levelled at businesses such as the barber shop in Netil Market as well as to the positioning of temporary architectural construction as a form of craft. Yet if these terms are becoming indicators of broad aesthetics, rather than descriptors of defined practices and products, this is in itself revealing. To me, what the loose usage of these terms suggests is that affiliation with craft or with pop-up is desired not only because of what doing craft or doing pop-up, in their purest sense, involve, but because of the value found in the narratives they offer. As the case of Netil Market shows, craft's pop-up geographies offer meaningful sites of labour to young people disenfranchised by economic crisis while at the same time playing into the prerogatives of developers and local governments by cheaply rebranding disused sites and normalizing flexible labour. Given the utility of these terms for (positively) narrativizing precarious urban conditions, their appeal in the contemporary economic climate is hardly surprising. Thinking about craft and pop-up together therefore helps to develop an understanding of how precarious urban conditions are being narrativized.

Pop-up is by no means the only geography in which the logics of craft production and consumption are visible. However, it is an arena in which the influence that craft's logics are having on the production and imagination of urban space is particularly clear. Thinking about pop-up culture as part of the craft economy can open up new ways of understanding craft's imaginary and, as this chapter has demonstrated, can elucidate what is at stake politically in craft's influence over cities.

Notes

1 All quotations from Sarah relate to an interview conducted in London Fields on 26 January 2015.

2 http://www.ofca.co.uk/

3 http://www.bellcontainer.co.uk/

References

Banks, M. (2010), 'Craft labour and creative industries', *International Journal of Cultural Policy*, 16 (3): 305–21.

Banks, M., Gill, R. and Taylor, S. (2013), *Theorizing Cultural Work, Labour, Continuity and Change in the Cultural and Creative Industries*, London, New York: Routledge.

Bratich, J. Z. and Brush, H. M. (2011), 'Fabricating activism: Craft-work, popular culture, gender', *Utopian Studies*, 22 (2): 233–60.

Butler, T., Hamnett, C. and Ramsden, M. J. (2013), 'Gentrification, education and exclusionary displacement in East London', *International Journal of Urban and Regional Research*, 37 (2): 556–75.

Colomb, C. (2012), 'Pushing the Urban Frontier: Temporary uses of space, city marketing, and the creative city', *Journal of Urban Affairs*, 34 (2): 131–52.

Dawkins, N. (2011), 'Do-it-yourself: The precarious work and postfeminist politics of handmaking (in) Detroit', *Utopian Studies*, 22 (2): 261–84.

Deslandes, A. (2013), 'Exemplary Amateurism, thoughts on DIY urbanism', *Cultural Studies Review*, 19 (1): 216–27.

Duman, A. (2012), 'Dispatches from the frontline of gentrification', *City*, 16 (6): 672–85.

Eatworkart. (2015), *eatworkart*. [Online] Available at: http://eatworkart.com/about/what-we-do/ (accessed 07 July 2015).

Ferreri, M. (2015), 'The seductions of temporary urbanism', *Ephemera: Theory & Politics in Organization*, 15 (1): 181–91.

Gauntlett, D. (2011), *Making is Connecting: The Social Meaning of Creativity, From DIY and Knitting to YouTube and Web 2.0.* Cambridge, Malden: Polity Press.

Gill, R. and Pratt, A. (2008), 'Precarity and cultural work: In the social factory? Immaterial labour, precariousness and cultural work', *Theory, Culture & Society*, 25 (7–8): 1–30.

Gov.uk. (2013), Meanwhile use lease. [Online] Available at: https://www.gov.uk/government/ collections/meanwhile-use-leases-and-guidance-for-landlords (accessed 19 August 2015).

Graziano, V. and Ferreri, M. (2014), 'Passion without objects young graduates and the politics of temporary art spaces', *Recherches sociologiques et anthropologiques*, 2: 83–102.

Gregson, N. and Crewe, L. (2003), *Second Hand Cultures*. Oxford and New York: Berg.

Harris, E. (2015), 'Navigating pop-up geographies: Urban space-times of flexibility, interstitiality and immersion', *Geography Compass*, 9 (11): 592–603.

Harrod, T. (2013), 'Visionary rather than practical': Craft, art and material efficiency, *Philosophical Transactions of The Royal Society*, 371 (1986): 1–12.

Harvie, J. (2013), *Fair Play*. Hampshire: Palgrave Macmillan.

Henninger. (2015), Office for Crafted Architecture, http://www.ofca.co.uk/. (accessed 01 February 2016).

Hracs, B. J. and Leslie, D. (2014), 'Aesthetic labour in creative industries: the case of independent musicians in Toronto, Canada', *Area*, 1 (66–73): 46.

Jakob, D. (2013), 'Crafting your way out of the recession? New craft entrepreneurs and the global economic downturn', *Cambridge Journal of Regions, Economy and Society*, 6: 127–40.

Luckman, S. (2013), 'The Aura of the analogue in a digital age, women's crafts, creative markets and home-based labour after Etsy', *Cultural Studies Review*, 19 (1): 249–70.

Luckman, S. (2015), *Craft and the Creative Economy*. New York: Palgrave Macmillan.

Luckman, S., Gibson, C. and Lea, T. (2009), 'Mosquitoes in the mix: How transferable is creative city thinking?' *Singapore Journal of Tropical Geography*, 30 (1): 70–85.

Martin, C. (2012), 'Controlling flow: On the logistics of distributive space', in A. Ballantyne and C. L. Smith (eds.), *Architecture in the Space of Flows*, London and New York: Routledge.

Martin, C. (2013), 'Shipping container mobilities, seamless compatibility, and the global surface of logistical integration', *Environment and Planning A*, 45: 1021–36.

Mathews, V. and Picton, R. M. (2014), 'Intoxifying gentrification: Brew pubs and the geography of post-industrial heritage', *Urban Geography*, 35 (3): 337–56.

McRobbie, A. (2013), 'Fashion matters Berlin; city-spaces, womens working lives, new social enterprise', *Cultural Studies*, 27 (6): 982–1010.

Mould, O. (2014), 'Tactical urbanism: The new vernacular of the creative city', *Geography Compass*, 8 (8): 529–39.

Parker, M. (2012), 'Containerisation: Moving things and boxing ideas', *Mobilities*: 1–20.

Potter, L. and Claire, W. (2013), 'Neoliberal Britain's Austerity Foodscape: Home Economics, Veg Patch Capitalism and Culinary Temporality', *New Formations: A Journal of Culture/Theory/Politics*: 155–78.

Schenll, S. M. and Reese, J. F. (2009), 'Microbreweries as tools of local identity', *Journal of Cultural Geography*, 21 (1): 45–69.

Schreiber, C. and Treggiden, K. (2015), *Makers of East London*. London: Hoxton Mini Press

Sennett, R. (2008), *The Craftsman*. London: Penguin.

Sharma, S. (2014), *In the Meantime, Temporality and Cultural Politics*. Durham and London: Duke University Press.

Sjöholm, J. (2013), 'The art studio as archive: Tracing the geography of artistic potentiaity, progress and production', *Cultural Geographies in Practice*, 21 (3): 505–14.

Theworshipfullittleshopofspectacles. (2015), *theworshipfullittleshopofspectacles*. [Online] Available at: http://www.theworshipfullittleshopofspectacles.com/handmade-frames/ (accessed 24 August 2015).

Thomas, N. J., Harvey, D. C. and Hawkins, H. (2012), 'Crafting the region: Creative industries and practices of regional space', *Regional Studies*, 47 (1): 75–88.

Thrift, N. (2008), 'The material practices of glamour', *Journal of Cultural Economy*, 1 (1): 9–23.

Tonkiss, F. (2013), 'Austerity urbanism and the makeshift city', *City: Analysis of Urban Trends, Culture, Theory, Policy, Action*, 17 (3):312–24.

Walker, Daniela. (2015), 'The hipster is dead, let's start an anti-authenticity movement' *Marketing Magazine* available at http://www.marketingmagazine.co.uk/article/1366143/hipster-dead-lets-start-anti-authenticity-movement (accessed 01 February 2015).

Warhurst, Chris and Nickson, Dennis. (2009), 'Who's Got the Look?' Emotional, Aesthetic and Sexualized Labour in Interactive Services', *Gender, Work & Organization*, 2009, 16 (3): 385–404.

WeAreArrow. (2015), WeAreArrow. [Online] Available at: http://www.wearearrow.com/about/ (accessed 18 August 2015).

PART FIVE

Technology, innovation and craft

17

Knitting and crochet as experiment

Exploring social and material practices of computation and craft

Gail Kenning and Jo Law

Hand-crafted textile production has a close but often tense relationship with technology and mechanization. Needles, hooks and frames have been used to extend techniques that had developed from knotting and hand weaving. Industrialized textile production transformed hand-crafted processes and techniques by formalizing repeatable actions as logical expressions, thus enabling them to be performed by machines. These algorithmic and iterative processes were central to the development of the mechanized punch-card operations of the weaving looms of Jacques de Vaucanson, and their subsequent refinement by Joseph-Marie Jacquard (Williams 1991). Charles Babbage and Herman Hollerith went on to adapt such approaches in the creation of computing machines, developments which shaped the social and material practices of both hand-crafted textiles and computational technologies.

This chapter investigates how processes are transformed and potentialities arise when hand-crafted constructed textiles and computational technologies are used in concert. It explores resonances between craft activities such as knitting and crochet and computer programming to show how they impact and extend our understanding of materiality and process as social practice. The chapter focuses on two distinct projects: the introduction of computational media to tertiary media arts students through practices of knitting and an experimental art research project that attempts to evolve crochet lace patterns (commonly known as doilies) using computational media.

Technology of our time

The need for craft to adapt, change and engage with the technologies of the present has long been recognized and is an ongoing concern. Walter Gropius, in the *Bauhaus Manifesto*, calls for artists, designers and architects to 'turn to the crafts' in their engagement with new technologies to develop new processes of making (Frayling 2011, p. 87). Janis Jefferies claims that craft gains authenticity through its connection with the everyday and is invested with the materialities of the now (Jefferies 2011). Richard Sennett argues that, as craftspersons, by engaging with machines of our own time we relate to technology as producers rather than consumers and, in doing so, gain a deeper understanding of the connection between what we use and what we make (Sennett 2008).

Sennett analyses the evolving relationship between makers and machines in his book *The Craftsman*, where he examines the role that machines play in material culture and suggests that 'sound judgement about machinery is required in any good craft practice' (2008, pp. 105–6). For Sennett, machine technologies are capable of reproducing human labour and replacing the maker, as shown when Vaucanson's loom stood in for the labour of silk weavers. However, he also suggests that technologies can offer unforeseen possibilities and potentialities by extending human capacities, exemplified by the production of new material forms and social practices as a result of the developments in glass and paper making during the Renaissance. Sennett's view of the machine can be seen as one of optimism, reflecting the technological blossoming related to the 'culture of freedom' of the mid-twentieth century, rather than the command-and-control approach to technology arising from the military industrial complex of the Second World War (Castells 2010). He suggests 'a machine, like any model, ought to propose rather than command' (2008, pp. 105–6). Like Sennett, Walter Benjamin before him argues that modern technologies have the potential to positively transform our relationship with the objects we make and our lived experience. Tracing the transformation of *Handwerk* (artisan labour) into *Kunstwerk* (artwork) through mechanical reproduction technologies, Benjamin advocates for a further transformation from the 'authored valuable' into the 'non-auratic multiple' of *Kraftwerk* (Leslie 1998, p. 8). Esther Leslie explains that the 'technical multiple does not squash out authentic experience but translates it into object-forms … appropriate for a modern age' (1998, p. 8). For Leslie as for Benjamin, both the objects and the tools of making are transformed in the process.

The impact of technology on our lived experience and relationship with objects has been explored by new media theorists, such as Marshall Mcluhan, whose concept of remediation was revisited by Jay David Bolter and Richard A. Grusin. They suggest that not only do technologies borrow, re-purpose, reuse and extend existing technologies, but also practices and processes remediate existing practices and processes, content and form (Bolter and Grusin 1999; McLuhan and Zingrone 1995). The creation of the transformative multiple object, as identified by Benjamin and Leslie, is just part of the transformative practices that repeat, recreate and extend existing social and material practices. It is by borrowing this framework of remediation that we can examine, compare and contrast the material and social processes of constructed textile practices such as knitting and crochet with those of digital and computational technologies. In doing so we can show how these practices mutually inform and are transformative as identified by Benjamin, and can extend as suggested by Sennett. We argue that the relationship between materiality and maker, and the (re)socialization of technologies is key to this transformation.

Extension through material practice:
Knitting as a computational medium

Knitting creates stretchy fabric by forming an interconnected loop of continuous yarn using two needles. Archaeological findings of nåelbinding[1] date back to around 300 CE, while artefacts from the eleventh century confirm weft knitting[2] as a well-developed technology by the second millennium. By the fourteenth century, knitting had spread from the Middle East through Islamic Spain to Europe, where it became firmly established. Unlike crochet, its mechanization in the late sixteenth century (beginning with William Lee's invention of the stocking frame in 1589) has come to define the practice of knitting. Knitting has evolved in response to mechanization. Materials changed from wool and linen to cotton in manufacturing. Technology was employed in the form of steam engines, which automated and accelerated the production process. The craft practice was also transformed by the availability of cheap labour. Since mechanization, hand-knitting and machine-knitting have come to define each other technically, socially, culturally and economically. Hand-knitting in the West during the war and depression years of the early twentieth century, for example, was taken up as a response to crisis, creating a sense of social cohesion through making. Knitting developments in the second half of the twentieth century were impacted by further technological innovations (dye chemistry, synthetic materials, programmable knitting looms), changing social conceptions of hand craft, and economics. In the twenty-first century, there has been a resurgence of hand-knitting as a reflexive activity, aesthetically conscious, politically aware and technologically integrated form of social movement (Bratich and Brush 2011). In this context knitting, as a socialized material technology, presents a model for exploring the relationship between art, technologies and the material world.

Situated within a tertiary media art curriculum, the subject 'Computational Media' is an introduction to computer programming in the creative arts disciplines. The student body is composed of undergraduates from the media arts, media and communication, and computer science programs. The aim was to develop 'an understanding of the material conditions of digital media and encourage exploration of its creative possibilities'. The subject had focused on the principles of programming through different languages and scripts (including C++, Java, Javascript, Processing, Command Line, HTML, CSS) employing mixed modes of learning (online tutorials, set readings, tests). The initial attrition rate was high as students perceived computer programming to be difficult (regardless of their actual experience), and often could not conceive of how programming fitted within the creative disciplines. Introducing knitting was an experimental approach in response to the concerns raised but, more importantly, to find new ways to explore computational media through technological, material and social perspectives.

The subject begins by focusing on 'human computing'.[3] This approach requires students to abstract and express information through codified language, for example, in designing a physical semaphore system, translating visual information using coded audio signals, (re)creating Sol Lewitt's artworks using his published instructions, or knitting.[4] Students then focus on digital computing using *Processing,* an open source programming language (Reas and Fry 2014). Technologies such as 3D printing, CNC routers and Arduino are also introduced as students are asked to explore concepts of iteration, repetition and variation using media of their choice. The aim is to increasingly build students' understanding of the significance of physical contact with materials and processes,

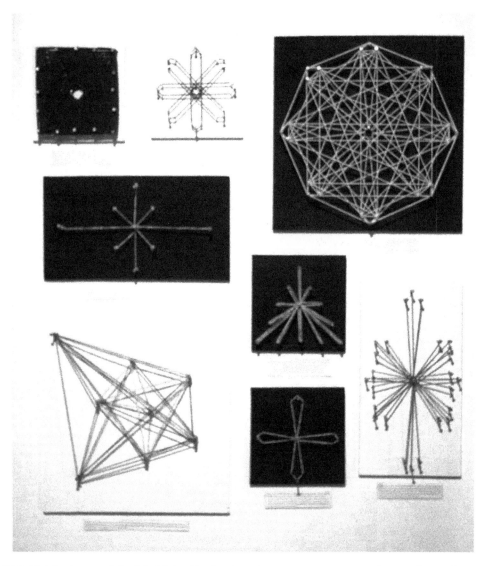

FIGURE 17.1 Project work by Madeleine Pitt for the subject 'Computation Media', exploring the concept of programmable iterations using strings and nails to create patterns.

even digital ones. Such approaches to learning are exemplified by Rudolf Steiner in his instructions to teach young children knitting and crochet. Arguments have also recently emerged about the importance of teaching material construction as part of the science, technologies, engineering and mathematics curricula through traditional craft such as sewing (Vesko 2015). Activities such as crochet and knitting can be explored procedurally through repetition, iteration, logics and loops. Furthermore, they can be formalized and transcribed as communicable and transmissible programmes, described mathematically and expressed as algorithms (Belcastro 2012; Taimina 2009). Thus, algorithms, which are frequently taught as abstract concepts, can be accessed directly in the handling of physical objects.

In the media arts curriculum, students are introduced to knitting through its commonalities with computer programming. This involves looking at the exploratory use of knitted, crochet and lace forms in contemporary art and design, and exploring how knitting and crochet engage with programming, mechanical and computational technologies.[5] Students begin by learning to cast-on and complete a simple knit stitch using 8-millimetre needles and worsted weight yarn. They are supported by online videos and physical demonstrations and assistance from tutors. Having mastered the basic knit stitch, students are encouraged to examine the construction of other stitches and decode extracts from simple knitting patterns verbally or as graphic representations. This process highlights the similarity of the abstract and expressive forms used in computer programming and in knitting, both processes being reliant on loop, iteration and logic. Students are made aware of knitting as an enactment of programming where constraints are experienced materially and physically.[6]

Technologies extend: Crochet Simulacra

The *Pattern as Process* experimental art research project uses digital and computational media to explore and extend crochet lace pattern forms. It begins by exploring the physical techniques and material constraints of this form of pattern making and then investigates crochet lace simulacra as text, diagram and code (Kenning 2015a, b; Kenning 2009). The origins of the crochet technique, which uses a simple metal or bone hooked tool to manipulate cotton, silk or woollen threads, is contested and according to some sources no more than 200 years old. However, its origins can be seen in similar techniques that are estimated to be more than 1000 years old. The crochet technique is evident across a range of cultures, but is primarily associated with eighteenth-century Irish lace and the production of doilies (Williams [1991] 1995). The subsequent popularity of crochet lace making was impacted by social and economic factors, trade agreements, the influence of fashion, and trends in hobbies and pastimes.

The crochet technique was thought to be more adaptable, have less structure and be less restrictive than techniques such as bobbin lace or knitting (Kenning 2015a, b). It could be used to mimic the appearance of other labour-intensive techniques, such as needle lace, and was used to recreate existing patterns made using such time-consuming methods more quickly and economically. For these reasons, the crochet technique was believed to offer the maker greater creative freedom. However, while the creative potential of the technique has been frequently recognized, a hegemonic pressure to conform, as is apparent in many craft practices, means that the basic doily form has not changed significantly in the past 200 years (Kenning 2015a, b). Furthermore, the flexibility of the technique and the lack of limitation on scale, size and pattern form meant that it was difficult to mechanize and so was impacted little during the industrial era. This contributes to the perception of a stasis in the development of the pattern form (Kenning 2009). So, if mechanization had little impact on the crochet lace form, what impact can computation and digital media have?

The *Pattern as Process* experimental art project investigated how the crochet technique could be reformulated in a digital environment to potentially extend the pattern-making process and produce pattern forms that had not been seen before (Kenning 2015a, b). After a series of investigations that involved physically making crochet patterns with threads, followed by frame-by-frame animations to create digital representations of crochet lace, computer code was used to generate a series of crochet lace simulacra. Viewers were able to see the stitch formation, modularity and developmental path of each pattern as it appeared as an onscreen animation. Changing and randomizing variables in the code, in relation to stitch, size, colour, position and shape patterns were generated, challenged the concept of what a doily was or could be.

Basic rules were applied to each of the crochet lace simulacra such as the calculations defining the size, type and stitch position were based on the last stitch made, and each stitch was generated one at a time. Under these set of rules some patterns appeared as only slight variations of traditional crochet lace doilies. However, if the increase or decrease in the value of a variable during the computation process was large, and the number of iterations significantly increased, extreme variations in the pattern form could be observed. For example, crochet lace simulacra were not limited by size and pattern forms frequently 'strayed' 'off-screen' as the position of a stitch was computed to be beyond the confines of the selected screen size. Similarly, whereas a small number of discrete motifs can constitute a crochet lace pattern made from physical threads, digital crochet lace simulacra might be made up of thousands of discrete motifs, each consisting of just one stitch (Kenning 2009). Crochet lace simulacra then could appear to be, for example, a kilometre wide or made up of 100,000,000s of discrete stitches.

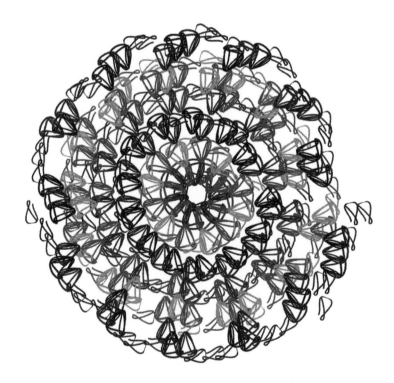

FIGURE 17.2 Digital crochet lace simulacra showing minimal variation.

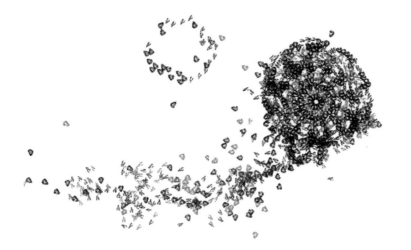

FIGURE 17.3 Crochet lace simulacra be made up of millions of stitches.

The experimental art research project shows that while crochet lace patterns may be limited by social and hegemonic pressure, changing materiality and social practices can facilitate experimentation and challenge our understanding of what crochet lace patterns are and can be.

Craft: Socializing technologies

The exploration of crochet and knitting with computational processes and practices underlined how these crafts operate technologically, materially and socially. These craft practices are in Sennett's terms learned and practised skills of cooperation and social acts of civilization (2008; 2012). The significance of 'doing something' together is recognized in the inclusion of knitting in primary and secondary curricula (LeJevic and Powell 2012), in the coming together of craft groups (Kenning 2015a, b), and can be reactivated in relation to digital and computational media.

In using knitting practices to teach computer programming the principal objective is to develop 'an understanding of the material conditions of digital media' and the concept of programming as an everyday social practice of abstraction and expression. Formulating a knitting pattern creates a diagram, a model or a construction blueprint and is akin to computer programming. The formulation of this expression must be activated through a direct engagement with materials. Likewise, computational media is explored as a way of thinking and a process of construction. It has a material practice and is analogous to other material practices. Here, Benjamin's *Kraftwerk* is useful for understanding the 'material conditions of digital media'. In reference to pottery, Benjamin suggests that as a technological, social and material object, a pot holds traces of the world within which it is made, that is, the textures and technologies from which it is produced. Likewise, the construction methods, tools and materials used in handcrafted textiles can be physically decoded from the resultant artefact by an experienced practitioner. So too computational and digital media are imprinted with material practice and social conditions of the making processes.

Engagement with computer technologies on a material level – at the level of code – is an inherently social and political act that shifts users from the position of consumers to that of producers (Rushkoff 2011). In teaching code as craft, students are impacted by the social conditions of practice. The knitted scarf or crocheted doily of the newly taught textile practitioner is akin to 'Hello World!', which is invariably the first program executed by a new coder.[7] These acts are acknowledgements of the crafts' traditions. In choosing a programming language a coder inherits and contributes to preexisting social norms and conventions. The coders' relationship to code, and to coding, 'despite appearing "merely" technical' is where 'technical knowledge-practices overlap with imaginings of sociality, individual identity, community, collectivity, organisation and enterprise' (Mackenzie 2006). In this environment learners are part of the wider environment: the online forums, societies of practices and the localized peer assistance of the offline classroom. Introducing knitting as social practice and computational craft draws attention to the social dimensions of coding.

In contrast the *Pattern as Process* research project draws attention to the agency of digital technologies and computational processes to challenge our understanding of the technological, material and social practices associated with craft, craft activities, craft processes and the craft object. It reveals how handcrafted artefacts and processes while not necessarily bounded by their materiality and the physical technique employed may be subject to social practices that impose limitations through hegemonic pressure. In the research project the experimental and computational processes used seemingly disregarded the hegemonic social practices that reward and celebrate conformity and tradition. While the pattern forms generated in the research project were not beyond the reach of the social practices that impact and shape technology and material practices, they were able to more closely explore the potentialities of the rules and logic of the crochet technique.

Engagement with digital machines push the boundaries of techniques and forms. Working with the core materials of digital media – codes – both the craft form and the techniques of making are transformed. In this way, established traditions of craft practices can continue to develop with machines of our own time. Significantly, this extension of tradition re-socializes technologies in the remediation of hand craft and extends social and material practices through the potential remediation of computation processes in hand craft.

It is evident in both projects that aspects of existing social and material practices associated with craft-based textile activities inform and are informed by digital media practices. Perceptions of knitting and crochet remain largely gendered. While manipulating the knitting needles and yarn was a challenge for many students engaged in the media art curricula, more male students were vocal about their own lack of dexterity and inability to undertake the task, whereas females students more frequently offered anecdotes about being taught craft activities by older female family members or at school. Reversed gendered attitudes are apparent in the use of computational media. Thus, the experimental approaches discussed in this chapter suggest that further research is needed in relation to addressing gender inequalities in relation to both hand craft and digital technologies (Buechley and Mako-Hill 2010; Buchholz et al. 2014). Understanding how craft and technological practices can mutually inform is key in the development of a form of making that moves beyond artificial gendered boundaries and explores making as simultaneously technological, material and social practices.

The connection between constructed textile practices such as crochet and knitting and computational programming requires further theorization. These projects show how constructed textile processes and techniques can be (re)located alongside contemporary research into pattern behaviours, pattern forms and pattern matching that draw on evolutionary and emergent possibilities and extend research in relation to other fields such as mathematics, science and engineering (Taimin a 2009; Wertheim and Wertheim 2013). The physical processes of traditional knitting and crochet foreground the existence and importance of inherent, changing and evolving material and social practices in computational and digital media. This research brings to the fore issues of craft and technologies beyond the now tired analogue/digital dichotomy.

Conclusion

Benjamin's *Kraftwerk* engages the technical reproducibility of modern technologies to restore to the process the bodily rhythms, mechanized by industrial production machines, through tactility and togetherness. Leslie writes, 'Technical reproduction … institut[es] new potential for a familiarity between receivers and producers, once more in the form of collective experience' (1998, p. 9). This is the socialization of haptic technologies. The strong parallels between communities originated in the use of digital technologies such as copyleft, open source and the creative commons, and that of craftivism, knitting circles and the maker movement, are no coincidence. As Sennett argues, 'The capacities our bodies have to shape physical things are the same capacities we draw on in social relations' (2008, p. 290). Craft as practice engenders a social dimension that is capable of (re)generating the shared rhythms, shared times and shared knowledge of the new commons for the distributive and contributive communities of craft practitioners who work together.

Sennett's account of the machines reminds us that for the contemporary craftperson 'working with machines rather than fighting was the radical, emancipatory challenge' (2008, p. 118). By remediating computational media through the technologies of knitting and crochet, and vice versa, this chapter responds to the call to engage with the technologies of our own era: to discover new ways of making by 'turning to the crafts', to create and embrace the imprint of *Kraftwerk* and to discover the everyday that is invested with the materiality of the now. This remediation has the potential to transform the relationship between materiality and maker, and their practices as social technologies.

Notes

1 Nålebinding is a technique of creating fabric using a single needle. It is distinct from both crochet and knitting, and predates both.

2 Weft knitting is created using a single continuous yarn creating rows of interlinking loops. The common hand knitting technique is weft knitting.

3 The subject curriculum from 2013 was principally written by Jo Law with contribution from Etienne Deleflie and co-taught with Etienne Deleflie and Mat Wall-Smith from 2014. Enrolments between 2013 and 2015 range from sixty to ninety students per year.

4 Knitting was chosen because Jo Law had learnt it as an adult and teaching other tutors provided a good understanding of the learning process. In addition, it required minimal equipment and materials.

5 Students were introduced to Dave Cole's *The Knitting Machine* (2005), Siren Elise Wilhelm's *365 Knitting Clock* (2010), Gerard Rubio's *Open Knit* (2014–), and Mar Canet and Varvara Guljajeva's *Knitic* (2009–), and Gail Kenning presented her research, works and practices (Kenning 2015).

6 Material contact is significant: the effectiveness of the workshop relies on the hands-on participation of all students in learning to knit regardless of whether they succeed or fail in creating a piece of knitted fabric.

7 There is some debate about the origin of 'hello world'. However, it is often the first piece of code that programmers learn. (http://www.thesoftwareguild.com/blog/the-history-of-hello-world/)

References

Belcastro, S. (2012), 'Adventures in mathematical knitting', in M. Pitici (ed.), *The Best Writing on Mathematics 2012*, Oxford & Princeton: Oxford University Press & Princeton University Press.

Bolter, J. D. and Grusin, R. A. (1999), *Remediation: Understanding New Media*. Cambridge, MA: MIT Press.

Bratich, J. Z. and Brush, H. M. (2011), 'Fabricating activism: Craft-work popular culture, gender', *Utopian Studies*, 22 (2): 233–260.

Buchholz, B., Shively, K., Peppler, K. and Wohlwend, K. (2014), 'Hands on, hands off: Gendered access in crafting and electronics practices', *Mind, Culture, and Activity*, 21 (4): 278–79.

Buechley, L. and Mako-Hill, B. (2010), 'LilyPad in the Wild: How Hardware s Long Tail is Supporting New Engineering and Design Communities', P2P Foundation, 13 October. Available online: http://p2pfoundation.net/How_Hardware%CA%BCs_Long_Tail_is_Supporting_New_Engineering_and_Design_Communities (accessed 9 September 2015).

Castells, M. (2010), *The Rise of the Network Society* (2nd ed.), Chichester; Malden: Wiley-Blackwell.

Frayling, C. (2011), *On Craftsmanship*. London: Oberon Books.

Jefferies, J. (2011), 'Loving attention: An outburst of craft in contemporary art', Buszek, Ma. E. (ed.), *Extra/ordinary: Craft and Contemporary Art*, 222–43, Durham: Duke University Press.

Kenning, G. J. (2009), 'Pattern as Process: An Aesthetic Exploration of the Digital Possibilities for Conventional, Physical Lace Patterns', PhD Thesis., College of Fine Arts, University of New South Wales.

Kenning, G. (2015a), 'Creative craft-based textile activity in the age of digital systems and practices', *Leonardo*, 48 (5).

Kenning, G. (2015b), 'Fiddling with Threads': Craft-based textile activities and positive well-being. *Textile: The Journal of Cloth and Culture*, 13 (1): 50–65.

LeJevic, L. and Powell, K. (2012), 'Knitting Curriculum: Storied Threads of Pre-service Art Teaching', *Journal of Curriculum Theorizing*, 28 (1): 175–90.

Leslie, E. (1998), 'Walter Benjamin: Traces of craft', *Journal of Design History*, 11 (1): 5–13.

Mackenzie, A. (2006), *Cutting Code: Software and Sociality*. New York: Peter Lang.

McLuhan, M. McLuhan, E. and Zingrone, F. (1995), *Essential McLuhan* (1st ed.), New York: Basic Books.

Reas, C. and Fry, B. (2014), *Processing: A Programming Handbook for Visual Designers and Artists* (2nd ed.), Cambridge, MA: The MIT Press.

Rush, M. (2005), *New Media in Art*, London: Thames & Hudson.

Rushkoff, D. (2011), *Program or be Programmed: Ten Commands for a Digital Age*, Berkeley: Soft Skull Press.

Sennett, R. (2008), *The Craftsman*. New Haven: Yale University Press.

Sennett, R. (2012), *Together: The Rituals, Pleasures and Politics of Cooperation*, London: Penguin Books.

Taimina, D. (2009), *Crocheting Adventures with Hyperbolic Planes*, Wellesley: A K Peters.

Vesko, S. (2015), Creating Craftier Engineers: Why students should learn to sew in STEM classes. *Slate*, 10 June. Available online: http://www.slate.com/articles/technology/future_tense/2015/06/stem_classes_should_include_lessons_about_low_tech_crafts_like_sewing.html?utm_campaign=trueAnthem:+Trending+Content&utm_content=557a523f04d3012a28000001&utm_medium=trueAnthem&utm_source=twitter (accessed 9 September 2015).

Wertheim, M. and Wertheim, C. (2013), Hyberbolic crochet coral reef. Retrieved 20/4/16, 2013, from http://crochetcoralreef.org/about/index.php

Williams, R. (1991, Reprinted 1993, 1995), 'The Industrial Revolution 1780-1880', in M. Ginsburg (ed.), *The Illustrated History of Textiles*, xvii–xx. London: Studio editions ltd.

18

Towards new modes of knowledge production

Makerspaces and emerging maker practices

Angelina Russo

In mid-2014, US president Obama hosted a Maker Faire[1] on the lawns of the White House in Washington, DC.[2] The Maker Faire is a proprietary event by O'Reily Media, primarily designed to showcase makers who are exploring new forms and new technologies. Maker Faires have become synonymous with innovation and experimentation across science, engineering, art, performance and craft. On the same day, the global energy corporation Chevron announced a US $10 million commitment to ten new FabLabs in the United States.[3] A FabLab is a small-scale workshop which is equipped with digital fabrication technologies and is made available to individuals through a membership system. The term is proprietary to MIT's Centre of Bits and Atoms, which began the programme of publically available infrastructure in 2001.[4]

These two events signalled that 'maker' activities were no longer seen as solely part of a broader American history of individual ingenuity often expressed as 'tinkering' (Tocchetti 2015), but rather that they had become central to a new generation of innovation where making skills would lead a regeneration in manufacturing practices and processes. If this grassroots convergence of analogue and digital making processes and practices could attract the support of the president of the United States and a global oil company, then digital transformation at the level of both design and manufacture would necessarily require a reconfiguration of knowledge production and exchange in order to scale beyond the maker community and into the broader innovation system. Such a shift in the ways in which products are conceptualized, manufactured and communicated would suggest that purposeful design be embedded within new making processes: from the proposal and inception phases, through the duration and onwards into the long-term aftermath of new products and services.

This chapter posits that to achieve this transformation in this innovation ecosystem, it is vital that pathways to access are provided to both digital fabrication facilities and training programmes that build engagement and collaboration between makers, researchers and communities

(Quinlan 2015). This is particularly important in the handmade design and craft sector, where changes to traditional models of knowledge production, and the dissemination and the ethics of consumption, are examples of what Rosner and Ryokai (2009) suggest are increasingly common partnerships between people and technology for the creation of 'personally meaningful things'. If this is the case, then such processes must be captured and documented to achieve a long-term understanding of what new modes of knowledge production will entail for the future of making practices in increasingly digital environments.

The issue of how making practices can simultaneously demonstrate the public value of small-scale social enterprise, the business opportunities afforded SMEs at medium scale in regard to skills regeneration and the large-scale and commercializable outputs of collaborative innovation within the context of digital fabrication remain under-investigated worldwide. Therefore, this chapter will explore two central questions:

a *What innovations must occur in maker expertise so that designers and craftspeople can engage most productively with emerging digital fabrication practices?*

b *How can these new making practices be embedded all the way through new modes of knowledge production in order to achieve innovations in product development, distribution and promotion?*

By pursuing these two questions, the chapter aims to connect maker expertise and practices to the knowledge and skills required to enable designers and craftspeople to emerge as leaders in new modes of collaboration, research and pedagogy that drive networked, decentralized and digital production cultures (Dougherty 2012). Central to my exploration of these questions is the argument that new types of encounters with often unlikely partners and knowledge systems, both old and new, must be explored in order to achieve the objectives of this new innovation ecosystem.

Increasingly, the ability to successfully create, manufacture, distribute and promote creative artefacts (including physical products such as clothes, bags, shoes and digital products, such as video games, software apps and so forth) is underpinned by three central and overlapping activities: creative artefact/service production by skilled practitioners, their connection to and participation in a networked society, and their ability to develop complex and novel forms of reciprocity. Such forms of contemporary practice are iterative in their reliance on personal expertise, civic participation and a genuine commitment to knowledge sharing. As a result, new forms of creative production are often better situated within environments with a vested interest in engaging in all three activities. It is no accident then that as large commercial entities are finding new ways of distributing and promoting maker cultures, cultural institutions such as museums, libraries and galleries are beginning to contribute to the innovation ecosystem by establishing test beds for the creation of new relationships between makers and the broader innovation ecosystem. Moreover, innovations in digital fabrication such as 3D printing have the potential to lay the groundwork for future design-driven manufacturing practices, returning 'making' to advanced industrial economies currently suffering economically and socially from its displacement overseas (Lindtner and Li 2012).

The first part of this chapter therefore explores commercial places of making, recognizing the important role that global distribution networks have played in creating a democratized distribution of knowledge (Anderson 2012; Dougherty 2012). This section of the chapter explores how such entities have supported a return of manufacturing to the global West via highly localized, customized industrial 3D rendering and printing. The second part considers the role that participants and institutions play in supporting the development of new knowledge as it relates to maker practices and activities. It recognizes that the bulk of creative work undertaken across Australia (and in other Western nations) is represented by micro-enterprises (Arts 2014). Therefore, for these makers to access infrastructure, support and new knowledge, the creation and maintenance of large knowledge networks becomes ever more crucial. It is within this context that partnerships with cultural institutions as a catalyst for broader engagement and product development are discussed. It is intended that, taken together, these two parts demonstrate the value of both commercial and institutional partnerships in the maker enterprise.

Commercial places of making

The success of early commercial digital content distribution sites such as *Flickr*[5] and *YouTube*[6] and bespoke design-centric services such as *ReadyMade*[7] and *Design it Yourself*[8] relied on fundamental transformations in the creation and distribution of primarily digital or digitized content in order to achieve critical mass in a novice online audience. Sites such as YouTube often used the convergence of creativity with user-generated demand to their advantage. For instance, the YouTube business model[9] offers a lucrative return to creators who can attract a large audience to their video uploads. Once a certain viewer number is achieved, advertisements are added to the beginning of the content and creators receive profits from the number of views of both. By contributing to the promotion of their own content, creators play an important role in the revenue creation of the product. Clearly this partnership asks of the creative an entirely new type of literacy, one which brings them together with their audiences in order to explore and promote traditional and new media forms.

One of the most successful commercial examples of the convergence of physical products and digital distribution has been Etsy,[10] an online handmade goods (as well as raw materials and vintage items) selling platform launched in 2005 to both enable small-scale makers to establish an online presence and to learn (through the training provided) about the 'long tail' (Anderson 2007) possibilities inherent in this new convergent e-commerce space.[11] For more than ten years, Etsy has pioneered the value of networks in the process of creating and promoting goods to their communities, and in doing so has established itself as what could be described as a 'cultural authority' in the dissemination and ethics of contemporary small-scale, artisanal production and consumption.[12] This important differentiator – the link between commodity and culture – is in keeping with Kopytoff's description of commoditization as process. He suggests that the production of commodities is both cultural and cognitive; that is, commodities must not only be produced as objects, but also be culturally marked as being a certain kind of thing (Kopytoff 1986). It is these cultural markers which differentiate objects and activities, legitimizing them as the product of culturally valuable processes (the handmade) or essentially tradable and expendable commodities (mass-produced items).

It is interesting to note, then, that in their drive to establish themselves as both a commercial success and a sector leader, Etsy have partnered over and over again with the cultural sector, offering regular community evenings at local museums,[13] supporting special event markets,[14] creating opportunities for new product development in partnership with cultural institutions,[15] supporting the promotion of digitised artefacts to 'inspire both amateur and professional creatives around the world to manipulate and transform the original images through their work'[16] and ultimately winning a Smithsonian Cooper Hewitt National Design Museum Design Award[17] for their strategic use of design in their company mission.

This is an important partnership in the space of creative production. Museums offer trusted authoritative environments through which to explore new models of collaboration, knowledge production, dissemination and communication: to gather culturally diverse experiences and propose new models for co-creation and collaborations. By partnering with the Smithsonian to support community events and to create new product opportunities, Etsy demonstrated their willingness to contribute to social well-being and economic growth and, in doing so, demonstrated their commitment to maker communities while operating a successful commercial enterprise in a global market.

As a testament to their success, in April 2015, Etsy was able to launch itself onto the stock market achieving a valuation of US $3.5 billion.[18] This contested move brought with it debates about whether a company built on small-scale independent producers could deliver long-term shareholder profits.[19] In the midst of this debate, a more cautionary tale has arisen – artisanal sellers are increasingly frustrated by the company's decision to enable mass-manufactured items to be sold on its platform. This seems to be a direct response to the establishment of Etsy Manufacturing[20] – a service which draws small-scale designer-makers into a production and/or professional manufacturing context and promotes their manufacturing abilities as a fee-for service to other designers. While still in its Beta form, Etsy Manufacturing has the potential to radically transform the artisanal arena, offering both the conceptualization and the production of bespoke goods at small-to-medium scales such that creative producers are able to extend their reach into broader markets at a broader scale.

Yet Etsy Manufacturing has found itself with a larger and more highly attuned networked distribution platform as its competitor; in October 2015, Handmade at Amazon[21] was launched. With its twenty-year-old global network and approximately 285 million active customers versus Etsy's 22 million, Handmade at Amazon has the potential to radically transform the artisanal marketplace. Interestingly, unlike the path which Etsy has taken with Etsy Manufacturing, Amazon Handmade promotes itself as 'factory-free',[22] an assertion which, on the surface, offers assurance that the artisanal quality of its products will remain. It would appear that this insistence on 'factory-free' has arisen from a well-documented history of Etsy's less-than-effective definition of 'handmade'.[23] Over the years both buyers and sellers have expressed their frustration with the fluidity of the term and it would appear that Amazon Handmade is attempting to reframe that discussion to their advantage.

Beyond the definitions, there seem to be issues with the Amazon Handmade business model. Barker (2015) defines five characteristics which the two platforms share and explores whether creators benefit as a result. They are: Amazon is expensive (in specific comparison both to Etsy and to online selling in general); Amazon plays a very large part in the individual's pricing structure (something which Etsy does not involve itself with at all); the central tenet of Amazon is that it provides a marketplace of readily accessible, moderately priced items (the antithesis of the handmade product creation and manufacture ethos that underpins Etsy); Amazon owns the selling platform and, with it, the customer database (this is particularly antithetical to the small business owner trying to build up their own customer database); and, beyond the lack of definitions regarding handmade, Amazon has no history of supporting this community. It stands to be seen whether the venture will be successful.

As Whitehead (2016) suggests, Handmade at Amazon is structured such that their audience analytics is held by a third party with a potentially vested interest in securing these data for their own gain. As Handmade at Amazon has yet to establish itself fully, it is difficult to predict how these concerns may evolve, but suffice it to say that the sheer scale and power of Amazon may yet create a new transformation in the maker manufacturing and distribution market. Certainly what is already evident is that Handmade at Amazon has positioned itself not as a leader in the *handmade* arena but as a powerful, global *distribution* platform, thus doing away with the specific community and institutional partnerships that have enabled Etsy to position itself as a thought-leader in the sector.

Participatory supporters of making

In 2010, Botsman and Rogers (2010) made claim to a phenomenon in participation which had arisen as a result of evolving practices made possible by social media. They suggested that the notion of 'Collaborative Consumption' was made possible because participatory, networked media had connected previously disconnected individuals and global communities resulting in new economies, new communities and new forms of cultural exchange. They offered that the drivers for these changes were the convergence of two ideologies: a recognition that the way in which we live our lives was no longer sustainable and that individuals could benefit from, and therefore had a vested interest in, offering contributions to online communities. This assertion was in keeping with the OECD's 2007 characterization of the participative web as being driven by increased participation and interaction (OECD 2007, p. 8), and reflected O'Reilly's earlier attempt to clarify the distinctive features of the participative web, namely his belief that the key feature of Web 2.0 (social media) was its exploitation of collective intelligence (O'Reilly 2005). The capabilities described by O'Reilly and the programming practices and infrastructure built upon them provided the foundations and the impetus for Web 2.0's 'architecture of participation'.

Early examples of O'Reilly's collaborative participation could be seen in his creation of online design services which embedded broader networked interactions and which were poised to transform innovation in the design sector. His most successful was (and remains) the US-based Maker Media,[24] a global multiplatform distribution network which connects makers to each other and to new partners. Maker Media launched *Make* magazine in 2005 quickly followed by the first Maker Faire in 2006, as well as Maker Shed stores. For this reason, O'Reilly Media can be heralded as the company that 'jumpstarted' the global maker movement. The Maker Media influence has spawned a generation of co-creation, multiple user-participation design sites such as redesignme,[25] 99designs,[26] designbay[27] and Kluster[28] which linked designers with external partners and potential clients in public forums. Such systems recognized the value of co-creative collaborative networks in the further development of products or services.

Yet, for all their systematic partnering, these smaller subsets of online participation were not the enduring platforms of collaborative production or consumption. As designers and creative producers began collaboratively developing products online with the aim of enhancing sustainability in communities and strengthening social bonds in urban contexts, it became clear that the end users, stakeholders, audiences or 'the crowd' were to become the linchpin to future commercial success. As a result, while the models for online participation in the support and purchase of products became evermore clarified,[29] the ways in which makers either led projects or built capacity by increasing networks remained limited. It was into this complex conundrum that the notion of crowdsourcing (Howe 2009) would grow to become an embedded practice of distributed problem-solving which would drive significant audience participation in the development, manufacturing and promotion of new products and services. Crowdsourcing could harness the creativity of an online community to collect, evolve and rank ideas and contributions in a public forum. This would result in changes to the ways in which audiences connected with organizations and individuals, creating new ways in which participants were to be considered partners within the design process.

Today, crowdsourcing underpins design testbeds such as Kickstarter,[30] a global online forum which offers budding entrepreneurs the ability to market test their design solutions and raise funds towards the next stage of product/service development, whether that be manufacturing, distribution or promotion. Kickstarter is now the global leader in a market of multiple crowdsourcing sites which attempt to reconfigure the relationship between audiences and small and medium enterprises. The key to the Kickstarter platform is that it offers evidence of the potential take-up of small-scale products along with the possible longer-term loyalty of the distribution market, thus reducing the risk for small-scale designers and makers. Kickstarter asks potential project creators to upload enduring and endearing digital content such as videos which will capture audience attention – images and ideas which will lead them to 'pledge' to support the further development of a product or service. In seeking pledges, Kickstarter entrepreneurs develop a ready-made audience base and preliminary sales, both of which, when analysed, provide invaluable potential audience data prior to major (and risky) investments in product development. From the deceptively simple Prepd Pack – The Lunchbox Reimagined[31] ($25,000 goal – at the time of writing funded @ $606,990 with 5,571 pledgers and 17 days to go – 9 February 2016) to potentially less-successful campaigns,[32] Kickstarter and other crowdsourced funding sites provide evidence of the emergent symbiotic relationship necessary in order to ensure that making practices are embedded all the way through new modes of knowledge production.

Institutional supporters of maker culture

While commercial successes such as Etsy and Kickstarter have reconfigured relationships between makers and audiences, they have done so with specific commercial outcomes at their heart. Participatory learning has enabled them to establish themselves as sector leaders, but, as Handmade at Amazon demonstrates, this commitment to knowledge production can recede into the background once global scale has been achieved. Within this context the central tenets of the maker movement, namely the willingness to create and share new knowledge, could potentially disappear over time. However, unlike commercial entities, cultural institutions have demonstrated their commitment to participatory learning, particularly in the development of digital literacies which contribute to the semiformal and informal learning environment.[33] This has occurred in tandem with the notion of public value and community well-being facilitated by museums being factored into major policy goals alongside health, education and the economy (Ander et al. 2011). Scholars have addressed how participation in cultural production and distribution lends weight to community engagement (for example, Kidd 2011), while others have sought to interrogate the value of museums engaging in well-being initiatives (Ander et al. 2011; Association 2013), yet the question of how museums might emerge as leaders in this process through a repositioning of their own practices remain unanswered.

As a starting point, museums have a long history of engagement through scholarship which has developed through participatory research and culminates in collections, skills and knowledge which provide a basis from which to encourage audiences and visitors alike to experiment and produce new works. Proceeding from this basis, the support of maker cultures within the museum must thus first meet the remit of scholarship and then seek to connect and collaborate with their communities through that scholarship. Finally, it must link this investigation with the dissemination of knowledge through learning programmes. Historically, this role was achieved by re-conceptualizing the museum from Temple or Forum and into an 'agora'.[34] That is, a space – both physical and virtual – which established dialogue through collections and brought those collections to the public through exhibitions and publications. In this way the museum formalized the relationship between the centrality of curatorial knowledge in the cultural contract between audience and institution.

Therefore, to consider the maker culture within museums, we must consider both the scholarly and the operational encounters which occur within these sites of investigation. Operationally, establishing museum-led makerspaces offers access to facilities such as computing, data modelling, 3D printing and prototyping, which allows individuals and museums alike to conduct research and disseminate the results of that research simultaneously. It is possible therefore that the theoretical and practical drivers which underpin the development of maker communities can be formalized and tested within cultural institutions. Museums have a global reach, extensive public outreach and education programmes, and highly committed networks and partnerships which offer further collaborations and relationships. Additionally, museums are highly connected and invested in government policy and therefore have the ability to test new practices and advocate in public forums. This allows them to focus discussion on how to creatively engage collaborative networks in the development of new products, services and experiences, particularly in the public and social innovation sectors. Therefore, making which is inspired by, made within and promoted through the cultural sector has the potential to offer new models for future end-user engagement in product and service development.

Made in the Museum: Museums as creative incubators

The notion of making through or with a cultural institution is not new. Such processes are often described and presented through exhibitions, public programs, education and outreach. What makes the potential role of the institution of the museum distinct in the case of maker communities is the reciprocal relationship which can be established – one where both institution and maker contribute to broader questions and together achieve a scale that results in new design solutions. As we have seen, participation in the maker realm extends across multiple technologies and sites, yet the extent to which this transformation affects their pedagogical underpinnings has yet to be fully determined.

If cultural institutions are to build mutual understandings in future communities and to inspire creative engagement through informal learning, then they too will need to find new ways to engage with a radically transformed learning environment. In the future, the complexity of digital literacy will extend to access and familiarity with high-level technological fabrication tools such as 3D printers, robotics and 3D modelling–based applications. Such technologies, while increasingly available at the domestic level, will necessarily require support by larger institutions if small-scale makers are to have access in order to develop their skills and future products and services.

An example would be the Smithsonian's Cooper Hewitt National Design Museum's (CHNDM) innovative exhibition entitled *Design for the Other 90%*,[35] which provoked discussions around the ways institutions and individuals address poverty through design innovations. The objects selected for the exhibition were examples of technologies that could be re-considered to achieve design solutions to provide low-cost effective solutions to benefit poor and marginalized communities. Projects which illustrated these central tenets included 'World Bike Prototype'[36] designed with high carrier capacity; the 'Solar Home Lighting System',[37] a wireless solar power system designed for rural and peri-urban users in India; and the 'Katrina Furniture Project',[38] which created furniture-making workshop facilities that used the storm debris to build furniture while building local economic and social capacity.

Design for the Other 90% (2007) offered a window into how maker communities could use their practices to explore broader social issues leading to national and international advantage and demonstrated how small-scale maker activities in the social innovation realm could be distributed and promoted in partnership with the museum to mutual benefit. *Design for the Other 90%* presented a unique example of how museums can use second-generation web or the 'participative web[39]' to connect communities and individuals to achieve a 'greater good' through innovative design solutions.

Another way in which this could occur can be seen at the New Museum in the United States, which, in 2014, opened a new facility called NEW INC[40]: the first museum-led incubator. This not-for-profit initiative offers co-working space, incubators, accelerators, connections to networks and privileged access to curators, to collection materials and to partners. Central to this is the idea of the museum as a cultural incubator, embedded in education and working with the community. NEW INC positions itself as a cultural institution and a civic leader: it establishes forums, drawing people together to discuss big issues in contemporary society. It offers an example of how cultural institutions can catalyse engagement in the world and participation in culture to educate through making. As this chapter is completed, the Australian Centre for the Moving Image (ACMI) in Melbourne, Australia, has just launched a new co-working space ACMI-X, which in some aspects mirrors the resources and infrastructure offered by NEW INC and Mahuki. The Innovation Incubator[41] has just opened at Te Papa, The National Museum of New Zealand.

The pedagogical underpinnings of the NEW INC initiative (with its focus on art-related start-ups and digital artists) suggests a focus on 'STEAM' education, that is, educational approaches which bring together science, technology, engineering and mathematics (STEM) and bring in 'the arts' (science, technology, engineering, the arts and mathematics – STEAM) as access points for guiding student inquiry, dialogue and critical thinking (EducationCloset 2014). Central to this encounter is the ability for students and educators to co-create through reflective processes occurring around the iteration of concepts and outcomes. Such iterative processes often require multidisciplinary knowledge, particularly when exploring non-discipline specific problems. Therefore, in considering the museum as creative incubator, it would appear that partnerships can be created which explore how 'making' and 'tinkering' (Tocchetti 2015) are processes which contribute to broader learning in STEM education.

Following on from these early examples, we are witnessing multiple projects which explore the connection between makers and museums while emphasizing collaborative relations as a source of content creation to create social change.[42] Yet, somewhat like the Etsy example cited earlier, for makers to achieve greater scale, they require specific skills in collaborative networking and strategic environments where they can test this interaction without being exposed to high commercial risk. Museums provide these environments and, perhaps for this reason, are increasingly making tentative steps into a new space, one where they provide the infrastructure, scholarly engagement and privileged access to their collections, networks and resources in order to support innovative participant maker initiatives. Emergent research across the sectors of education, museum studies, design and communication suggests that there are three central themes which would coalesce around the notion of museum as creative incubators: skill development, convergent literacies and DIY citizenship.

Skill development

In the early days of crowdsourcing, service design[43] became a convergent area of practice where design services became consumer products. Design practices which had previously relied on trusted, physical relationships built over time, for instance, graphic design and web design services, were challenged by the now global opportunities afforded by new digital platforms. Innovations such as Quirky[44] and Elancers[45] (now Upwork) provided, for the first time, a global marketplace, where clients could connect with hundreds or thousands of designers by uploading a brief and calling on designers to respond. Unlike the traditional practice of securing a design firm to provide graphic design collateral, these new platforms enabled clients, designers and makers to connect with global audiences in the development and promotion of their products and services. Within these forums individuals could gain and promote their agency by uploading their portfolios and user comments of their works. This public-facing global workforce could then confront issues of sustainability, social inclusion and accessibility to create systems and services as required. Makers had become a commodity, and those who were best able to explain the maker processes were able to mobilize both latent and real literacies to create new pedagogies for creative prototyping.

This was made particularly visible in the Shapeways Marketplace, where designer/makers began to offer their products and establish their global credentials by embracing customization.[46] Today, designers/makers upload their designs and offer customized manufacturing of their creative artefacts based on materials which have been tested with the specific design. Thus, the designers/

makers' digital literacy and ability to manipulate both the design and the final manufactured object has become an important commodity in the offer of their services. The greater the customization they can offer, the more valuable the service becomes. As service design often straddles commercial and social sectors, its ability to develop and strengthen the knowledge and expertise in the practice of innovation offers an intriguing encounter through which to host and support exploratory collaborative design services. This has already been tested at a commercial and institutional scale through MuseumMade,[47] a global online retail environment that draws together museum products from around the world to sell them in a single platform, but it remains under-developed in relation to maker activities and outcomes.

Convergent literacies

Communities of making have grown exponentially as individuals have increasingly sought to extend their own knowledge by connecting with others online. Platforms such as Ravelry[48] or Instructables[49] explore the relationship between handmade design as a space of social production and one of participation in DIY citizenship supported by online engagement. In both cases, audiences share their 'maker' knowledge by uploading replicable patterns which others test and rate. For instance, Instructables currently hosts the pattern and documentation to build the first 3D-printed electronic circular knitting machine. The documentation for this machine, designed by artists Varvara and Mar, has been made available to a global audience, thus establishing local knowledge and innovation with global networks. By hosting this documentation, Instructables reconfigures the relationship between innovation and commercial production by making 'the social act of sharing' (Wolf et al. 2013) central to knowledge dissemination. Instructables have established their credentials as a platform which supports a granular and hard-won need to catalyse maker activity. Their platform allows for multigenerational knowledge exchange, acknowledging this as an appropriate space through which to explore how makers can contribute to global economies and the impact of this collaboration on local industries. Partnering with makers in this way, Instructables offers highly skilled crafting individuals and communities a forum through which to explore the sustainability of their processes while it promotes and makes visible its underlying tenets of inclusion and intergenerational learning (Maidment and Macfarlane 2011).

DIY citizenship

The notion of DIY citizenship seems to occur and reoccur as each new digital transformation is announced (Media et al. 2014; Hargraeves and Hartley 2016; Hawkes 2001; Russo 2011; Hartley 2000; Daily 1999). As digital platforms have become more sophisticated, DIY citizenship has extended to the convergence of physical and virtual objects and has been framed by notions of critical making (Ratto and Boler 2014). This is in keeping with Bell, Wakeford and Fischer (2008), who illustrate the ways design can address issues of social justice and allow individuals and communities to plan and improve their own lives.

Throughout these paradigmatic shifts, the role of cultural organizations as authoritative environments through which to explore questions of citizenship through the reinvigoration of traditional skills with a broad range of digital literacies has remained. For instance, institutional collaborations with social designers[50] offer a unique community through which to explore large-scale issues of future DIY citizenship. In these instances, social design practices focus on improving well-being by considering how design decisions impact on all users throughout the product or service lifecycle. Such considerations are central to institutional remits as both custodians of traditional cultural practices and leaders in the interpretation and contextualization of such practices. Cultural institutions are thus well positioned as forums for the discussion of an 'active' and critical making process. Similarly, 'design as activism' (Bell, Wakeford and Fischer 2008) communities are thus appropriate partners for explorations into collaborations with museums: as their breadth of concern for environmental, civic and social issues are often manifest and illustrated through cultural collections. Across multiple areas of investigation, it would appear that, as Ting (2015) asserts, 'the notion of DIY citizenship signals a shift in the possibilities of civic and political participation in which citizens assume active roles as social interventionists' (2015: 294–95).

Conclusion

This chapter has been offered as an illustration of some of the ways in which new places of making are linked to new modes of knowledge production and emergent creative practices. From FabLabs through makerspaces and to cultural and creative incubators, each site-specific exploratory space challenges our understandings of encounters between practice and knowledge production. The chapter has aimed to demonstrate how, when and where we, as audiences, have come to accept the dynamic of these encounters. At the same time, it has held a lens to our understanding of the granularity of these encounters, the complex and subtle practices that form them and the ways in which we grapple with their novel outcomes.

The projects introduced go some way to demonstrating the opportunities for increased value and benefit derived from these encounters, often formed through collaborative co-creation and multiplatform distribution. They offer cases for conceptualizing the creative learning afforded by strategically linking existing cultural resources with entrepreneurial individuals. These cases provide preliminary evidence of the types and location of new knowledge made possible by establishing an ecosystem of interdisciplinary creators, appropriate infrastructure and attenuated forms of engagement. It is perhaps no accident that these early examples demonstrate characteristics of what Gibbons et al. (1994) would call Mode 2 learning, that is, a commitment to socially distributed, application-oriented, transdisciplinary knowledge production that offers a way of both conceptualizing and framing interdisciplinary problems relevant to contemporary society (1994, p. 9). While these cases have aimed to expose the complexity of their encounters, they have yet to provide substantive evidence of the potential for strategically networked maker production beyond the scale of the individual. As we move towards scaling these encounters, we cross a conceptual threshold from maker to manufacturer. In doing so, we must consider the challenges that will arise, particularly as we extend maker practices into a broader commercial and cultural ecosystem.

It is impossible to consider the dynamics of these opportunities without understanding the wider context of professional and production manufacturing in our age. Therefore, these cases, irrespective of whether they are enduring examples of how the thresholds between maker activities and broader manufacturing might be established, provide us with a taste of how expansive and distributed this sector will become. As a result, any mechanism for developing or distributing these encounters must accept other existing platforms, and should ideally seek to bring them to draw them out and connect them to each other, thus building sustainable and economically viable pathways through new knowledge production. Shaping of the physical environment of the future FabLabs, makersspaces and cultural/creative incubators will necessarily be informed by digital cultures and digitality, information-seeking practices, maker and manufacturer expectations, novel partnerships and the ways in which all forms of media come to distil and communicate these practices to a broader audience.

The chapter began by offering that digital transformation at the level of both design and manufacture would necessarily require a reconfiguration of knowledge production and exchange, research collaboration, product development, distribution and promotion. It has been my intention to describe an arc which could credibly address the two central questions by offering museums as trusted authoritative cultural environments which could support creative activities as the catalyst for the development of new forms of emergent maker practices. In doing so, the complex relationships between makers, manufacturers, institutions and audiences have been investigated. They have been explored while considering the possibility of how these relationships become part of an extended ecosystem of makerspaces – beyond individual spaces and into the virtual realm where others encounter our products and services and, in turn, those creative artefacts become the extension of the makerspace, both physically and virtually, expressed as individual and collective experiences across multiple platforms online. The mechanics of these encounters for the basis of the proposition for this chapter and their investigation provide us with a framework for planning future social experiences where we can rehearse some of the rudimentary basics for the programming of future maker spaces. The future has yet to be made.

Notes

1 Maker Faire is the proprietary name for a showcase event developed by Maker Media. Maker Faire gathers together people who enjoy learning and sharing their knowledge. www.makerfaire.com

2 https://www.whitehouse.gov/nation-of-makers

3 http://www.fabfoundation.org/2014/06/the-fab-foundation-launches-new-fab-labs-in-the-us-with-generous-grant-from-chevron/

4 https://www.fablabs.io/

5 www.flickr.com

6 www.youtube.com

7 http://www.readymade.com/

8 http://www.papress.com/other/designityourself/index.html

9 http://www.investopedia.com/articles/personal-finance/032615/how-youtube-ad-revenue-works.asp

10   www.etsy.com

11   http://larchmontchronicle.com/crafters-decorate-shoes-gift-boxes-at-museum-workshop/

12   Brotherhood of St Laurence – Mapping the Clothing Manufacture Industry

13   http://larchmontchronicle.com/crafters-decorate-shoes-gift-boxes-at-museum-workshop/

14   http://www.leeds.gov.uk/Events/Pages/etsy-made-local-leeds-christmas-market.aspx

15   https://blog.etsy.com/en/inspired-by-the-american-museum-of-natural-history/

16   http://www.theglobeandmail.com/life/fashion-and-beauty/fashion/want-to-add-fine-art-to-your-own-
     designs-this-museum-and-etsy-let-you-do-it-free/article20644892/

17   http://www.smithsonianmag.com/smithsonian-institution/cooper-hewitt-gets-crafty-honors-etsy-
     national-design-award-180951273/?no-ist

18   http://www.theaustralian.com.au/business/technology/the-markets-a-hard-art-for-etsy/news-story/
     71871f25bf412b462b9cbcca44936fa1

19   http://www.theaustralian.com.au/business/technology/the-markets-a-hard-art-for-etsy/news-story/
     71871f25bf412b462b9cbcca44936fa1

20   https://blog.etsy.com/news/2015/etsy-manufacturing-opens-to-designers/

21   http://www.businessinsider.com.au/data-on-amazon-handmade-is-etsy-killer-2015-10

22   http://www.businesswire.com/news/home/20151008005326/en/#.VhbTgLRVhBc

23   http://www.luckybreakconsulting.com/blog/the-problem-with-selling-on-handmade-at-amazon/

24   http://makermedia.com/

25   http://www.redesignme.com/

26   http://99designs.com/

27   http://www.designbay.com/

28   http://www.kluster.com/buy/features

29   For instance, sites such as eBay which rely on maintaining a good reputation as a seller,
     or Amazon, where independent book reviews contribute both to the general knowledge
     surrounding products and to the sale of those products

30   https://www.kickstarter.com/

31   https://www.kickstarter.com/projects/prepd/prepd-pack

32   https://www.kickstarter.com/projects/1819959388/the-box-bike-collective-all-purpose-cargo-
     bicycles?ref=nav_search

33   http://www.dream.dk/?q=en/content/welcome

34   Duncan Cameron's classic 1971 article, The Museum: A Temple or the Forum

35   http://other90.cooperhewitt.org/

36   http://www.designother90.org/solution/worldbike-prototype/

37   http://www.designother90.org/solution/solar-home-lighting-system/

38   http://www.designother90.org/solution/katrina-furniture-project/

39   'Participative web' can be dated from shortly after 2000, although the term Web 2.0 was not
     coined by Tim O'Reilly and Dale Dougherty until 2004.

40

41   http://www.stuff.co.nz/business/78980970/Te-Papa-invests-1m-in-Mahuki-business-innovation-hub

42   See for instance Mahuki @ Tepapa The National Museum of New Zealand http://www.mahuki.org/

43   http://www.service-design-network.org/

44 www.quirky.com

45 www.elancers.com

46 http://www.shapeways.com/product/SNLF5VPCF/spilled-tea-ring-size-6?li=related-items-km&optionId=55454096

47 http://www.museummade.com/

48 www.ravelry.com

49 http://www.instructables.com/

50 www.socialdesignsite.com

References

Ander, E., L. Thomson, G. Noble, A. Lanceley, U. Menon, and H. Chatterjee (2011) 'Generic Well-Being Outcomes : Towards a Conceptual Framework for Well-Being Outcomes in Museums', *Museum Management and Curatorship* 26 (3): 237–59.

Anderson, C. (2007), *The Long Tail: How Endless Choice is Creating Unlimited Demand*, London: Random House.

Anderson, C. (2012), *Makers: The New Industrial Revolution*. New York: Random House.

Australia Council for the Arts (2014), *Arts in Daily Life: Australian Participation*. Canberra: Australian Government.

Barker, L. (2015), 'The Problem with Selling on Handmade at Amazon', *Lucky Break Consulting.* http://www.luckybreakconsulting.com/blog/the-problem-with-selling-on-handmade-at-amazon/.

Bell, B., K. Wakeford, and T. Fischer. (2008), *Expanding Architecture. Design as Activism*. New York: Metropolis Books.

Botsman, R., and R. Rogers. (2010), *What's Mine is Yours: The Rise of Collaborative Consumption.* New York: Harper Business.

Daily, The. (1999), 'Critical News Making and the Paradox of "Do-It-Yourself News ."'

Dougherty, D. (2012), 'The maker movement', *Innovations: Technology, Governance, Globalization* 7 (3): 11–14.

Gibbons, M., C. Limogoes, H. Nowotny, S. Schwatzman, P. Scott, and M. Trow (1994), *The New Production of Knowledge: The Dynamics of Science and Research in Contemporary Societies.* London: Sage.

Hargraeves, I., and J. Hartley, ed. (2016), *The Creative Citizen Unbound How Social Media and Diy Culture Contribute to Democracy, Communities and the Creative Economy.* Bristol: Policy Press.

Hartley, J. (2000), 'Sound and citizenship', *International Journal of Cultural Studies* 3 (2): 153–9.

Hawkes, J. (2001), *The Fourth Pillar of Sustainability: Culture's Essential Role in Public Planning*, Melbourne: http://www.culturaldevelopment.net.au/community/Downloads/HawkesJon(2001)TheFourthPillarOfSustainability.pdf

Howe, J. (2009), *Crowdsourcing: Why the Power of the Crowd Is Driving the Future of Business.* New York: Crown Business.

Kidd, J. (2011), 'Review Article Challenging History : Reviewing Debate within the Heritage Sector on the 'Challenge' of History', *Museums and Society* 9 (3): 244–8.

Kopytoff, I. (1986), 'The cultural biography of things: Commoiditization as process', in *The Social Life of Things: Commodities in Cultural Perspective*, edited by Arjun Appadurai, 64–91. Cambridge: Cambridge University Press.

Lindtner, S., and D. Li. (2012), 'Created in China: The Makings of China's Hackerspace Community', *Interactions* 19: 18–22.

Maidment, J., and S. Macfarlane (2011), *Crafting Communities: Promoting Inclusion, Empowerment and Learning between Older Women*, London: Routledge.

Museums Association (2013), '*Public Perceptions of – and Attitudes to – the Purposes of Museums in Society*'. London.

O'Reilly, T. (2005), 'What Is Web 2.0 Design: Patterns and Business Models for the Next Generation of Software', *Tim O'Reilly and John Battelle Answer the Question of 'What's next for Web 2.0?'* 1–15.

OECD. (2007), 'Working Party of the Information Economy. Participative Web: User-Created Content', Paris. http://www.oecd.or/dataoecd/57/14/38393115.pdf.

Pang, L. K. (2012), *Creativity and Its Discontents: China's Creative Industries and Intellectual Property Rights Offenses*. Durham, NC: Duke University Press.

Quinlan, O. (2015), 'Young Digital Makers. Surveying Attitudes and Opportunities for Digital Creativity across the UK', London: www.nesta.org.uk.

Ratto, M., and M. Boler, eds. (2014), *DIY Citizenship Critical Making and Social Media*. Cambridge, MA: MIT Press.

Rosner, D. K., and K. Ryokai. (2009), 'Reflections on Craft: Probing the Creative Process of Everyday Knitters', in, Proceedings of the seventh ACM conference on creativity and cognition. Berkeley, CA: ACM. 195–204.

Russo, A. (2011), 'Transformations in cultural communication: Social media, cultural exchange, and creative connections', *Curator: The Museum Journal* 54 (3): 327–46.

Ting, T-Y. (2015), 'Book Review. DIY Citizenship: Critical Making and Social Media, Edited by Matt Ratto and Megan Boler', *The Information Society* 31 (3): 294–5.

Tocchetti, S. (2015), 'Diybiologists as ' Makers 'of Personal Biologies : How Make Magazine and Maker Faires Contribute in Constituting Biology as a Person', *Journal of Peer Production* (2): 1–10.

Whitehead, S. (2016), 'Why Isn't Anyone Talking About the Most Frightening Part of Amazon Handmade?', *The Huffington Post*. http://www.huffingtonpost.com/shannon-whitehead/why-isnt-anyone-talking-a_1_b_8288806.html.

Wolf, P., P. Troxler, P-Y. Kocher, J. Harboe, and U. Gaudenz. (2013), 'Sharing Is Sparing : Open Knowledge Sharing in Fab Labs 1 Knowledge Sharing in the Global Fab Lab Community : A Literature Review', (Hess 2008): 1–11.

19

The post digital

Contemporary making and the allure of the genuine

Keith Doyle, Hélène Day Fraser and Philip Robbins

Material Matters is an active research centre operating from within the Intersections Digital Studios of Emily Carr University of Art + Design. It explores the interchange of new digital fabrication technologies, legacy material ecologies and traditional material production processes through design and craft practice–led methodologies. As digital content creation technologies develop, they are becoming increasingly accessible and broadly capable of creating numerous alternate pathways for visualization, prototyping and material production. 3D printing plays a significant role within this endeavour. As an emergent production technology, it has experienced explosive growth in scale, distribution and application. A rapid vertical industry consolidation has also led to widespread lateral proliferation of cost-effective means to adapt and employ this technology. This expansion, coupled with the enthusiastic uptake from an engaged, open source-minded community, has catalysed a generative, socialization of knowledge, markedly lowered the barrier to personal application and greatly broadened the base of expertise. While the increased proliferation of cost-effective 3D print technologies worldwide might indicate a looming saturation of innovation, new avenues and methods of making continue to emerge. As a site of active material inquiry, Material Matters pursues a diverse range of conceptually interlinked research projects that apply this new personal production platform to more traditional methods of making; this chapter examines some of our most recent work.

Local versus distributed

We are exploring the implications of pairing this new and seemingly complementary technology – additive manufacturing (more commonly known as 3D printing) – with traditional methods of making found in ceramics, glass, metal casting and textile production. Our work seeks to develop meaningful new pathways to making through a hybridized digital/analogue workflow, conflating the efficiencies within these new digital opportunities and the inherent strengths of legacy process/ knowledge. Seen as a symbiotic method rather than a rigid choice between a local or distributed material knowledge, our work examines how this new technological means can interconnect, reconnect and carry forward legacy processes rather than simply supplanting or displacing them. This route has led to the creation of interstitial artefacts, things that exist somewhere between the handmade and the digital, and somewhere between local and distributed centres of knowing. As researchers and creative practitioners we confront these points of fissure and friction, exploring pathways that intersect, diverge and reconnect, affording the opportunity to develop new material authenticities.

The craft economy (local)

At its core the craft economy is built upon very particular forms of production; craft processes require high levels of skill and an intimate, tacit knowledge of materials and methods by an experienced practitioner. Craft production's high degree of technical knowledge and material specialization, over time, forms a tightly linked synthesis of material, process and individual. Craft production comes to embody an individual; the mark of the maker, and an ethos; the embrace of material and method.

Though craft production is emblematic of an individual's technical mastery, it also fosters a distinct irony. A craft object is highly localized in its fabrication, highly individualized, produced for consumption in low numbers and indelibly associated with an individual practitioner. This apparent anti-mass production, regional, egalitarian economy has tended to produce expensively unobtainable, elitist objects directly at odds with the innate premise of their production; this greatly narrows crafts' accessibility. It was this paradox that undermined the Arts and Crafts Movement of the 1880s for then, as now, if a craft object cannot attain a high enough market price to justify the skill, time, materials and effort to produce it, it teeters on the edge of economic viability. For craft production, this has proved to be a pervasive and persistent problem.

Additive manufacturing (distributed)

Additive manufacturing technologies, a process of a successive layering of material to make a 3D object, are built upon an extremely fluid digital infrastructure that allows for a level of public participation and interaction that is unprecedented. Powerful computer systems, affordable, full-featured 3D modelling programmes and high-speed communication networks allow for the design, production, sharing and refinement of any aspect of 3D printing architecture (Robbins, Doyle and Day Fraser 2014). An open source–minded community is driving the consolidation and subsequent re-contextualizing of knowledge connected to making, and a new paradigm is subsequently developing through the easy combining of legacy production with digital means. Further, Open Source Appropriate Technology (OSAT) (Pearce 2012) and the widespread search for increasing economy in material cost, selection and ecological impact are rapidly re-defining what it means to have a sustainable small-scale personal production platform (Robbins, Doyle and Day Fraser 2014).

Making do

As makers in contemporary society we have the opportunity to reposition our expertise, to ask ourselves how we might re-situate and re-contextualize local *making* knowledge through distributed personal production platforms. Contemporary reflective approaches in both design and material practice act as a means to identify an evolving connection between new digital and established analogue processes. We are aware that how we approach our craft and craft's implicit relationship to the individual ultimately affects the way objects are perceived (Nimkultrat 2010). In this context of concurrent digital/analogue methodologies, authenticity is achieved through reproduction and serialization by the maker, incorporating an implicit reflexive process of fluid design and manufacture by re invention or copy, made real and made material. Fluid processes of 3D digital design and rendering on the screen enable a particular knowledge of the artefact – literally, the knowing inside and out. When craft sensibilities and local knowledge in legacy processes are also applied, they stabilize and lend cultural import to 3D-printed interstitial objects. Using this technology to create in a manner that is both pertinent and genuine to contemporary practice is, however, not always evident.

3D printing is a highly adaptable form-generation tool that is capable of producing remarkably complex objects in a wide range of materials. The direct production of form it facilitates is often decoupled from the manual skills and tacit material knowledge implicit to craft. This transition produces an unexpected, enticing but also problematic aesthetic phenomenon. For when 3D printing is used to its greatest capability – freely complex geometry – it produces objects that begin to look unsettlingly the same. These artefacts bear the hallmarks of the method and none of the maker. This is the very antithesis of an *authentic* process.

Making is political act. *Making* has evolved from early forms of contravention and disruption of the status quo (in the case of the open source movement itself; this is evident in the processes of hacking and hacktivism) (von Busch 2008). It has evolved to inhabit a new cultural norm, a new germane social enterprise starting with hactivist actions and movements (von Busch 2008), through the easy facilitation of new social-economies of scale centred on the creation and small-scale production and distribution of material goods (3Dhubs). Today's makerspaces are incubators of invention much like more established institutions before them. In contrast, however, they also serve to facilitate a meaningful cultural and material production that incorporates distributed technology and local expertise. OSATs (Pearce 2012), such as the personal 3D printer (Tinkerine *Studio Ditto Pro*, etc.), serve as fluid platforms for knowledge creation and expressive maker production. OSAT affords and underscores new social configurations whereby makers can determine the autonomous application of labour towards production through shared local resources and the mutual interest of the localized knowledge base (Shorthose and Strange 2004).

In addition to design intent, skill or technological capacity, many printed objects tend to be limited by budgetary considerations. This observation has affected our exploratory practice. Intent on lowering the cost and making the technology more accessible, we have sought to replicate and replace costly industry-based 3D printing consumables. A case study, detailed in 2014, outlined how we developed local criteria, which were then applied to a test regime designed to facilitate the replication of the required print medium characteristics (resolution, build density, reliability) (Robbins, Doyle and Day Fraser 2014). These cost-effective strategies have served as a seed, a nudge towards developing our own appropriate technologies, a new distributed knowledge, affecting the development of our own OSATs and research appliances. They have also led us to develop new refined methodologies for making.

The following section will detail our recent work along two avenues: ceramics and textiles. We will provide two case studies that highlight new OSAT printing developments at our labs and their relationship to ceramic-based processes (encaustic tile production) and textiles (extruded surface printing) as initial proof of concept work tying the inherent build quality of filament-based 3D printers with traditional woven/knit/sewn textiles.

Case study one: Digital encaustic tile production

One of the greatest signifiers of the craft marketplace is the direct lineage back to an individual maker and that maker's direct connection to an object's production. How is it possible to maintain this tangible, visceral allure and at the same time address the conflicting polarity between the rarefied, elitist object and the hegemony of the generic, mass-produced? We are situated at a time of interesting transition. The maker's means of production are in dynamic flux, rapidly shifting and scaling with novel production ecosystems in ascendancy. Technological means that until very recently required massive outlays of capital and the marshalling of armies of knowledge can now be purchased, placed upon a desktop and mastered within a remarkably short space of time. Machines can be made, reimagined and remade easily; their plans and parts shared effortlessly, their original purposes radically altered. Digital methods have come to encapsulate levels of skill previously acquired over a lifetime of diligence. Within all of this mechanical commotion, it is worthwhile considering where and how the maker's trace is located? How might we afford and retain legitimate links to a digitally mediated process? In the 1830s Minton & Co. began the industrial production of encaustic ceramic tiles with intricate, crisp, richly coloured and highly varied patterns inlaid into their surfaces. Minton tiles quickly became a mainstay of Victorian interiors, and a distinctly beautiful hallmark of a highly craft-conscious yet industrious era. Encaustic tile production forms the basis of this investigation into synthesizing a meaningful method from the hybridization of the emergent and legacy.

Encaustic tiles were produced through a multistep process that oscillates between the highly skilled and labour-intensive, to the semi-mechanical and semi-automated (see Figure 19.1). This process began with a repeating tile pattern carefully produced on paper. The pattern was then accurately reproduced in strips of sheet metal, bent and soldered to form closed cells. This collection of loose cells was then oriented, clustered and fixed into place, producing the tooling utilized in final tile production. This tooling acted as a precise multi-segment mould wherein various coloured liquid clay slips were introduced, backed with moist powdered clay, compressed under great pressure via hydraulic press, resulting in flat, stable, intricately detailed and brightly coloured tiles. The initial transition of this process, from paper pattern to soldered cells, required

FIGURE 19.1 L-R from top left (1) pigmented cement, (2) 3D-printed frame in tile form, (3) 3D-printed frame filled with tinted cement, (4) remaining form filled with damp cement, (5) the tile press, (6) tile removed from press. Photograph Philip Robbins.

considerable skill and care in order to replicate the original paper pattern seamlessly and create accurate metal cells that would register with other tiles regardless of their orientation.

The production process described above, from filling the cells to removal from the press, was quick and efficient, taking only a few minutes, but there was a distinct bottleneck. The initial preparation of tooling patterns was dependent on refined manual skills. The desired design complexity of patterns could easily run counter to available metalworking skill. To this day, this imposes a limit on the dynamics of the tooling and by extension the capabilities of the overall process. It is worthwhile to consider the contemporary opportunities and frictions here between traditional tooling (tediously exacting, laborious and somewhat creatively limiting); the manufacturing workflow (quick, simple and highly efficient); the requirements of an intermediate craft process (metalworking – constraining the overall process); and the insertion of digital workflows (affording a new type of efficiency and creative fluidity).

Fused Deposition Modeling – a form of additive manufacture (3D printing) – utilizes plastic filament to methodically recreate slices of an object, systematically extruding and depositing material layer by layer. This high fidelity process, driven by 2D or 3D data, can produce objects with very narrow cross sections and, as a result, can easily replicate the cell structures of encaustic tile's metal tooling (see Figure 19.2). Additionally, as initial patterns are designed and produced quickly, accurately and inexpensively, this vertically integrated process (2D sketch, translates to vector sketch, translates to 3D model, translates to 3D print), creates a highly fluid, iterative workflow enabling the reinterpretation of traditional designs as well creating new opportunities for pattern creation not possible through traditional methods alone.

FIGURE 19.2 Encaustic tile frame. Photograph Philip Robbins.

This considered form of re-skilling, or perhaps more accurately, skill-shifting, allows for design intents to be more easily achieved, or in fact expanded, without significantly compromising the place of the maker. By carefully positioning the entry and exit points of digital technology within a traditional craft, the 'authentic' material result of traditional process need not be radically altered. By placing the efficiency and elasticity of a digital method at the pinch point of a traditional craft distinctly new opportunities emerge.

Case study two: 3D printing and traditional textile substrates

Similar to the introduction of the sewing machine (in its day, once a new technology) and its indirect links to women's social and labour rights movements of the twentieth century, we are interested in the 3D printer's capacity to subvert existing strategies and assumptions pertaining to making. A segment of our work looks at the possibilities for redirecting the formal economies of commerce and growth towards more sustainable situations. Our approach to this domain has been to develop means of augmenting and amplifying novel qualities connected to existing textile technology and their derivative artefacts. Rather than supplementing the deep, layered, and nuanced expertise already connected to the production of textiles and textile based products, through autonomous labour we wonder what role additive manufacturing might play in potentially reframing elements of our making and consumption patterns. The three examples cited below are very early stage explorations in this domain connected to a current three-year research study: cloTHING(s) as conversation.

A textile is a flat surface/substrate that does not attain three dimensions (or form) until it has been manipulated through construction. In conventional modes of production (whether it be bespoke, small- or large-scale production), textile forms are built out of this flat plane. Fabric off the roll is manipulated via hand construction, or by applying machine and hand in tandem. More recent innovations in knitting and weaving technologies have facilitated the production of three-dimensional forms that are created directly as the cloth – the textile – is formed. It is significant to note that textile product construction, in whatever forms it may take, is inherently comprised of varying degrees of systemized and automated actions. It is a type of mutation scenario – the textile product evolves/grows/changes as it is passed from one stage of construction to the next. When a textile is manipulated, adjusted and given form through conventional methods of production that are inclusive of individual hands, the allure of the genuine as represented by hand making can be retained. When machine actions and/or the strategic rationale of production take precedence over possible choices and the insight of a skilled maker's intuitive/tacit actions, craft is lost.

Given this conundrum, 3D printers have the potential to act as a significant intermediary. 3D printing (additive manufacture) is situated in local knowledge and connected to individual decisions and implicit acts of making. The technology enables a dynamic fissure in contemporary society and offer up a means to truncate conventional routes of the mass-produced. For textiles, the sewing machine, is an early manipulator of form and subverter of conventional making actions (organized labour). Made available to the general public in the mid-1800's sewing machines (a mechanical technology) radically shifted the process of craft and in turn the processes of making (Mossoff 2009). While they are most commonly associated today with a proliferation of industrialization and mass production processes, sewing machines have also provided a novel small-scale personal production platform. When this technology was first introduced it acted to re-contextualize the local and, in the case of women, opened up new sites of political and financial autonomy (Binder 1987; Mossoff 2009; Sarioglu 2011). These latter impacts, we think, have connections to contemporary acts of individualized production occurring through the use of 3D printing, which likewise are shifting a paradigm of material production and are contingent on revisiting and revising existing social and political relations, a contemporary *Makers* tool.

With this in mind we have taken on a series of textile-3D printing explorations made up of open-ended acts of production that ply the digital, mechanical and intuitive. Initial 3D printing of polylactic acid (PLA) filament directly onto preexisting textiles was executed using an OSAT RepRap printer (Pearce 2012). These studies provided us with a series of low relief details (a cup, a star, a polka dot pattern) attached to the textile substrate. Some of the initial testing provided examples of hard/soft connections that were fairly durable, others less so. The movement and manipulation of the textile substrate and the subsequent displacing/dislodging of the printed forms were all noted. Hard form (such as a cup printed directly on to a textile) and scale (the relative dimensions of the printed artefact) affected use and imagined possibilities. As designers this insight led us to reconsider the potential future use applications of the newly formed artefacts.

Beyond the material qualities of the artefacts themselves, we are keenly interested in the integral dialogic process of building these tests. We have been tracking conversations between individuals speaking about craft and making. Traces of these conversations (intuitive mark making) have been illustrated and translated into digital pattern and numerical code (NC) which are replicated and repeated to create more complex patterns and motifs that often resemble lace. The digital retains a differential over the analogue process in this case as the craft of lace and the continuity of thread is replaced by a different pattern altogether (NC) that is comprised of seemingly random stops and starts in the construction of the 3D print model. Unlike conventional lace making, the digital interface (and code) picks up and deposits the heated filament (also a thread) in a non-linear, asynchronous yet connected manner. Notions of the craft of making and sequences that facilitate the making of meaningful stuff are subverted.

In parallel with our work using OSAT filament printing, a case study has emerged concerned with printing a more symbiotic soft and pliable medium – silicon – onto a textile substrate. Fabric types tested have included: wool melton cloth, hemp/lycra blends, unbleached canvas, a cotton waffle weave, and a double weave containing spandex, porous and foamy technical fabrics and waterproof technical fabrics. Initial explorations involved the application (through pressure) of varied thicknesses along simple trace-lines. Here we were simply looking to effectively apply silicon as bonding agent in combination with fabric. A second set of explorations encompassed testing simple vectors on the silicone printer, creating simple closed loop designs that the printer can execute in one pass, and developing a series of operations to generate G-Code that the silicone printer could recognize. Interestingly, this approach emulated the thread of lace making more appropriately than before. Once a reasonably quick workflow had been developed and fine-tuned, further testing began with different types of fabric and materials focusing on pre-stretched fabric, tactility and porosity and the possibility of welding layers of fabric together using the printed medium.

As noted previously, these textile-based explorations do not seek to supplant making connected to traditional production. They have, however, greatly broadened our creative scope and allow us to begin modelling means of transforming a measure of the economic condition of production. By placing the advantages of 3D printing within an existing workflow, it has ceased to act as an autonomous agent but rather as an enabling tool that maintains the status of the craft maker within newly streamlined production.

Conclusion: Social forums for knowledge mobilization

What does it mean to act as makers in contemporary society? What does it mean to re-situate and re-contextualize local *making* knowledge through a distributed personal production platform? We are exploring the implications of pairing a new and seemingly complementary technology, namely additive manufacturing and 3D printing, with others, with peer networks and with traditional methods of making. Our work seeks to develop meaningful pathways to making through hybridized digital/analogue workflows not in isolation, but rather as autonomous actions in new social configurations.

A highly successful public forum has leant an increased profile to Material Matters' interests and successes over the past few years affording opportunities to explore distributed knowledge

FIGURE 19.3 Detail of the pressed encaustic tile's surface. Photograph Philip Robbins.

within informal economies of peers and will continue to do so well into the near future. This ongoing series of explorations is grounded in a strategy aimed at providing a context for the OSATs and act as an outreach to our own personal communities, while sustaining ongoing face-to-face public and industry-focused knowledge transfer. The events are structured as a series of formal presentations given by experts and enthusiasts integrated with informal networking opportunities.

Making is a political act. *Making* has evolved. How we approach our craft and craft's implicit relationship to the individual and outward to the community ultimately affects our perception of objects and artefacts. In this context of a concurrent digital/analogue methodology, authenticity is achieved through the *makers*, own autonomous labour of reproduction and serialization, as invention or copy, made real, or made material through an implicit reflexive process involving others, and ourselves.

References

Binder, R. (1987), Did she donkeystone her doorstep?: The Victorian ideal of domesticity and the reality of working class women's lives,10 March 2016. Available from: http://digitalcommons.colby.edu/cgi/viewcontent.cgi?article=1026&context=seniorscholars.

Mossoff, A. (2009), The rise and fall of the first American patent thicket: The sewing machine war of the 1850s, 10 March 2016. Available from: http://papers.ssrn.com/sol3/Papers.cfm?abstract_id=1354849.

Nimkulrat, N. (2010), 'Material inspiration: From practice-led research to craft art education', *Craft Research*, 1 (1): 63–84.

Pearce, J.M. (2012), 'The case for Open Source Appropriate technology', *Journal of Environment, Development and Sustainability*, 14 (3) 2012.

Robbins, P., Doyle, K. and Day Fraser, H. (2014), 'Lowering Barriers to Uptake, Diversifying Range of Application, Carrying Forward Legacy Processes' *NIP30: The 30th International Conference on*

Digital Printing Technologies and Digital Fabrication, 2014 (Hardcopy), conference proceedings, Vol. 30, September 2014.

Sarioglu, A.I. (2011),' 'My faithful machine: The role of Technology in Daily life the case of Singer Sewing Machine in Turkey' (Doctoral diss., Middle East Technical University).

Shorthose, J. and Strange, G. (2004), 'The New Cultural Economy: The Artist and the Social Configuration of Autonomy', *Journal of Capital & Class*, Winter 2004, 84, (3).

von Busch, O. (2008), 'Fashion-able. Hacktivism and engaged fashion design. School of Design and Crafts'; Högskolan för design ochkonsthantverk.

20

Crafting code

Gender, coding and spatial hybridity in the events of PyLadies Dublin

Sophia Maalsen and Sung-Yueh Perng

Introduction

Female-friendly coding groups are part of the rapidly expanding hacker and maker movements that experiment with alternative forms of production and innovation (Meyer 2013; Rosner 2014). Specifically in terms of software hacking, they have a long history of tinkering with technology for the pursuit of openness, freedom, transparency and the democratization of science and technology (Coleman 2013; Lindtner 2015; Maalsen and Perng 2016). While other hackerspaces and makerspaces have become popular in the past decade, spaces that are dedicated to women working on software or hardware projects are relatively new. In these spaces, organizers and participants make room for the diversity of ideas, genders, goals and practices, and in the process they seek to redefine themselves and their relationships with technology (Fox, Ulgado and Rosner 2015).

In this chapter, we follow their work to provide an initial analysis of the gendering of subjectivities and the hybrid spatialities emerging from the work of organizing and participating in the monthly 'meetups' of PyLadies Dublin. PyLadies is a global movement that encourages women to code in the programming language of Python, regardless of their levels of skills, purposes of use and professional backgrounds (http://www.pyladies.com/). PyLadies has local chapters across the continents, in cities such as Bangalore, India, Seoul, South Korea and Rio de Janeiro, Brazil, but most of the local chapters concentrate in North America and Northern and Western European countries and cities. Our research led us to join the Dublin chapter, whose inaugural meetup was held in November 2013, going along to the meetups, as well as learning to code and act in such an environment. In addition to PyLadies, we draw upon our research on the closely related group, Coding Grace, which provides introductory tutorials for participants to learn and incorporate new programming skills into their own work.

There is an increasing discourse around code as craft and we contribute to this discussion. As for craft, 'code is about creativity … about engaging with coding as a form of expression and knowledge' (Salmond 2012). For Nafus (2012), engaging in the development of free and open source software is 'craft-like'. Writing software code scratches the programmers' itch of making, sharing, examining and improving the code by removing bugs in it, which motivates the programmers to become involved in such 'communities' and stay. Defining craft, 'an unwieldy beast of a phenomenon' to use Wagner's phrase (2008, p. 1; Jakob 2012, p. 3) phrase, is challenging, but as Wagner notes, it is more than just making, but encompasses the political (2012, p. 3). While technology is often posited as the antithesis of craft and the handmade, repositioning it as a tool for expression and political activism highlights its affinities with craft more broadly. This is perhaps best characterized by hackers and the process of hacking, which Coleman (2013, p. 98) argues, is a practice in which 'craft and craftiness converge'.

But while we situate coding as a craft we do so to additionally situate its role in knitting together and supporting a community of women that challenge the masculinity of computer programming – thus it is about both making and the political (see also Rosner and Fox 2016). The ethnographic component of the chapter illustrates how during the process of coding and regular meetups, participants develop a strong sense of community through a shared practice of coding. We focus on the practices and processes of making coding subjectivities and spatialites, and by thinking through them as craft work, our approach is similar to Costin's (1998, p. 3) observations on the ability of craft and crafting to create, maintain and communicate social identity and relationships through crafting practice and the craft objects produced. We pay particular attention to the technical arrangements, social relationships and material and informational spaces inhabited by Pyladies Dublin, which offers an interesting and fruitful case study as it intersects gender, relations of making and places of making, nested firmly within the social, physical, entrepreneurial and digital worlds.

Coding in gendered spaces

Crafting an inclusive coding/programming community is valuable work. Research has demonstrated what Corneliussen (2004) refers to as the hegemonic discourse of computing which creates different expectations of relations to computers based on gender (although see Lagesen 2008 for a discussion on different gendered relationships to computer science in Malaysia). Such discourse works to create subject positions in which men are expected to be more knowledgeable, interested and have greater expertise in computer science and to be interested in the technology itself, whereas women are not expected to share this fascination or experience (Corneliussen 2004, p. 175). This is despite the feminization of computer programming in the early days of computer science (Herbst 2008, p. 25). Additionally, 'men are associated with computer games, programming and technical tasks, while women are associated with communication, information and writing – tasks that can be described without references to technology' (Corneliussen 2004, p. 175). Indeed, Corneliussen claims that 'the connection between men and computer skills is so close, that being a man can function as a sign of computer competence' (2004, p. 177). Computer competence framed as masculine clearly has implications for power, for to 'question the masculinity of computers is questioning our image of masculinity itself: computers are power' (Coyle: 43 cited in Misa 2011. p. 12).

In this section, we look at the ways in which inclusive coding communities can help women challenge hegemonic discourses of computing and craft a programmer subjectivity with the help of groups such as PyLadies. Support communities for women within computing have been increasingly seen as a way to retain and recruit women within computing cultures (Gabbert and Meeker 2002), and thus redress the imbalance associated with gendered subjectivities. Toupin (2014) notes the increase in hackerspaces informed by a culture of openness but observes that they remain male-dominated spaces, with groups such as women and queers under-represented. Events which try to redress diversity within these spaces, such as women-only nights, are often considered controversial in their exclusiveness, which stands in direct opposition to an otherwise open source commitment to an espoused culture of openness (Toupin 2014). However, reflecting the hegemonic discourse of computing on a broader computing culture level, the 'openness' of hackerspaces is assumed rather than actual.

Despite this, the hegemony of computing discourse and hackerspaces can, however, be resisted and reworked. Toupin (2014) demonstrates various endeavours of creating safer and more inclusive spaces for those who do not fit and associate themselves comfortably with dominant hackerspace or computing cultures. Central in creating such spaces is to recognize that the subjectivities of these participants are not fixed; indeed Corneliussen (2004) details the complex strategies that men and women acquired to position their own subjectivities by negotiating assumed competences when legitimizing their presence in rooms that are of specific gender compositions (e.g. 'a more open room for women' or 'women in a room for men'). We can see similar reworking and crafting of relationships to computers, and programming and coding more specifically in the work of PyLadies, and another female-friendly computing space, Coding Grace. We can also see through these efforts to craft a computing community that is inclusive and which offers not only women but also men who do not fit the typical computer expert male subject position completely or comfortably, an opportunity to acquire computing confidence. In an interview, Vicky, the organizer of both coding initiatives, said:

Diversity for me initially is more trying to get women into Python as well as any technology but I want to widen the doors too. It doesn't matter what background you are from, culturally, gender wise, religion wise, just anyone who wants to learn should have an opportunity to learn. And they should not be afraid to go to technical events.

Technical events here encompass a variety of occasions, from workshops on specific programming techniques to the networking events for programmers. However, these events comprise predominantly white, male participants and can be an intimidating environment for women to attend, regardless of their coding skills. The predominant male presence, the conversation focus of competences and experiences, and the uncomfortable instances and conducts that constitute, or might lead up to, sexual harassment, all discourage females in terms of the participation in technical events and more generally their involvement in computing and other science and technology industries.

Yet crafting safe and inclusive environments is a complex process and can sometimes be hindered by agendas actually intended to encourage openness: the focus on a particular identified minority group may in turn exclude other groups by virtue of this specialized remit. For Vicky, for example, diversity and openness involve issues much broader than gender. During the interview she re-enacted a conversation she had with a company which potentially can provide sponsorships for events that she plans to promote as 'diversity friendly':

> 'Diversity, does that mean you are open to everyone?' I said, 'yes.' He said, 'but our remit is for women in tech.' I said, 'ok I will just keep it female friendly.' So we are not quite ready to call it diversity friendly, so when you explain diversity for me it is open doors to anyone who wants to come and learn so it is not gender only.

Vicky's aim to create open and diverse coding spaces in this instance is paradoxically restrained by initiatives to enhance gender equality within computing cultures. Diversity, being open to everyone, is perceived differently in the excerpt above and is significantly reduced in scope to the focus on 'women'. The broader diversity label challenges people's perceptions concerning for whom computing cultures are promoted and shaped, as was particularly the case when Vicky was sourcing event sponsorships from the private sector. At the same time, aligning with female-friendly remits is itself met with resistance from predominantly male programmers who see such events as divisive, as reflected in both Vicky's experience and Toupin's (2014) aforementioned work. Groups such as PyLadies and Coding Grace seek to build inclusive computing cultures; however, their work encounters resistance of the broader computing community which views female-friendly events as exclusive or divisive and hindered by perceptions and remits that narrow the scope of diversity.

Crafting an inclusive community is thus an ongoing and reflexive process. This process is dependent on the individuals within the community and the work they do to perform their subjectivity within computing cultures. As participants in PyLadies and Coding Grace learn to code, they rework and negotiate their own subjectivity in the process. Resisting the hegemonic discourse of computing and gender ascribed subject positions is however a continuous practice. Participants can learn to code and become a competent programmer but still feel unable to inhabit a subject position of computing competence. This is most evident in a conversation between Vicky and another participant. The participant has removed the pre-installed Windows to her laptop, which now runs on Linux and still encounters problems. As Vicky described,

> She fixed her own machine – she is working on Linux – and she is wondering what is going on. Basically she has been tinkering with her laptop, she has been coding, she has been going to tutorials, she is a coder but she just doesn't admit it. But she is compiling stuff away, doing this and that and she says she is not a programmer.

Inhabiting the position of 'programmer', or believing oneself to be a competent coder, is complex identity work. It becomes a *subjective* matter, or a matter of *subjectivity*. As Vicky continues to discuss, there is a multiplicity to coder subjectivity which influences how individuals see themselves as fully or partially being that subject. Some are more closely related to coding, including confidence, competence and experience, and others depend upon how individuals recognize the relationships between code, work and identity. The same participant does not see herself as a coder partly due to the fact that her day work does not involve much coding, and a similar situation applies to those who write code only as part of their work:

> She was saying in the work she does at the time she was contracting, there wasn't much coding involved and I think a lot of people have this perception that they are not coders. Researchers or data people say, I am not a coder.

But for Vicky, these are all valuable experiences of writing code and qualify these individuals as coders:

> You are a coder, you are writing Python code, you are analysing data, you are using libraries. You are writing code so you are a programmer! You could be other stuff as well, you are a data analyst, but you are a programmer because you code stuff. I think it is people's perception and herself, I tried to convince her that you are a coder!

These conversations show that maker identities (including programming/coding) are fluid and influenced by a subject's 'ability to use and extend tools, adopt an adhocist attitude to projects and materials, and to engage with the broader maker community' (Toombs, Bardzell and Bardzel 2014). The participant discussed above clearly demonstrates the traits listed by Toombs et al., but still has difficulty in accepting her subject position as oppositional to that prescribed by the hegemonic discourse of computing. Despite being able to write code, the participant still has difficulties in authoring/authorizing her identity as a programmer. Subject positions are therefore influential on an individual's computing competence; however, it also illustrates that these identities can be negotiated. This negotiation is a complex process and at times there are discrepancies between an individual's ability and their self-perception, but inclusive spaces such as PyLadies and Coding Grace can redress this imbalance and help the individual grow into their 'programmer' subjectivity.

Crafting hybrid coding spaces

In the case of PyLadies Dublin, organizing inclusive, friendly and supportive spaces for coding forms another aspect of their valuable work. The 'matters' produced through these spaces are the amalgams of programmers, gatherings, spaces and cultures that support one another in their engagements with a particular programming language and with the tech culture and industry more generally. These coding groups and spaces are in some ways comparable to a 'mobile sewing circle' where participants meet in person and embroider mobile phone text messages to make 'matters': the patchwork and the sharing and articulating of personal stories, experiences and concerns emerging as a result of engaging with each other's life, messages and sewing tools (Lindström and Ståhl 2012). For PyLadies the practices of documenting their code online, organizing gatherings that foreground mutual support, and making themselves available to each other, offering skills and providing encouragement, enhance wider, supportive and more collaborative engagement with technology. To demonstrate how such spaces and communities are developed, we build on an emerging field of studies that examine a variety of hackerspaces, makerspaces and DIY

Labs and their social, cultural, technological and economic significance (e.g. Meyer 2013; Lindtner, Hertz and Dourish 2014). In developing the analysis, we observe a wide range of informational, emotional, material and embodied practices that make PyLadies communities and coding spaces for developing alternative coding cultures.

PyLadies' meetup venues differ each month, and Meetup.com and Facebook pages are set up for event announcement and coordination. As participants, we look up event details from these pages before travelling together on train to find the venues. On a bright evening in June 2014, this research journey led us to the creative and historic quarter of Dublin. Arriving in Dublin and with a printed map in hand, we embarked on the walk that led us through the streetscape dominated by elegant four-story Georgian buildings in an area developed in the eighteenth century for merchant houses but now transformed into a bustling commercial quarter. The venue was in an incubator space in that quarter, converted from one of the terraced Georgian townhouses in a busy street full of niche retailers, and that was where we spent the next two hours, writing code together with our fellow programmers. Like this meetup, many other events are hosted by technology companies that are Dublin-based or have headquarters or branches here. But some of the venues were trickier to find compared with this pleasant short walk. It takes each participant considerable effort and determination to join because the meetup is after work, involves more than listening to talks, and requires actual code writing. Furthermore, these venues can be outside of the central area and difficult to reach by public transportation, adding onto the difficulty of travel during peak hours. Accordingly, participants are always in high spirit to see others joining them, and the sense of a 'coding community' grows as the members turn up to meetups recurrently while they move across Dublin each time they meet.

In addition to this conviviality, the material arrangements of the room and embodied interactions occurring there have been important to develop a distinctive, supportive atmosphere even though coding can be an individual activity. At a practical level, coding can be a very personal, considering that a programmer has to organize her own understanding and reasoning about life world situations, and translate them into software codes according to specific rules set by the programming languages being used. However, regardless of the different locations or layouts of the venue, PyLadies meetups often comprised of two or three tables joined together so that people could sit around them to form a 'group'. The group felt social and lively when participants were arriving. Sounds of greeting and catching up with each other infused a social element to the gathering. By contrast, when participants focused on their codes, the time in the room proceeded in a way that felt as if it ceased to exist, that it was not even noticeable. For these participants, it was because they were so engrossed into their thoughts, codes, fingers and screens, finding out how to do the syntax right or looking up additional information online. PyLadies has a shared project of building their own website and connecting it with the existing Meetup.com or Facebook pages. But contributing to the collective project is not a prerequisite to participate in the meetup. Instead, this common project is mostly intended for those who want to come along but do not have a specific individual project in mind. Indeed, the organizer has encouraged participants, repeatedly, to bring their own projects to the meetup, as long as they get to spend time on coding 'in a like-minded environment instead of … binge-watching tv episodes which seems to be the norm as folks want to chill and relax even though they plan to learn something new like coding' (Vicky, Personal communication). By seating the participants together but having both individual and shared projects at the meetups, these arrangements make flexible space to encourage participants to learn coding in their own ways and to give or receive help to troubleshoot problems during their engagement with new codes, as the following interlude occurring at the same meetup demonstrates.

To discuss technical problems in a shared space often means interruption to other participants, and it requires considerable embodied boundary work to create spaces for discussion and collaboration. As the meetup became quiet when participants started working on their projects, one participant broke the silence and stillness, very gently, and tried to ask the mentor a question. Immediately, she felt abashed for having to raise her voice, for sending it across the whole room during the initial, short exchange of words. Becoming really conscious about her 'intrusion' into their own, shared space, she moved herself to sit next to the mentor on the far side of the room, to continue their conversation. Even though other participants did hear the conversation, they did not seem to mind the discussion and carried on with their own projects. This short 'disruption' demonstrates the in situ practices of producing collaborative working spaces critical for sustaining the coding community. These spaces are not designated or fixed; instead they emerge and disappear when troubles occur and become fixed. They can be short, but can also linger when technical issues become followed by unanticipated but engaged discussion on issues not restricted to technical ones. For example, the issue of 'coding subjectivity' as we discussed above is a recurrent theme, and is one through which participants explore, as a group, their assumptions about the skills and identities associated with an appropriate 'programmer'. Accordingly, these highly negotiable and permeable boundaries between technical and social issues and between individual and shared issues matter for PyLadies' coding spaces because they foster skill and knowledge sharing and reflections on personal and social conditions in relation to male-dominant coding subjectivity.

Apart from such in situ practices, PyLadies participants also use an online collaborative note-taking tool to share their own project ideas, progresses and suggestions. These documents of project ideas and progresses act as more than archives, and become a dynamic place of project development facilitated by the support network of the Pyladies community. In the beginning, PyLadies tried to assemble necessary Python frameworks to build their own website, as well as for the beginners to learn the language. The online notes have detailed how to create and activate a virtual environment, set up Python modules, frameworks or libraries, and connect to Meetup. com's API to make the functions available on PyLadies' Meetup pages (e.g. RSVP an event) equally available in their website. These notes allow the participants to recreate the process outside of the meetup, or to catch up if they fall behind or could not participate in that particular session. In more recent meetups where participants work more on their individual projects, the provision of technical details can still be found. For instance, one of the participants has an idea of accessing and obtaining the data about available bikes from the bike-share scheme of Dublin Bikes, and visualizes and publishes the availability for its users. This attracts the interest of another participant who then goes on to find out where and how to access the data and how to parse the data obtained.

Taking into account the online, material, informational and embodied arrangements around PyLadies' spaces of coding, we argue that PyLadies itself is craft work that weaves together supportive software code writing practices and more inclusive spaces to 'widen the door' for those who only have restricted access and resources to programming. Finding venues and sponsorships to organize monthly gatherings can be repetitive, but still require careful and creative consideration to enhance alternative sociotechnical cultures and imaginaries around programming and to promote more supportive, collaborative, encouraging and transformative cultures. The spaces of coding emerge through participants engaging in individual projects, sharing knowledge and experiences among themselves, and motivating each other. In turn, they reconfigure coding cultures by crafting technically, socially and emotionally supportive spaces to work. The participants dedicate time to themselves to write code, develop mutual encouragement, provide company to each other, and lend helping hands only when necessary, highlighting that they are a group of competent, individual, female programmers. But they do more than produce code. The production of code also provides an opportunity to re-evaluate and reconfigure their sense of self. Through continual engagement in the group, participants learnt to not only code but to learn to identify themselves as coders/programmers, an identity that many initially felt unworthy to inhabit. In the process they have crafted a cultural shift, strongly aligning with the political aspect of craft. In this way, female coding subjectivities become inseparable from how they perform hybrid socio-spatial relationships around coding. The multiple places where coding and gatherings take place are reconfigured and become alternative 'geographies of display' (Wakeford 1999), ones that focus less on scripting gendered bodies and identities and instead demonstrate possibilities of hacking, diversifying and reconfiguring hegemonic coding culture, subjectivity and spatiality.

Conclusion

In this chapter we have explored the spatial, performed and gendered dynamics of crafting code and an inclusive coding community. Initially we had intended to address coding/programming as a craft and to attend to the dynamics that support that process. We discovered through our research that much more than code was being crafted. Through engaging with PyLadies and Coding Grace, participants have made, negotiated and reworked their subjectivities as coders and programmers, in the process not only gaining the skills to code, but also contributing to the development of an inclusive and supportive computing community. This process was, however, continuous and reflexive, with individual subject positions fluid and performed relative to the space. On a broader level these actions played out to build networks and links outside of the two female-friendly coding meetups. The organization of the events required partnerships with companies invested in increasing women's participation in computing cultures, and as such the location of the meetups was changeable, dynamic and fluid. The spatial dynamics of the meetups were an important element in providing a supportive coding environment. While positive steps had been made towards encouraging participation within computing cultures, there remained resistance to increasing diversity more broadly. As such, those involved with the groups see the project as far from complete. However, the case studies discussed here demonstrate that it is through the act of coding and participating in such spaces that individual subjectivities are reworked and remade, and that inclusive spaces are built, one event and one line of code at a time.

Acknowledgements

The research for this chapter was conducted under the Programmable City project, funded by a European Research Council Advanced Investigator award (ERC-2012-AdG-323636-SOFTCITY). We are grateful for the participants of PyLadies Dublin and Coding Grace for their encouragement and generosity along our research journey.

References

Coleman, E. G. (2013), *Coding Freedom: The Ethics and Aesthetics of Hacking*, Princeton, NJ: Princeton University Press.

Corneliussen, H. (2004), '"I don't understand computer programming, because I'm a woman!" Negotiating gendered positions in a Norwegian discourse of computing', in K. Morgan, C. A. Brebbia, J. Sanchez, and A. Voiskounsky (eds.), *Human Perspectives in the Internet Society: Culture, Psychology and Gender*, 173–82, Southampton, Boston: WIT Press.

Costin, C. (1998), 'Introduction: Craft and social identity', *Archaeological Papers of the American Anthropological Association*, 8 (1): 3–16.

Coyle, K. (1996), 'How hard can it be?', *Wired Women*, Seattle: Seal Press.

Fox, S., Ulgado, R. and Rosner, D. (2015), 'Hacking culture, not devices: Access and recognition in feminist hackerspaces', in *Proceedings of Computer-Supported Cooperative Work*, 56–68, Vancouver, BC, Canada.

Gabbert, P. and Meeker, P.H. (2002), 'Support communities for women in computing', *SIGCSE Women and Computing*, 34(2): 62–5.

Herbst, C. (2008), *Sexing Code: Subversion, Theory and Representation*, Newcastle: Cambridge Scholars Publishing.

Jakob, D. (2012), 'Crafting your way out of the recession? New craft entrepreneurs and the global economic downturn', *Cambridge Journal of Regions, Economy and Society*, doi:10.1093/cjres/rss022.

Lagesen, V.A. (2008), 'A cyberfeminist utopia? Perceptions of gender and computer science among Malaysian women computer science students and faculty', *Science, Technology, and Human Values*, 33 (1): 5–27.

Lindström, K and Ståhl Å (2012), 'Making private matters public in temporary assemblies', *CoDesign: International Journal of CoCreation in Design and the Arts*, 8 (2–3): 145–61.

Lindtner, S. (2015), 'Hacking with Chinese characteristics: The promises of the maker movement against China's manufacturing culture', *Science, Technology and Human Values*, 40 (5): 854–79.

Lindtner, S., Hertz, G.D. and Dourish, P. (2014), 'Emerging sites of HCI innovation: Hackerspaces, hardware startups and incubators', in *Proceedings of CHI*, 439–48, Toronto, Canada.

Maalsen, S. and Perng, S. Y. (2016), 'Encountering the city at hacking events', in R. Kitchin and S. Y. Perng (eds.), *Code and the City*, London: Routledge.

Meyer, M. (2013), 'Domesticating and democratizing science: A geography of do-it-yourself biology', *Journal of Material Culture*, 18 (2): 117–34.

Misa, T.J. (2011), *Gender Codes: Why Women are Leaving Computing*. New Jersey: Wiley & Sons.

Nafus, D. (2012), '"Patches don't have gender": What is not open in opensource software', *New Media & Society*, 14 (4): 669–83.

Rosner, D. K. (2014), 'Making citizens, reassembling devices: On gender and the development of contemporary public sites of repair in Northern California', *Public Culture*, 26 (1): 51–77.

Rosner, D. K. and Fox, S. (2016), 'Legacies of craft and the centrality of failure in a mother-operated hackerspace', *New Media & Society*, doi:10.1177/1461444816629468.

Salmond, M. (2012), 'Code as Craft', *Journal of the New Media Caucus*, 8 (1), http://median.newmediacaucus.org/spring-2012-v-08-n-01-caa-conference-edition-2012-code-as-craft/ (6 May 2016).

Smith, N. (1996), *The New Urban Frontier: Gentrification and the Revanchist City*. London and New York: Routledge.

Toombs, A., Bardzell, S. and Bardzell, J. (2014), 'Becoming makers: Hackerspace member habits, values, and identities', *Journal of Peer Production*, 5, available from http://peerproduction.net/issues/issue-5-shared-machine-shops/peer-reviewed-articles/becoming-makers-hackerspace-member-habits-values-and-identities/ (17 September 2015).

Toupin, S. (2014), 'Feminist hackerspaces: The synthesis of feminist and hacker cultures', *Journal of Peer Production*, available from http://peerproduction.net/issues/issue-5-shared-machine-shops/

peer-reviewed-articles/feminist-hackerspaces-the-synthesis-of-feminist-and-hacker-cultures/ (17 September 2015).

Wagner, A. (2008) 'Craft: It's What You Make of It', in F. Levine and C. Heimerl (eds.) *Handmade Nation: The Rise of DIY, Art, Craft, and Design.* New York: Princeton Architectural Press.

Wakeford, N. (1999), 'Gender and the landscapes of computing in an Internet café', in M. Crang, P. Crang, and J. May (eds.), *Virtual Geographies: Bodies, Space and Relations*, 178–201. London: Routledge.

Index